Advance Praise for *Sissy*

"When the political reality facing this country seems dark, we need shinier, sparklier thinkers in the public eye. With a signature style matched only by their wit, Jacob fits that bill perfectly."
—Alan Cumming

"Genderqueer and nonbinary voices are too often silenced in mainstream conversations about gender. It's why we need writers like Jacob Tobia, who offer us a more inclusive vision and provide readers living beyond the binary with reflections of themselves."
—Janet Mock

"*Sensational.* Gut-punchingly hilarious and full of heart . . . *Sissy* is guaranteed to make your mascara run from happy and sad tears alike."
—Tyler Oakley

"Dear men, please read this book. Whether you're sensitive, bold, gay, straight, pan, bi, creative, analytical, or don't even know who the hell you are, this book is a blueprint for healing our gender-based trauma from the inside out. It's brilliant and important and I couldn't put it down."
—Jay Duplass

"In a world full of digital noise, Jacob's words cut right to the heart. A Mindy Kaling meets Roxane Gay treasure, *Sissy* proclaims what we all know to be true: gender nonconforming people are a powerful part of the past, present, and future."
—Tommy Dorfman

"This is a book that every parent should read. We owe it to the next generation to raise children who celebrate gender diversity and are empathetic towards themselves and others; *Sissy* encourages just that."
    —Judy Shepard

"Jacob is a unique and inspirational voice for living your own truth. I love their personality and message, and I can't help but creep on their Instagram. ;)"
    —Gigi Gorgeous

"Gender nonconforming people like Jacob aren't just a passing phase or a cool fad, they're a fundamental part of our human family. Through embracing and empowering nonbinary people, we empower everyone to live a more authentic, glittering life."
    —Dustin Lance Black

"Jacob's energy, verve, and luminosity of self bring joy to so many, and I'm confident that *Sissy* will do the same."
    —Miss J Alexander

"It's not so much that Jacob's work has 'rescued' me—rather it's taught me that maybe there is something generative about remaining underneath, in the places and spaces and conversations that people avoid. It's this commitment to honesty—in its most visceral sense—that makes Jacob so exceptional and precious."
    —Alok Vaid-Menon

"Jacob's style, charisma, humor, wit and truth telling are authentic. . . . The world needs Jacob's voice, offering us all permission to be our truest selves."
    —Sara Ramirez

"Clad in clip-on earrings and towering heels, Jacob Tobia proves to be the Mary Poppins of gender nonconformity with *Sissy*, a memoir filled with penetrating insight into what it means to live a life between genders that will also make even the straightest, cissiest reader cackle. What a feat of femme multitasking! *Sissy* is a book that truly makes the anti-patriarchy, pro-genderqueer medicine go down in the most delightful way."
   —Meredith Talusan

"As someone who came out as gay while playing in the NBA, I can say firsthand that being yourself against all odds takes guts. Through standing up for gender nonconforming people and living their truth for all to see, Jacob is blazing a similar trail. This book is yet another step on Jacob's courageous road."
   —Jason Collins

"For any young person who's currently struggling with their gender, *Sissy* will be a source of strength, power, and much-needed laughs."
   —Jazz Jennings

Sissy

A Coming-of-Gender Story

Jacob Tobia

G. P. PUTNAM'S SONS

NEW YORK

PUTNAM

G. P. Putnam's Sons
Publishers Since 1838
An imprint of Penguin Random House LLC
penguinrandomhouse.com

Scripture taken from the Holy Bible, New International Version®,
NIV® copyright © 1973, 1978, 1984, 2011 by Biblica, Inc.® Used by permission.
All rights reserved worldwide.

LIBRARY OF CONGRESS CATALOGING-IN-PUBLICATION DATA

Names: Tobia, Jacob, author.
Title: Sissy : a coming-of-gender story / Jacob Tobia.
Description: New York : G. P. Putnam's Sons, [2019]
Identifiers: LCCN 2018041589 | ISBN 9780735218826 (hardcover) |
ISBN 9780735218833 (epub)
Subjects: LCSH: Tobia, Jacob | Gender-nonconforming people—United
States—Biography.
Classification: LCC CT275.T69 A3 2019 | DDC 305.30973—dc23
LC record available at https://lccn.loc.gov/2018041589

Printed in the United States of America
1   3   5   7   9   10   8   6   4   2

Book design by Elke Sigal

Penguin is committed to publishing works of quality and integrity. In that spirit, we are proud to offer this
book to our readers; however, the story, the experiences, and the words are the author's alone.

Sissy is a work of nonfiction. Some names and identifying details
have been changed in order to protect privacy.

For all the girls,
who deserve power
instead of cruelty.

For all the boys,
who deserve gentleness
instead of violence.

For all of us in between;
for all of us outside;
for all of us beyond.

And for my grandmother,
whose brooch sparkles on the lapel closest to my heart.

CONTENTS

Part III · Big Queen on Campus

Sissy

Introduction

I never really got to have a childhood. Or perhaps a better way to put it is that, as a feminine boy, my childhood was never really *mine*. My natural connection to my body, my comfort in my identity, my sense of security and safety were all taken from me before my earliest memories formed. They were pried from my hands, sometimes gently, occasionally violently: coaxed out of me through a combination of punishing isolation, public humiliation, and, when I managed to get things "right," acidic reward.

For the majority of my life, I assumed that everyone experienced life this way. I thought childhood was just *like that*, that we were all on the gender tightrope together, spending almost all our energy struggling to balance.

In some ways, that's true. Everyone struggles with their gender identity. Every boy, no matter how butch, struggles to fit in with the other boys. Every girl, no matter how femme, struggles to feel woman enough.

But my pain was different, and for the longest time, I didn't want to admit that to myself. It's easier to navigate society when you assume everyone else is hurting in the same ways you are. It's easier to be at peace with the world when you pretend you haven't been treated more unfairly than anyone else. Pretending like you haven't been hurt, like injustice wasn't done to you, is a viable short-term strategy for reducing your suffering. But at some point, the injury starts to catch up to you.

Gender-based trauma is less like a broken leg and more like a bad back. A broken leg is undeniable. A broken leg makes itself known within seconds. You stop walking on it, you call an ambulance, and you go to the damn hospital. You stop what you're doing, change the way you relate to your body for a few months, and prioritize recovery because you *can't not*. You can't walk again if you don't. The need for healing is acute.

A bad back (which I, at the ripe old age of twenty-seven, have) is different. It builds up over decades. It doesn't come from one traumatic incident, but instead from a lifetime of stress and minuscule damage. A bad back can go unnoticed for years.

But then you're on a run or lifting weights at the gym or throwing a Frisbee, and *kablam*—there goes your back. The pain releases. The years of tension break, all in a moment. The damage catches up to you.

The first time the damage of my childhood caught up with me, I was sixteen, sitting in my brother's old room flipping through TV channels. Watching reruns of a show I hadn't seen in years, I experienced something new: nostalgia. For the first time, I felt old. Well, perhaps *old* is a bit dramatic, but I felt like a chapter of my youth had ended.

I thought back to who I was at eight years old, when I'd watched the show for the first time. Even back then, I knew I was different. I just didn't know how to tell the world. Like that, years of repression dawned on me. For so long I'd been suppressing my identity. But all of a sudden, while channel surfing, the tension of holding my identity in had burst.

I went downstairs on that rainy December night, gathered my parents around the kitchen island, and came out as gay. My father's rejection was painful, my mother's fear rubbed me raw, but at least it was done. I thought the tension was gone. I'd had my one great setback and could now move on with my life.

Your first back injury shakes you and throws your confidence, but it often mends quickly. Within a few days, you tell yourself that you're better, that your back is fine, that it was a freak accident and won't happen again. You ignore the gnawing pain that lingers when you lay down at night.

And even though you're in denial about the severity of your problem, you change your behavior ever so slightly. You don't pick up heavy things, you stop doing sports or physical activities that you used to love. Those are only small sacrifices, right? And you're not *really* injured, are you? Going to the doctor is just a hassle, y'know? It's easier to accept that you can't do certain things, that certain things simply aren't for you.

Then one day, you aren't doing anything strenuous, you're just bending over to *pick up a damn noodle* that fell on the kitchen floor or twisting to *grab something from the back seat of your fucking car*, when *wham*—your back spasms again. And it's terrifying. Because it becomes clear to you that your back injury wasn't a one-time thing. You start to realize that there might be something deeper going on, something structural.

So the conversation changes, because it's not just that you can't go on a run or climb a mountain or take that Rihanna dance class you've always wanted to take. It's that you can't do your laundry, or reach for items in the cupboard, or grab a book from the bottom shelf. Suddenly, you can't *live a regular life*, and you have to admit that your injury is serious. That your pain is real. That you need to do something in order to heal.

For the longest time, I didn't realize the ways in which I was still hurting. After I came out as gay, I thought I was done, that wrestling with my identity was a one-time thing. I'd publicly declared my identity, dealt with some rejection, and could move on.

Then, two years later, when I was a senior in high school and the future loomed ominously on the horizon, my friends and I were hanging out when they posed a simple question:

What's the first thing you remember?

As my friends shared fond reminiscences of childhood, I sat with the question, perplexed by what was coming to me. My memories all seemed to center around my gender, around feeling out of place, isolated, or disoriented in my boyhood. At the age of eighteen, just as I was entering legal adulthood, I realized that it was not normal for all of my earliest memories to be of pain and confusion. Hearing my friends share happy moments and struggling to find a fond memory of my own, I was overcome with pain. During the course of a normal conversation, my injury was unleashed.

Spasms of residual trauma hit me one after another. I remembered sitting in a tree house with three girls from my preschool class, deciding what to play. We were all avid fans of the TV show *Sailor Moon*—a Japanese cartoon about five girls in sailor outfits who fought evil—and decided that we should pretend to be characters from the show for the day. My friend went around our group, asking each of us which character we wanted to be. I held my breath, hoping that no one else would want to be Sailor Mercury, my favorite character, who happened to be a girl.

But it didn't matter. When my friend got to me, she said matter-of-factly, "And Jacob can play Tuxedo Mask since he's the only boy!"

I remembered my heart sinking. It felt like an indictment, like a verdict. I didn't want to play a boy character that wasn't part of the core group of girls. I wanted to be one of the group like everyone else, but as the only boy, I had no choice in the matter. I couldn't play a girl. Feeling alone at recess, unable to be fully part of any group, is a prevailing theme in many of my earliest memories.

Another spasm hit me, this time as I remembered dress-up time in kindergarten. For most of my classmates, this was a vital space in which to explore identity, fostering creativity, theatricality, emotional development, and empathy. It allowed them the space that they needed to imagine their futures, who they could be, and who they might become.

For me, dress-up time was none of those things. During the course of my childhood, I came to associate dress-up time simply with a sense of longing. I longed to experiment with my gender. I longed to wear pink, to try on frilly garments, to envelop my body in sequins and cover my lips with bright lipstick. I longed to prance in a dress, to dance in a tutu, to flounce about in a tiara, queen for the day.

Instead, I was relegated to trying on oversize blazers, doctor's jackets, or construction vests. Through social pressure and gentle correction by teachers, I was steered away from anything with the slightest edge of femininity. Eventually, my options became so limited that I gave up dress-up time altogether, choosing instead to sit in a corner drawing quietly on my own, enviously watching girls in my class sport layers of tulle.

Sitting on my best friend's bed, I realized that I couldn't even have a regular conversation reminiscing with friends without experiencing pain. I realized that the damage ran deeper than I could've ever imagined. It was more extensive, more firmly rooted, than I could fully understand.

Even when we can no longer regularly function because our back is so bad, many of us *still* don't seek help. Instead, we lose faith that we will ever lead a healthy life. We leave our bodies unhealed. We relinquish, or are *compelled* to relinquish, the idea of health.

There are a million reasons why. For some, it's because we don't have the insurance/money necessary to see a doctor; for others, it's because we don't have the mental health necessary to properly value our body; for many, it's because we don't have either. We give up because we live in a world that only allows some access to healthcare. We give up because our bad backs make it harder to get good jobs. We give up because the world blames us for our disability. We give up because we don't know anyone else who has overcome their pain. We give up because we feel that, if we were only stronger, we could've conquered this. We give up because we internalize our trauma, we believe that it is our fault. We give up because we are alone and have no one to show us what recovery might look like. Without a community to rely on, we spiral further and further into injury.

When I first looked my gender in the face for real, when I first acknowledged my pain, it terrified me. It crushed me. There was just *so much* of it. It was *everywhere*. How could I possibly start to heal? My pain consumed me, hanging like a specter over my life, pathways of trauma seared into my neurons, the words *sissy* and *faggot* perpetually ringing, revisited again and again.

Instead of working to heal the pain, I became *accustomed* to it. I accepted that my life was going to be this way: that I was never going to have the kind of life my friends had, that I would never be able to enjoy things without pain droning in the background, that I was damaged beyond repair.

There were a few, precious periods of time when my pain eased. There were queer conferences where I found entire rooms full of people like me. There were tender moments in my dorm at Duke University, putting on lipstick with a friend. There were moments when I was onstage, performing in drag or performing as someone else, when I could sneak away from it. There was the summer I spent in Cape Town living with my gender nonconforming best friend, dressing up and hosting dinner parties.

But those moments felt few and far between. They were anomalies. And they never seemed to last.

So bit by bit, I gave up on living a healthy life. I gave up on having a partner, on having a family, on having a career that I loved. I gave up on enjoying sex. I gave up on having fun at parties. I gave up on the idea that I could ever feel comfortable in my body or look myself in the mirror. I gave up on everything. Floundering in the dark, I gave up on the idea that my life mattered altogether.

Then, after a failed attempt at relocating to Washington, DC, after college, I did the most stereotypical thing possible: I moved to New York. And while paying rent became much more difficult and street harassment became a part of my daily reality, I suddenly found myself *surrounded* by other people who were damaged in the same way that I was. People who'd endured decades of gender-based trauma but had moved forward anyway. It was mostly about *numbers*. Sure, I'd known other gender nonconforming people in North Carolina and we did our best to support one another, but I felt like there were never enough of us to comfortably fill a room. In New York I discovered an established *community* of people who had the same pain I did, who'd been injured as I had been, but refused to stop moving.

I found other gender nonconforming people who were willing to hold my hand as I took my first steps toward healing. I found people who were invested in helping me diagnose the pain I was enduring. I found people who held me when the therapy was too much. I found people who I couldn't scare off, no matter how intense things got. Recovery began to feel like a real possibility, even an *appealing option*.

And my world bloomed.

As a gender nonconforming adult, I am still recovering from how the world treated me when I was a child. But because of the love that has been shown to me by other trans and gender nonconforming people, I am much further along in my recovery than I once was. I'm leading a life that now feels vital. I have a dynamic career doing what I love. I have a community of queer people that envelop me in love nearly 24/7. I am opening up to the world about my journey. I am owning my truth. I am wearing sequins and leather anywhere that I please. I did my taxes on time this year, goddamn it.

Over the last few years, I have learned that healing from gender-based trauma is possible. It starts when you make peace with what was done to you. But it doesn't end there. Healing continues as you learn to claim that others should not have to endure what you have endured.

Eventually, the line between healing your injury and healing the world begins to blur. Your healing becomes uncontainable. It expands in every direction, radiating out of you and into the world. It unfurls to touch everyone you love, everyone who crosses your path. It becomes unstoppable, and ultimately, it transforms the world.

That's what impelled me to write this. Through the power of honest, sometimes snarky, often silly storytelling, I want to let my internal healing ripple throughout the world around me.

And this healing isn't just for gender nonconforming people. This healing is for everyone. Perhaps the greatest oversight of the trans movement thus far is that it has positioned gender-based trauma as something that only trans people experience. As a result, there are millions of cisgender, heterosexual people—particularly men—who have never coped with the trauma they've experienced, who don't even recognize their experiences *as trauma* in the first place. They've spent a large portion of their lives being told that they are not man enough if they do this or aren't masculine enough if they do that, and none of these imperatives are even recognized as gender policing. So many men remain trapped in a cycle of abuse that says you can't cry, can't recognize your pain, and must participate in cultures of violence. For many, participating in this cycle of abuse is even a badge of honor.

This book is particularly for them. In our world as it is today, it isn't a question of *whether* you've had gender-based trauma in your childhood. Everyone has had some. Rather, it's a question of what *degree* of gender-based trauma you've experienced, what degree of distance you felt from your body and your peers. We all need to heal on one level or another. Through sharing my experiences on the margins, I'm aiming right for the center, for the core of how gender hurts us all.

I don't believe my childhood had to be the way that it was. I don't believe feminine boys like me should have to spend so much time alone, alienated from boys and girls alike. I don't believe young boys who want to wear pink should be compelled to mute their heart's longing. I don't believe a child should have to sacrifice his love of unicorns in order to make friends and receive affirmation from adults.

Growing up, I didn't have the words *trans* or *genderqueer.* I didn't know that I even counted as trans until I was in my twenties. I didn't really have any positive ways of thinking about myself, my femininity, or my gender. Instead, I just knew that I was a faggot, that I was a sissy. For years, those labels haunted me, filling me with shame and embarrassment, dread and loathing.

But here's the remarkable thing about self-love: When you start to love yourself for the first time, when you start to truly embrace who you are—flaws and all—your scars start to look a lot more like beauty marks. The words that used to haunt you transform into badges of pride.

And so, at the age of twenty-seven, I adore the words *sissy* and *faggot.* I take pride in them. They are a cherished part of my history, a beautiful piece in my life's menagerie, transformed from lead to gold by the alchemy of self-discovery and self-acceptance.

I'm the shiniest, queenliest, sparkliest faggot that I can be.

I'm the most effervescent, gorgeous, dignified sissy that the world has ever seen.

I own it. I live it. And this book is, at least in part, the story of how that came to be.

A Quick *Man*ifesto

(Pun Intended)

I used to think that my gender was a voyage that needed a destination, but as I've gotten older, I've come to embrace that my gender is more like an onion. It doesn't have a center, a core, or a discernable middle. It's layer upon layer upon layer, veiled beneath a thin skin. Sometimes the act of peeling apart the layers, of chopping them up and processing them, can make your eyes sting. Uncovering a new layer can even make you cry. Sometimes it's smelly work. But each layer is meaningful, and with enough time and proper preparation, each layer is delicious.

Here's the thing. This isn't a book about a self-actualized trans person who knows everything there is to know about their gender; this isn't a book about a demure, polite queer person who's here to teach you Transgender 101; and this certainly isn't a book about a queen who's got everything figured out.

In fact, this book is a rebellion against a mainstream, classical trans narrative that's, quite frankly, gotten a little repetitive. This far past the Trans Tipping Point™* the Trans Narrative© has basically been distilled into something of a Mad Lib™. It generally goes like this:

My Classical, Binary Transgender Story

I was born in the wrong body. The doctors told my parents that I was a _____ [boy or girl], but I always knew that I was the opposite of that. I grew up in a _____ [small/medium/big] _____ [town/city/village/suburb] in a _____ [nuclear/single-parent/conservative/dysfunctional] family. I told my mom that I wasn't a _____ [boy/girl], I told my dad that I wasn't a _____ [boy/girl], but no one believed me.

cue dramatic Lifetime Original Movie music

I spent years hating myself, thinking that something was wrong with me. I became more and more depressed. _____ [Troubling story of depression/suicide/self-harm/abuse. You owe it to the audience, even if you're not *really* ready to share it yet].

---

* "Transgender Tipping Point," is a now infamous phrase that was coined by *Time* magazine on its June 2014 cover, the one with Laverne Cox (which, wow, did she look *good*. Her portrait on that cover was *fire*). The phrase signified a monumental shift in the public consciousness about trans people. One moment, trans people were seemingly invisible; outcasts living on the fringes of society. The next moment, we were *everywhere* and *celebrated*. It felt like a miracle at the time, but strikes me as kinda sad now, if only because I was naïve about the whole thing. I thought the trans tipping point meant that we were done. I thought the trans tipping point meant that being trans wouldn't be so difficult anymore. I thought that the trans tipping point meant that trans people would be accepted and affirmed *everywhere*. The term is powerful, but for me it's become a bittersweet reminder of my long-lost optimism, an optimism that *seriously* miscalculated the amount of work that lay ahead.

Then one day, I got the courage to come out.

_____ [Dramatic story about coming out to your parents. You have to start with the story about when you came out to your parents, even if it's not what you want to talk about. Focus on all the terrible things they said to you.].

I was rejected by many people in my life. _____ [More trauma]. _____ [And even more trauma, because that's the only way that people will try to understand you or take this seriously]. _____ [Maybe just one more traumatic story for good measure? If the audience isn't crying, you're not doing your job as a spokesperson.].

That's when I decided that I needed to transition. I started hormones and had a _____ [breast augmentation/reduction]. Then I did the really hard thing and got "the surgery" to make sure that my genitals aligned with my identity. And don't even get me *started* on body hair! It takes so long to _____ [grow/get rid of].

cue "Firework" by Katy Perry.
*This is the part where you should tear up a bit**

Now I'm living as a _____ [man or woman] and I couldn't be happier. I reintegrated into the gender binary and "fixed the problem," so now I'm a _____ [man/woman] just like you! I am so happy now that my body finally aligns with what heterosexual society expects a _____ [man's/woman's] body to be. Now I can be a normal person and live as a full part of society.

Thank you for listening to me and hearing my authentic truth [smile so that you don't seem threatening]. Trans people are just like you!

Over the last few years, I've heard this narrative reiterated ad nauseam in national news outlets, documentary films, fundraising materials, and Facebook posts alike. It seems to be the only trans narrative that cisgender* people want to hear; the only trans story that cisgender people can comprehend. Quite frankly, I'm exhausted by the limits of the cisgender imagination.

Let me be clear. There isn't anything inherently wrong with this narrative. It's like chocolate ice cream: it's delicious, delightful, widely appreciated, and pairs well with countless toppings. But if you walked into an ice cream store and they *only* had chocolate ice cream, you'd feel like there was something missing.

The classical binary narrative is still a transformational and deeply worthwhile story. There are many, many trans people for whom this classical narrative *is* true, and those trans people are just as self-actualized, powerful, and beautiful as anyone else. It is still courageous and radical for trans people to tell that story and claim that truth as theirs.

But it is not okay for cisgender people to take that story as *the* trans story, because that narrative simply isn't true for all of us. No one trans story is better or inherently more "radical" than another, but that hasn't stopped cisgender media culture from deeming certain trans stories to be more valuable than others. Those of us who don't fit the classical narrative end up either having our stories edited and reedited until they fit, or end up having our voices silenced.

And that's fucked.

At its best, this narrative is just an *oversimplification* of the trans community. At its worst, this narrative is used as a tool—reinforced by cisgender editors, curators, movement leaders, and gatekeepers—that continues to pressure trans people into fitting into one of two binary genders. By showing how *desirable* it is to be gender conforming and

---

* If you don't know what the word *cisgender* means by now, that's probably because you *are* cisgender, bless your heart!

"pass" as a man or as a woman, this narrative reiterates the idea that gender nonconforming trans people are less-than and should be lucky to be treated as the gender with which we identify.

Through diagnosing the classical trans narrative—and through detailing how my own story and worldview differ from it—we can come to a deeper understanding of why this book is a timely and *oh so needed* challenge to people who believe that there's only one trans story to tell.

The first thing that's challenging about the classical trans narrative is that *it glamorizes trauma.* As trans people, our stories are not valued if they are gentle. We can't just wake up, realize we feel differently about our gender, and take it day by day. We can't try on lipstick, like it, think about it for a few weeks, and decide to wear it more. We can't be low-key. Being trans has to be a *big deal.* It has to be this *massive* thing that defines you. We have to burn for years, neglected and abused, before coming out dramatically. Otherwise, why should our identities be taken seriously? Too often, the world demands that we *earn* our transness through our trauma.

I refuse to tell my story in those terms. My trauma is no longer what I define myself by, and it has taken a lot of therapy, self-love, and depression naps for me to get to that point. I define myself by a set of different virtues: the fact that I am a decent writer, the fact that I am a resilient person who has found healing, the fact that I am goofy as hell, the fact that after decades of being understood by everyone as white, I'm finally beginning to explore what it means to be an Arab American, the fact that I was eating my grandmother's hummus *way* before white people decided hummus was cool.

What also frustrates me about the classical trans narrative is that it depends on trans people *existing solely in the man-woman binary.* Fitting into the gender binary, being a "real woman" or a "proper man," has been baked into almost every facet of trans storytelling. Your body and the sex you were assigned at birth are poised as the enemy, as the dragon that must be slayed, as the Ring that must be hurled into Mount Doom, as

He Who Must Not Be Named. At the end of the story, you have overcome your body to truly fit into the gender binary again. Fitting into the gender binary propels the rising action, the climax, the falling action, the denouement. Without the gender binary, many might feel that trans storytelling wouldn't hold water.

Sorry, but I'm not going to use the binary idea of "coming into my manhood" or "earning my womanhood" to orient you. This isn't about any singular conquest, because as it turns out, trans storytelling gets *better* without the gender binary as the goal. The story opens up. Free from proscriptive binary boundaries, we are able to tell stories that don't come with an inevitable conclusion, and the possibilities become as endless and varied as the world around us. I'm bored of our culture's obsession with binary-oriented storytelling. It feels like being stuck in missionary position, when all I really wanna do is *ride*.

Another thing I want to challenge about proscribed trans storytelling is that it demands *consistency of identity*. As trans people, we're supposed to say, "I've always known I was a girl" or "I've always known I was a boy." We're supposed to say that we've always had a rock-solid identity and sense of self; otherwise, our identity seems weak, uncertain, *fallible*.

There are many things that I have always been. I've always been clumsy, I've always had trouble with group sports activities, I've always been a bit of a stage queen, and I've always made it a point to eat ice cream on at least four different occasions each week. There are many things that I've always known about myself, but my gender just isn't one of them. I didn't know that I was a girl. And forgive the double negative, but I wasn't sure that I *wasn't a boy*, either. I just knew that gender was kinda stupid and that I wanted to play with Barbies, get dirty in the creek behind my house, *and* kiss the blue Power Ranger real bad.

As people, our identities change over our lifetimes. This applies to transgender and cisgender people alike. Everyone has a gender that evolves. Even if you identify as a woman, *what it means to be a woman* is never the same from day to day. Or, if you identify as a man, the way that your manhood manifests will be different throughout your life. The idea that *gender is consistent* is a flawed premise to begin with. By resisting convenient labels and embracing authentic ambiguity, I want to challenge the tenet that gender must be consistent and immediately legible to others. This is a story about the messy parts, the rough edges, the chunky bits of the stew.

But perhaps the most exhausting thing about the classical trans narrative, and the thing that most strongly violates my personal pet peeves, is that it's not *funny*. Within the way that we are accustomed to talking about gender, there seems to be no place for humor. We have to take gender *seriously*, because gender is not a laughing matter.

Well, I beg to differ. Gender is *not* serious, or at least, it shouldn't be. Taking our own gender or the gender of others too seriously results in a world where gender must be rigid, must adhere to consistent rules and regulations. This is detrimental to basically everyone, because it stops us from having fun with our gender presentation and sense of self. If "being a man" and "being a woman" are always treated as serious things, we perpetuate a world in which human possibility is confined.

That's why, in these pages, I've tried to let loose and have a little fun. I'm giving you permission to laugh not only with me, but *at* me, because I refuse to take my experience with gender too seriously. I refuse to talk about my childhood confusion without also laughing at how dramatic I am. I refuse to talk about my father's initial rejection without giggling at how silly his mannerisms are. I refuse to talk about the fact that I'm trans without also talking about the fact that I am a hot, overachieving mess of a human.

Don't think of this book as an epic journey. It's not. Instead, think of this book as you would a good sex party. There are rich interactions with countless individuals. Each moment is complex, beautiful, and passionate. There is pleasure in the pain and pain in the pleasure. And half the time, especially in the beginning, you really aren't sure what to do with your genitals.

Oh, and *one more* thing (sorry). The trans narrative perpetuated by mainstream media *fucking sucks* because it rarely acknowledges history or community. It implies—or, at times, outright says—that this whole trans thing is new. That the trans experience is a product of the modern world. As if trans people haven't been around for all of recorded history. As if gender nonconformity isn't as old as gender itself. As if precolonial and indigenous cultures across the world didn't have rich traditions of honoring gender nonconforming, trans, and two-spirit people. As if every trans person on the planet doesn't owe our present freedom to the struggles of generations of gender nonconforming and trans folks who came before.

It (callously) suggests that we claim our identities in a vacuum, solely through our own courage and audacity. Not only is that inaccurate, it's just plain fucked up. No trans person exists in a vacuum. Even before we *first hear* the word *transgender* or the term *gender nonconforming*, we are born into a world that has been painstakingly, albeit chaotically, built for us by our trans elders. Even before *we know their names*, our trans and queer elders have paved the way for us. Against insurmountable odds, they found a way to survive in the wilderness; oftentimes learning by trial and error; leaving behind field guides and hand-drawn maps and hastily scrawled notes about which berries will kill us and which berries are oh-so-yummy to eat.

The struggle to feel self-actualized in your gender, to feel that your gender is fully *yours*, is a fundamentally human struggle. No matter what labels we use to describe ourselves, everyone has their own journey to gender authenticity. The more we share our journeys, the more we challenge the static structure in which we are told to understand ourselves, the greater freedom we find to celebrate ourselves as we are. In a moment when the conversation about gender norms has never been more nuanced or more heated, I'm doing my best to stand as a beacon, a well-adorned, glitter-encrusted lighthouse providing direction, warning, and much needed light to all the sexy sailors and pirates who want to plumb my depths.

We deserve more expansive portrayals of trans lives. It's time for trans folks with the messiest identities to step up to the plate. It's time for gender nonconforming and nonbinary trans people to get the mic. It's time for trans people of color to shape the story. It's time for low-income and rural trans people to guide the narrative. It's time for disabled trans people to set the course. It's time for indigenous trans people to get the whole damn stage.

And while I can't claim to represent all of those perspectives,* I'm proud to stand up as a trans weirdo and claim that it's time for something different, something out of the box, something with fewer cobwebs. This book is a fabulous fuckup in terms of communicating a universal, easily understood trans experience. This book is a glorious failure in terms of communicating the truth of gender in conveniently digestible, bite-size pieces. But I'd like to think that's what makes it perfect.

Here's to hoping that you agree.

---

* You have to buy their books, too (budget permitting). Buying one trans book and calling yourself informed is like buying one bottle of wine and calling yourself a sommelier.

PART I

Kiddo

Chapter 1

The Girls Next Door

*A*s a child, I had absolutely no shame about my gender or about my body. None. Just zero. To the degree that it was kind of a problem.

To illustrate this, my mom loves to tell me a story, one that I don't consciously remember. There are a lot of stories like that. Our childhood memories are fickle, flighty birds; always flapping around and morphing and transmogrifying. They're like one of those floating dandelion tufts that blow by you when you stand in a sunlit field. They run away if you so much as breathe; to catch them requires the greatest delicacy, the most serene approach.

This isn't one of those memories. Thankfully, I didn't have to catch this one, because my mom won't let me forget it.

The story goes like this. When I was around three or four years old, after I'd already been potty trained and learned to pee standing up, my parents would frequently catch me peeing outside. And by "outside" I don't mean "far back in the woods behind a tree where no one could see me," I mean "straight up in the front yard in plain sight of the neighbors." It wasn't that I was an exhibitionist or that I was deviant or anything—I was just doing what came naturally to me. And when I was playing outside and found myself with a full bladder, what came naturally to me was dropping my pants right where I was and relieving myself.

When you think about it, there really isn't a logical reason for human beings *not* to pee outdoors. Pooping outdoors (something I never did unless I was camping with the Boy Scouts) is another matter, because it's an issue of sanitation, but peeing outside is completely natural and harmless. Urine is a naturally sterile fluid, it doesn't really damage anything, and it certainly can't transmit any diseases. In urban areas, like New York City, it makes sense not to pee outside, because there are just too many people and the city already smells enough like piss. But in the suburban sprawl of Cary, North Carolina, the reason I wasn't supposed to pee outside came down to one thing: modesty.

We expect children to be modest with their bodies. We culture our children to be ashamed of nakedness, but there's nothing natural about that. Most kids have no problem whatsoever running around the neighborhood buck-naked and giggling. I was no exception to this rule.

One day, my mother caught me, and she was not thrilled about it. Her edict was simple: "Jacob, you are not allowed to pee in our yard!"

The next day, she sent me outside to play, but not without a reminder.

"What did we talk about yesterday, Jacob?"

"Don't pee in our yard."

"Yes. Thank you. Now go play."

Twenty minutes later, when my mom came outside to check on how I was doing, I was nowhere to be found. She checked the front yard, looked over to our neighbor's house, and circled around back, where she found me standing firmly in our neighbor's backyard, peeing.

"Jacob! Get back here! What did I tell you?!"

"You didn't say anything about peeing in our neighbor's yard!" I exclaimed, triumphant.

From this story, you should learn two things about me. One, I am the worst type of smartass, and I learned to mobilize my intelligence to get what I want from literally before I can remember. Two, shame about who I am or about my body did not come naturally to me. I had to learn to be ashamed of my body and my identity. And even when others insisted that I should be ashamed, I did my darnedest to ignore them and live a shame-free life.

In the glimmers I remember, the first few years of my childhood were lived without shame. I could freely relate to my body and, without fear of reproach, my gender.

My femininity came as naturally as my masculinity. As a child, I simply wanted it all. I was a precocious, smart, fast, energetic little fucker, and baby, I wanted all the gender I could get. In "quintessential" little boy style, I wanted to run around screaming in the front yard. I wanted to play in the dirt and get in mud fights. I wanted to splash in puddles and roll in the grass and be filthy and smelly. I wanted to frolic in the woods and find sticks that could serve as swords, then fight with them. I hated playing coordination-based sports because I didn't naturally enjoy competing for things, but I adored using my body and getting it dirty. I loved playing with bugs; I thought spiders were the coolest animals. I fancied lizards and would chase blue-tailed skinks around the deck whenever I saw them, trying to catch them and take them up to my room to live with me. I also liked snakes.

But for every ounce of masculinity, of rough-and-tumble boyhood, there was an ounce of femininity. My gender was balanced tit for tat.

For every romping excursion in the woods, I equally wanted a glamorous tea party with some dolls. I loved coloring and doodling and sparkles and feathers. Arts and crafts were my favorite, and I would spend hours diligently decorating a Popsicle stick wreath or adding glitter poofs to a drawing for my mom to put on the refrigerator. I excelled at gymnastics and relished seeing how gracefully I could move my limbs. I loved to dance, to shake my body all over and feel the beat and move my hips and kick my legs and spin in circles. I loved fairies and witches and princesses and wizards alike. I wanted to wear pants and dresses, bow ties and skirts. I wanted Barbies and an Easy-Bake Oven to accompany my science kit and bug collection. And for most of my early childhood, the part that I struggle to remember, I had no shame about what I wanted.

The older I get, the crueler I feel memory has been to me. I had one period in my life where my gender did not come paired with shame and expectation, a brief window of three or four years that I can now hardly recall. I almost feel as if gender-based trauma is what activated my memory itself, because my ability to remember coincides almost perfectly with my inability to express my gender safely.

As an adult, I am attempting to revive that early part of my consciousness. I am attempting to resurrect the dead memories of this blissful period, Lazarus-like, from their crypt. I want them to have legs. I want them to walk again. I want them to dance. Some days, the good days, I feel that I am an archaeologist excavating a beautiful Pompeiian mosaic buried under volcanic ash. Other days, the hard days, I am both Eve and Adam, groping about in the wilderness, trying to get back to Eden. It will likely take the rest of my life to return to a gender that is free of shame. I will spend the rest of my life trying to resurrect who I was when I was four. But perhaps this is what we all do? Or at least, this is what we all *should* do.

The memories I have of my life pre-shame are scarce and beautiful. Back then, my two best friends were girls from my neighborhood, Katie and Paige. Katie lived in the house next door, and Paige lived up the road a bit. When I was very young, I could venture freely back and forth to Katie's house, but if I wanted to see Paige, I had to schedule a play date and be escorted by a parent.

Katie's and Paige's houses were my sanctuaries. There, playing one-on-one, I could just be a girl for a while. I didn't have to feign any masculinity that didn't feel natural. I didn't have to worry about my older brother's judgment or my parents' concern about what my femininity meant. With Paige and Katie, I could simply be. Playing dress up, playing house, playing with dolls. I didn't have shame about my gender and, equally important, Katie and Paige didn't, either. If anything, it made me cooler than other kids. The fact that I could gender shapeshift was sort of awesome. I had a "boy's body," sure, but I was at home being a girl, and at that age, Katie and Paige simply thought that was neat.

Katie's house was the most special, because her mom, Mrs. Bullock, could not have been more affirming and sweet toward my childhood femininity. Their whole house was a font of feminine energy, especially compared to my own.

In my house, I was inundated with a sedate sort of masculinity that came from the rest of my family.

There was my mom, who was pretty much a tomboy growing up—a virtue that would later bring us closer together. When I began to explore my gender in my young adult life, my mom innately understood on some level, because she, too, had been gender nonconforming when she was a kid. Even as an adult, my mother only wears lipstick to church, wears light blush and mascara on a daily basis, but *never* eyeliner, and would choose capris over a dress any day of her life.

Some of her favorite memories of her childhood came from running around with my grandfather doing "boyish" things. He taught her how to drive stick shift and how to mow the lawn. They'd throw a football around in the back yard before my mom ran off to play tackle football with the neighborhood boys. He'd drive her to the Dan River Mills Chemical Manufacturing Plant, where he was the manager, and let her skateboard around the plant with no helmet on.* One weekend, my grandfather took my mom to a fire tower; they climbed it and had a picnic together at the top. My mom's childhood was tomboy bliss until

---

* When I sent this manuscript to my high school Gay-Straight Alliance advisor, she was quick to note that *no one* wore helmets in the 1960s or 70s. So I guess this wasn't as badass as it sounds?

the age of twelve or thirteen, when my grandmother pulled her out of a baseball game to tell her about periods, about how she needed to stop roughhousing with the boys.

There was also my dad, who grew up in a Catholic Lebanese immigrant family of seven in Cleveland, Ohio. As a young man, he worked at the Ford factory during the summers alongside my grandfather, until he got his dual PhD in toxicology and pharmacology. This gave him a combination of nerdy masculinity (in the science-PhD way) and grumpy masculinity (in the repressed-Midwestern-Catholic way).

He, too, had a few gender nonconforming attributes, ones that I've only come to appreciate later in life. When I was a child, my dad was often the one who did the laundry, bathed us, made us dinner, cleaned the house, cut our nails, and did so many of the other myriad details that are usually relegated solely to mothers. My mom did those things, too, but from the outset, my parents had a very gender-equal partnership when it came to managing the household; something that shouldn't be taken for granted in early 1990s suburban North Carolina. It was unusual enough that some of our neighbors even poked fun at my dad for doing what was understood at the time as "women's work." When they did, he'd just shrug his shoulders and keep doing what needed to be done. He didn't relate to the work as feminine *per se*—they were just tasks that had to be taken care of—but he almost completely rebuffed the idea that a man shouldn't do housework, and that put him way ahead of the pack. In the words of one of my neighbors: "he didn't give a fuck who thought it was 'weird'!"

And then there was my brother, Matt, who was three years older and a typical antiauthority guitar-playing skater type from an early age. When we played with LEGOs together, I would build castles and spaceships, and he would build spaceships and race cars. We agreed on spaceships.

This mundane, practical masculinity was reflected in every aspect of our house, from the less-than-cute interior decorating to the pragmatism of our clothing. I don't begrudge the fact that our house wasn't immaculately decorated or that our shirts weren't always on trend—if anything,

I think it's awesome that my mom and dad didn't care too much about aesthetics, especially my mom. She grew up in Virginia in a generation where women were expected (or really *obligated*) to beautify the home and beautify the self, and I love that she rejected that imperative and focused on other things. I've always admired that about her, though she'll likely be embarrassed that I wrote about it in a book.

But the relatively quotidian furnishings and masculine energy of my house combined to make the Bullocks' house totally enchanting. Mrs. Bullock is about as feminine as they come. She applied full makeup almost every day, had her hair done regularly, and wore dresses and heels and jewelry that my mother wouldn't even have tried on for fun. And unlike my house, the Bullocks' was dominated by feminine energy that poured from Katie, her older sister, Betsy, and Mrs. Bullock herself, outshining Mr. Bullock. Where our house was plain, the Bullocks' was well decorated. Where our house was practical, theirs was tasteful. Where our house was masculine, theirs was perfectly femme.

For a feminine child like me, the Bullocks' house was a sanctuary and a laboratory folded into one.

Mrs. Bullock was in an ideal position to encourage and comfort me. She was like a cool aunt who would let me eat all the candy I desired and then send me home without having to deal with the short-term sugar high or long-term health consequences. I could be as feminine as I wanted at her house, and she was totally fine with it because she didn't feel the same pressure my parents felt to ensure that I was a "normal boy." She affirmed my femininity in the simplest of ways: She let me do what I wanted. If I wanted to put on a tutu, I did. If I wanted to put on makeup, I did. If I wanted to decorate cookies with bright pink sprinkles, I did. If I wanted to wear her shoes, I could (as long as I didn't try to walk up and down the stairs in them).

In many ways, Katie and Paige were the sisters I never had. If I'd had an older sister instead of an older brother, maybe I would've figured things out a bit earlier. I would've had ready access to jewelry and dolls and bright colors and someone whose hair I could braid. But I also would've been a demon little sibling to any older sister, because you know I would've stolen her stuff constantly. I would've been that little sibling who, when their sister got a new dress, would've snuck into her room, put it on, and run around the neighborhood in it before she had the chance to wear it first. I would've been that little sibling who stole her makeup and then claimed it "just disappeared" or that she'd "left it at the neighbors' house" or something. It's probably good that I didn't have an older sister, because I would've been a monster. Well, *more* of a monster.

The freedom I got from Mrs. Bullock was a freedom my parents didn't know how to give me. From the time I was about five, my parents began to feel real pressure to teach me the rules. They were never abusive or violent or unkind about it, but I was a smart, more-emotionally-intelligent-than-average kid, so they didn't have to be. All it took to curtail my feminine behavior was the slightest look of disappointment when I reached for the "wrong" item of clothing in the dress-up bin, or the subtlest hesitancy when I asked if I could get another Barbie set for Christmas. The smallest gestures and emotions became significant currency. As soon as I was old enough to perceive gender policing, I began to abide by what it told me to do.

When I enrolled in preschool, things got worse. While my parents policed my gender gently, my peers at school were ruthless. If I insisted on coloring in a picture of a fairy or a pony, the boys and girls alike would glare. If I appeared too interested in the girls' dress-up bin, I would be met with looks of disapprobation.

By the time I was six, Mrs. Bullock's house went from being *one* of the places I could safely express my femininity to being *the only* place I could. But this, too, would not last.

When my older brother started elementary school, things changed radically for me. In elementary school, children take the task of gender policing upon themselves. In an environment of increasing independence, first and second graders use gender as a primary tool of establishing social power and position. Children who conform to masculinity or femininity, who excel at "being boys" or "being girls," are granted social status, and those who can't or won't perform their gender roles correctly are immediately ostracized. Across the board, from teachers and principals to pop culture and TV shows, this behavior is not only permitted, but *encouraged*. Gender, matched only by ethnicity, body type, and family income, incites bullying, and becomes the primary indicator of who belongs and who is an outcast.

When my brother learned this behavior, he brought it home with him, and my life became hell. All of a sudden, boys and girls were radically different people. All of a sudden, who I was was not okay. All of a sudden, in my own home, I went from being a person to being a *sissy*.

Sissy was the first gender identity I ever really had. It was the first word that was ever applied to my difference. Before *gay*, before *transgender*, before *genderqueer* or *nonbinary* or *gender nonconforming* or *GNC*, *sissy* was the first word the world ever gave me. And it was imparted to me with such shame. A scarlet letter. My cross to bear.

The moment this label was placed on me, it burned. My brother, along with the rest of the kids in my neighborhood, my teachers, my preschool classmates, and my parents, began bullying me for my femininity. Along with other boys from the neighborhood, he reiterated over and over again that it was not okay for me to be friends with girls, that hanging out with girls made me liable to get cooties, that spending time with girls was grounds for social isolation and reproach.

My brother and his friends communicated this message in a number of ways. They would mock me for my mannerisms, for the way I spoke, for the way I held my wrists or moved my body as I walked. They would mock me for skipping or dancing or being too nice or coloring too well or sitting in the incorrect position or singing too loudly in choir. Once I'd been marked as a sissy, everything was fair game. My every behavior, every mannerism, every inclination was put under a public microscope, available to all for interrogation and inspection.

My mom wasn't stupid. She could plainly see what was happening. She could see that the water around me was beginning to heat up, that it'd soon be boiling. She knew the world was becoming increasingly hostile to her effeminate, sensitive, creative son. And she, like every parent of a gender nonconforming child, faced a horrible choice: She had to choose between affirming me and keeping me safe from harm.

While this choice was made iteratively, almost daily, my strongest memory of it is from Halloween 1997, when I was six years old.

Like every Halloween, my mom took me to the Toys"R"Us* near our house to pick out a costume. As I stared down the wall of costumes, which was easily three times taller than me and over forty feet long, I felt a little out to sea. Spread around me were countless identities, ideas, possibilities-of-self to experiment with for one night only. I could be a princess surveying my realm, a firefighter facing down an inferno, a scientist exploring outer space, or I could be something stupid like a pumpkin or a ladybug or whatever.

I mean, no offense, but why do children go as pumpkins for Halloween? It's such a Hufflepuff choice, not to mention a pretty arbitrary vegetable. You get *one night* to be as extravagant as you'd like, as daring as you want, and something compels certain children to say, "I wanna be a *gourd*. That's just *who I am*."

It's not that children shouldn't dress up as vegetables. I'm a vegetarian and I love vegetables, so obviously I think that children dressed as vegetables are adorable. It's just that I believe children should be able to dress up as vegetables *any day* they want to; they shouldn't have to waste

---

* Rest in peace, Toys"R"Us. ☹

their precious, once-a-year Halloween costume on it. Parents should just be able to say, "Okay, it's Tuesday. You know what that means, Stephanie? Time to dress up like your favorite item from the produce aisle!" Stephanie shouldn't have to wait until Halloween for that. Stephanie should get to dress up like a tomato any day she damn well pleases. Anyway.

As I stood there, facing the great wall of identities offered by Toys"R"Us, one costume stuck out to me above all others: I wanted to be Pocahontas more than anything in the world.

Now, let me preface this story with the following: If you think that I am *in any way* endorsing cultural appropriation by writing this, you should just stop reading. I swear to Goddess,* if I hear about *any one of you* reading this passage and deciding, "Okay, yeah, great, the moral of this story is that Jacob thinks it's awesome for white people to dress up as Native Americans for Halloween, so I'm gonna go do that," I will use the power of the internet to find out where you live and throw so many eggs at your house that it becomes a giant omelet. Or if you're vegan, I will throw *so much tofu* at your house that it becomes a giant *tofu scramble.* The point of this passage is *not* that white people should dress their children as Native Americans for Halloween. That's basically the opposite of the point here. *Capisce?*

All that being said, it was 1997. I was six years old and hadn't quite developed my political consciousness about cultural appropriation or the colonization of the Americas and subsequent genocide of Native American people at the hands of white settlers yet. I also didn't know *multiplication,* so I had some stuff to work on.

What I *did* know was that Pocahontas was, by far, the most badass Disney princess. Keep in mind that Disney's transgender-butch-lesbian

---

* God is a woman, by the way. Likely a transgender woman of color, according to contemporary biblical scholars (i.e., me, my friends, and Ariana Grande).

masterpiece *Mulan* wasn't released until a year later, or else I would've obviously gone with that (equally problematic) costume.

The similarities between who Pocahontas was and who I saw myself as were uncanny. She wore dresses. I wanted to wear dresses. She loved running around in the woods and singing. I loved running around in the woods and singing. She talked to trees. I *also* talked to trees.

So in that toy store aisle, I took a deep breath and conjured up all the courage I could muster. The inevitable question was posed by my mom: "So, who do you want to be for Halloween this year?"

I paused, turned to her, and managed to squeak out, "Pocahontas, maybe?"

The silence was deafening. You know when you tell someone you're in love with them, and within two nanoseconds, before they can even utter a word, you know they don't reciprocate? This was like that. I knew, from the moment the words left my lips, that it wasn't going to happen.

My mom paused and let out a deep sigh as her gears turned. How could she explain to me what I needed to know? How could she tell me what I needed to hear?

If we'd grown up in a different world, in a more perfect universe, in an alternate, less racist, less misogynistic reality, perhaps that would've been the moment when she would pause, collect her thoughts, and cautiously say what needed to be said: "I know you are more feminine than the other boys. I know you love dresses and flowers and playing with your grandmother's jewelry. And I love that about you. There is absolutely nothing wrong with who you are, and I will support you no matter what. But I also want to help you understand the world you're growing up in. You are growing up in a world where many people—your brother, your father, your classmates, your peers, random strangers on the street, you name it—are going to be hostile toward you because of your femininity. People are going to spend most of your life making you feel less than. Knowing that, I want to help you make an informed decision. Would you rather go as a more socially acceptable costume, like a pumpkin or some equally stupid vegetable, thereby avoiding the torment of your peers? Or are you ready to put on a dress and bravely face the world? Whatever you choose, I will support you and love you and hug you when it feels like too much. Okay?"*

But in our universe, instead of saying all that, she simply turned to me with a quiet look of concern and sheepishly asked, "What about going as a boy character from the movie?"

If we lived in a better world, I would've turned to her and replied, "Really, Jane? Are you *serious* right now? You want me to go as John Smith, the asshole colonizer? I mean, I *know* the Disney version of the movie makes his ethical position sort of 'debatable' or whatever, but we all know that is some propaganda bullshit. Are you *seriously* suggesting I walk around the neighborhood dressed as a genocide-perpetrating white dude?"

We didn't live in that world. So, defeated, I turned to her and simply said, "Okay. But I want to go as another boy from the movie, not John Smith."

Looking back on that Halloween, I missed the mark. If I'd known then what I know now, the solution would've been obvious: I should've just gone as Grandmother Willow.

She doesn't *have* a gender. She's a tree.

Later that year, my maternal grandfather passed away from complications from a brain tumor. His death was expected, but still felt sudden

---

* In a more perfect world, that would've *also* been the moment when she'd say, "Look, honey, I know you resonate with the character of Pocahontas, but we already live on stolen land and you are not an indigenous person, so it would be very insensitive for you to wear someone else's culture as a costume."

"Certainly, Mother," I'd respond. "You're absolutely correct. My teacher taught us about the land theft and subsequent genocide of Native American nations in kindergarten last week as part of our People's Herstory class, so I shouldn't go as Pocahontas. But could I go as another Disney princess instead?"

for my parents when it happened. My parents decided I was too young to attend the funeral, so instead of traveling to Danville, Virginia, I went next door to stay with the Bullocks.

When they explained to me what was happening, I was off-the-walls excited. Yes, I was sad my grandfather had passed away, and I was going to miss seeing him, but at that age, the idea of death didn't feel too real yet. What *did* feel real was the idea of *a two-day sleepover at the Bullocks'—with girls!!!* In kindergarten, "no sleepovers with boys and girls" was ground zero of the gender binary. It was, far and above everything else, the most important rule. And I was breaking it!

Though I was just going next door and the Bullocks had a key to our house, my parents insisted I pack a few basics so I wouldn't have to run back and forth to grab things. The juxtaposition between my mother's grief and my giddiness must've been striking. I did my best to rein in my giggles and jitters, but a rambunctious child can only do so much to contain their excitement.

My parents walked me next door, rang the doorbell, and shared a somber hug with Mrs. Bullock before she took me inside.

To this very day, it was the best staycation I've ever had. Though I didn't really understand what was happening in the existential terms of our fragile human mortality, Mrs. Bullock assumed I was devastated. She did her utmost to cheer me up, which basically meant I got to queen out for two whole days. Katie and I played dress up ad nauseam, we played with Barbies for *hours*, and I didn't have to look over my shoulder, anxious that my parents would walk in at any moment. We slept in the same room and got to giggle and have movie marathons and do all the fun things girls did together when they had sleepovers on TV shows. We even took a bubble bath together (with our bathing suits on, of course), and Mrs. Bullock let me *paint my nails*. I got to wear blue nail polish for twenty-four whole hours before Mrs. Bullock took it off to send me home. She knew my dad would be less than thrilled if I showed up back at the house like that.

What was so radical about the sleepover was that it totally went against the grain of everything else I was learning in my life at that time. Everywhere else, the messages I was receiving were all about how girls and boys were different and couldn't be left alone together. About how girls and boys had different "parts" and needed to be kept separate. About how boys were one thing and girls were another thing entirely. About how men and women needed to act differently because that's what everyone said. Everything was about difference, and the more easily you could discern and perform your given role, the more praise, affirmation, and love you received from the world.

Chief among this (mis)education was a fixation on the body. Male and female bodies were euphemized to the extent of comedy. Because the words *penis* and *vagina* were deemed too "mature," I was instead taught to say "wee-wee" or "pee-pee," which, when I think back on it, have low-key radical potential, because the terms were gender neutral. Boys had pee-pees, girls had pee-pees, boys went wee-wee, girls went wee-wee: It was all the same, shrouded in the language of body shame.

In practice, however, the terms were not used radically. Instead, it was made very clear to me that girls' pee-pees and boys' pee-pees were *very* different, but that difference was never properly explained. As a kid, I wasn't shown diagrams of a boy's pee-pee and a girl's pee-pee, and I was chastised for asking about it—something I did with some frequency.

Because I was an implacably curious child, I was perplexed by the difference between girls' pee-pees and boys' pee-pees. At that age, I made a very natural assumption: The physical difference would explain everything. The difference in our pee-pees would explain why boys and girls *had* to act differently. If I could simply compare the two, I might figure out their alchemy, and all this "act like a boy" gender stuff might finally start to make sense.

When I look back on it, I realize that the way I was taught about genitalia was akin to learning mythology. Through its magical, determinative power, my pee-pee explained everything that I had to be. The mystical, *other* type of pee-pee explained why I couldn't play with Barbies or like the color pink. Genitals had the ability to tell us everything about who we were, about how we should function in the world. They determined the future.

I hoped that, some day, I would figure out what the fuss was all about. I thought that if I could just see a girl's pee-pee, and maybe another boy's pee-pee, I would be able to understand everything about how gender worked.

I got my chance to bridge this mystical divide at one of my brother's baseball games. Baseball games were generally the worst. I hated going to them more than anything in the whole world. Playing in them was humiliating, because I was awful at baseball, but I would've taken that humiliation over the boredom of watching my brother's team play any day.

There was one baseball field that wasn't so bad, because it had a playground nearby where the younger siblings could congregate while our older siblings smashed things with bats, caught balls, threw the bases around, scored innings, danced in the outfield, and did whatever else you were supposed to do during a game of baseball.

One day, shortly before my seventh birthday, I ran off with two other little siblings—Maddie and Ian—to go play. After a few minutes of swinging from the monkey bars, going down the slide, and sitting atop the jungle gym, we were already bored. To pass the time, we got to talking. Out of the blue, Maddie brought it up.

"My parents say that boys' pee-pees are different than girls' pee-pees," Maddie blurted out.

"Duh. Everyone knows that," I responded, matter-of-factly. I didn't like it when other kids implied that they were smarter than me.

"Yeah, I know everyone knows that!" Maddie didn't like it when other kids implied they were smarter than her, either.

Ian corroborated. "Yeah, I heard that, too."

"Have y'all ever, I dunno, seen what the other kind of pee-pee looks like?" I inquired.

"Yeah, I saw my dad's once on accident when he was getting out of the shower," Maddie bragged, cavalier. "My mom's, too. They're pretty different. Boys' hang down and are funny looking, girls' are a lot smaller and prettier."

"That's interesting," Ian commented.

"Huh," I added.

There was an awkward pause after that. We stood there uncomfortably, but I think we all knew where things were heading. Maddie, who was a year older, finally had the courage to say what we were all thinking.

"I'll show you my pee-pee if you two show me yours."

"Ew, gross!" said Ian. He was trying to ruin this.

"I don't think it's gross," I said. "We could just show each other for a second. And no touching!"

"Won't we get in trouble?" Ian was such a wet towel.

"Not if you don't tell anybody, stupid!" (Maddie for the win.) "You don't have to if you don't want to, Ian, but Jacob and I are gonna go do it."

Maddie and I exited the jungle gym and went over to a nearby tree. Ian squirmed for a moment, but ultimately felt too left out not to join. We circled around the tree, looking over our shoulders to make sure that no parents were walking over.

Maddie took the reins, because Ian and I were too nervous. "On the count of three, we drop our pants for three seconds, okay?"

"Okay."

This was it.

"One."

I was finally going to figure out why boys and girls were so different.

"Two."

This was going to explain *everything.*

"Three."

We dropped our pants. For three brief seconds, we looked around, then pulled our pants back up.

I could not have been more disappointed by what I saw. For all the weight adults seemed to give them, our bodies were nothing fascinating. We all just kinda had some skin and some other stuff down there. Ian and I looked more similar, I guessed, but Maddie didn't look all *that* different. It was still skin and stuff. I don't know what I'd been expecting to see, but I'd thought that looking at a girl's pee-pee for the first time would be like Adam and Eve eating the apple. I had imagined that this whole "being a boy" thing would finally make sense, that the difference between who I was and who girls were would feel somehow justified.

Instead, I was more confused than ever. If our bodies were supposedly so different, if we were supposedly so opposite, why wasn't it more dramatic? Why didn't Maddie have, like, some kind of magical portal down there? Or something shiny and crazy? Or tentacles or a claw or pincers or dragon fangs or wings or something cool like that? It was just a bunch of skin!

I felt ripped off. I realized, for the first time, that sometimes adults just make stuff up when they don't know how to explain what's really going on. I'd seen a girl's pee-pee, but I was livid that it didn't *explain* more. Like any good scientist, I left my successful experiment with more questions than answers. If boys and girls didn't look all that different, then why did people seem so insistent that we *act* differently?

To top it all off, our moms were yelling: Apparently, we had to go back to watching our brothers' stupid baseball game.

This newfound knowledge didn't help to ease the masculine expectations placed on me. If anything, it made them feel like even more of a burden. Ignorance was bliss, and unfortunately, I was no longer ignorant.

By the time I was in second grade, the bullying had gotten pretty bad, and the only way I made it through was by being the teacher's pet. In elementary school, my teachers (who were all women) played a vital role in supporting and nurturing me, in recognizing my femininity—the fact that I was a gentle, sweet, creative, artistic, kind little kid, as opposed to a raging ball of aggression like most boys—and affirming it. My second-grade teacher and I were so close that she invited me to attend her wedding the year after I was in her class. I was a dream to teach because, in addition to being bright, I was desperate for my teachers' affection and support—affection and support I couldn't get from my peers.

But by the summer after second grade, the bullying went from being quiet, surreptitious stuff to being overt, ruthless, and cruel. As my brother prepared to start middle school, his hormones were picking up, and he was becoming more and more aggressive in his masculinity. So were his friends at school and the other kids in the neighborhood.

Growing up, I'd managed to come into ownership of a grand total of one Barbie. I knew it was dangerous to have, that I would be *done for* if word got out in the neighborhood. So I did my best to keep it hidden from my brother and the other kids. I only played with it when I knew I could be alone, when the door was closed and no one was watching.

One day, when I came back inside from playing in the woods behind my house, I heard peals of laughter coming from upstairs. Unknowingly, I went to see what was so funny. When I got to the top of the stairs and looked in the playroom, I was horrified. In my brother's hands was my Barbie.

"Look what *we* found," they taunted. "Oh, and we gave her a little haircut." I looked at her head, and to my horror, her long blond hair was almost entirely gone, cut and pulled out in reckless chunks.

The gates of hell opened, transforming me into a demon. I charged toward my brother, screaming.

"GIVE IT BACK! GIVE HER BACK!"

I grabbed at my toy and managed to get a grip on it, but was disarmed by a swift jab to the stomach. I recoiled in pain and lunged again, but my brother and the other boys dodged out into the hallway.

"You want your Barbie back, Jacob?" they teased.

I stormed out of the playroom; it quickly became a game of keepaway. The boys took over while my brother snuck off to the bathroom. He came back holding a container of floss high over his head. "Give me the Barbie," he commanded.

By then, I was too exhausted to fight. I'd given up, and try as I might to stop the tears, I'd started to cry. The only thing worse than being a boy who played with Barbies was being a boy who *cried because of his Barbie*. I knew I had to get out of there before I broke into full-on sobs. I ran out of the house and hid under the deck, where I could finally let out what I was feeling.

A few minutes later, I came back in with my game face on. I couldn't let them know they'd gotten to me. Walking up the stairs, to my horror, I saw that they'd wrapped a piece of floss around my Barbie's neck and hung her from the banister—a brutalized effigy of my femininity. I wanted to cry all over again, but I knew that they were likely hiding around a corner, waiting to ambush me with more taunts when I reacted with weakness.

So I didn't react. I didn't even finish walking up the stairs. At the age of seven, I simply turned around, walked calmly back downstairs, fetched a pair of scissors, cut my mutilated Barbie free, took her back to my room, and locked the door behind me.

I tried not to tell my parents about it; the only thing worse than being a sissy was being a sissy *and* a tattletale. But at that age, I was shit at containing my emotions. Later that day, my mom asked me what was wrong, and the truth burst out of me before I could stop it.

"Matt destroyed my Barbie," I croaked, eyes welling up, shame and devastation rearing their heads in equal part.

"He *what?*"

"He cut off her hair and then his friends hung her from the banister." The tears finally broke.

"He *what?*" she fumed, in shock.

We walked up to my room together, grabbing my Barbie from under the bed. All tattered, chopped hair and deformed plastic, she looked terrible.

"Oh, sweetie," my mom cooed, holding me, "I'm so sorry. I'll be right back."

My mom stormed into the other room. I couldn't hear the precise verbiage of the dressing-down she gave my brother, but my mom doesn't yell very much, so the fact that I could hear her voice booming through the walls at all meant that my brother was in deep shit. I cradled my Barbie, her dented face gazing back at me.

A few minutes later, my mom came back with my brother in tow.

"Matt has something he'd like to say to you, right, Matthew?"

"I'm sorry," my brother grumbled, lackluster and embarrassed.

"And?"

"And," he mumbled begrudgingly, "I have to go with you to the store to help you pick out a new one."

In a world that delivers very little justice for gender nonconforming kids, *that felt good.*

Unfortunately, even after my brother shopped with me, the bullying and public shaming didn't relent. After they targeted my toys, my brother and the boys in my neighborhood began going after the fact that I was friends with girls. They went from making subtle jokes about it to aggressively making fun of my friendships. Ironically enough, they would make fun of me by suggesting I had crushes on the girls I hung out with. It was cruel because it was so obviously not the case.

Oh, where are you going Jacob? To hang out with your girlfriend *Paige?*

Are you in love *with her? You must be, because you hang out with her so much. Do you want to* kiss *her? Or are you hanging out with her because you're a girl, too?*

It was relentless. Each time I hung out with Paige or Katie, I had hell to pay. In the beginning, I tried to resist their taunts, thinking that if I could just ignore them, they might go away. They didn't.

Jacob and Katie sitting in a tree, K-I-S-S-I-N-G. First comes love, then comes marriage, then comes the baby in the baby carriage.

Oh, Jacob, you still like coloring books? You're such a girly girl.

You don't want to play football? What are you, a sissy? Oh yeah, you are.

Why do you like crafts so much? Only sissies know how to braid.

As summer progressed, things just got worse. This time my brother's friends at the YMCA summer program were to blame. When they saw my brother's attitude toward me, saw that I was already vulnerable, they began piling it on. I became pretty much the sole target of the fifth-grade boys. The taunting was endless.

One week, they targeted my shorts. At that point in my life, I preferred wearing running shorts—the kind that hit you mid-thigh—instead of basketball shorts—the kind that went over the knee. It felt like one of the few feminine things I could get away with. Maybe I couldn't wear skirts, but at least I could wear cute shorts. I walked onto the bus one day and they started singing, in front of everyone:

> *Who wears short shorts?*
> *Jacob wears short shorts!*
> *Who wears short shorts?*
> *Jacob wears short shorts!*

I lashed out, yelling at them to shut up, to stop it, but the more I protested, the more vicious they became.

Oh, look at those legs!

Damn, Jacob!

Wow, they're so short.

Yeah, they almost look like girls' shorts, y'know?

When I realized that fighting back only made it worse, I crawled to the back of the bus, sat down, pulled my knees to my chest, and burned with equal parts anger and shame.

The next week, it was no longer my shorts that were the issue—it was my body. My brother's friend Joseph led the charge on that one, originating the taunt that would haunt me for the rest of the break.

One day on the playground he walked over to me, looked me up and down, and said, "Jacob, your belly is getting awfully big. Are you *pregnant*?!"

I froze.

I had a little potbelly as a kid. It's just how my body was naturally shaped at the time. I still kind of have one, if you look closely, but I know how to dress around it more effectively now.

"How many months are you? You look like you're going to pop any day now!" He reached for my stomach. "Can you feel the baby kick, Jacob?"

I lunged backward, smacking his hand off my stomach. I was molten lava.

"SHUT UP, JOSEPH!" I screamed at the top of my lungs. "JUST SHUT UP!"

By then, the entire group was watching.

He rubbed it in. "Oh, sorry, I know how cranky girls get when they're *pregnant*."

That was it. I hurtled forward, fists at the ready. When I was about to get to him, I had a brief moment of doubt. What would happen to me if I actually punched him? I was in karate, sure, but could I really punch a *fifth grader*?

The moment of doubt cost me my hit. Joseph extended his arm, caught me on the top of the head, and began pushing me backward as I flailed my arms, desperately trying to land something. I lunged forward one or two more times, but it was no use. I backed off and Joseph stood there, a smug twinkle in his eyes. I'd done exactly what he'd wanted. I'd taken the bait. I'd let him get to me. I'd lost my cool, and he looked that much stronger for it.

Why no one ever intervened to help me, I'll never quite know. Why none of the counselors noticed that I was being brutalized, I can't quite say. During my adolescence, adults never seemed to help me. They never seemed to care. Something about the "boys will be boys" mentality, I guess.

That day, I decided I would never lose my cool to a bully again. I decided I'd have to find another strategy to overcome them. So, for the rest of the summer, I just took it. I let them say whatever they wanted to. I became stone, went spiritually comatose, let go of the idea that I deserved to be happy.

Third grade was the year that everything snapped. I'd decided that enough bullying was enough, and if I couldn't be myself without being tormented, I'd simply be no one. I voluntarily cut off my friendships with Paige and Katie. I stopped wearing the cute shorts I loved. I stopped being vocal or outspoken around the neighborhood kids. I stopped spending time with kids my own age almost altogether. I played video games with my neighbors every now and then, but I remember spending day after day reading alone in my room or longingly watching the other kids bike up and down our road.

To top it off, that year I lost the consistent kindness of having a good teacher. My third-grade teacher was mean, addicted to Diet Coke, and the proponent of a tough-love strategy that was wholly inappropriate for dealing with third graders. Where I needed a kind mentor, I received a stony disciplinarian. Where I needed affirmation, I received criticism. Where I needed warmth, I received only ice.

I wish that I had some poignant story about the moment I officially gave up on being feminine, about the moment I gave up on feeling happy in my skin, about the instant when I decided that the shame of being gender nonconforming was finally too much, but I don't think gender works like that.

When I was a kid, I didn't know how to handle all the anger I felt toward the world. Whenever I got really angry, when my emotions got intense enough, I didn't punch somebody or take it out on other kids. Instead, I directed my anger inward. I destroyed things I loved, things I'd made. One day, my mom made me so mad, I went straight up to her room, took a clay pot I'd made for her in art class, and smashed it to smithereens. Another time, I got so mad that I ripped all my favorite drawings from my sketchbook and tore them to shreds. I had nowhere to turn my anger, so I turned my anger on myself. Self-destruction was the only coping strategy I knew, the only one that didn't seem to get me in trouble.

I want to acknowledge that I'm breaking my promise not to make this book too heavy. I'm going to go a page or two without cracking a joke. I don't mean for this to be unduly grave, but it's the only way I know to honor this time in my life.

Because self-destruction was the only coping mechanism that made sense to me at the time, at the age of eight, I often thought about killing myself. And I'm not talking abstractly. I'm talking vivid fantasies of suicide; fantasies that I never told my parents about; fantasies that I never told *anyone* about until I sat down to write this book.

When I was pushed to the brink of loneliness and gender agony as a third grader, when I didn't know how to communicate with the adults in my life about what was going on, I channeled my anger at my own body, my own existence. When the world made who I was feel impossible, I began to see my own body as an impossibility. For years of my life, I told myself this was normal. That kids just thought about killing themselves sometimes. That every third grader had experienced that. In order to move on with my life, I had to normalize it. *And besides*, I told myself, *it's not like I ever really tried anything.*

While it's true that I didn't make a real suicide attempt at that age, I am horrified by the memories that come back to me. I remember lying in my childhood bedroom for hours, fantasizing about what it would feel like for a knife to enter my wrists. On the rare occasions that I was alone in the house, I remember pulling our biggest knife out of its holder and staring at it for a few minutes. I remember running a butter knife along my wrist, careful not to leave a mark, just to see if anything would happen, just to see how it felt, scratching my skin.

I'm not sharing this with you to be dramatic. I'm not sharing this with you to suggest my life has been the most difficult or that I've overcome the most adversity. I'm not sharing this with you because I feel this trauma is what makes my story matter or makes *my* trans experience any more important than anyone else's. I'm not even sharing this with you because I feel this experience makes my story unique. On the contrary: Contemplating suicide at a very early age isn't remarkable for a trans child. So many of us did.

I'm sharing this with you because I want the world to understand that depriving a child of the ability to express their gender authentically is life threatening. I'm sharing this with you because I want you to understand that gender policing is not some abstract, intellectual concept; it is a pattern of emotional abuse that came from every direction and singularly robbed me of my childhood. I'm sharing this with you because I want you to understand that telling a boy not to wear a dress is an act of spiritual murder. Most of all, I'm sharing this with you because it is true, and things that are true need to be said.

There is a fable about frogs that I remember hearing as a kid. If you toss a frog into a pot of boiling water, it will realize that it is in danger and immediately hop out. But if you put a frog in room-temperature water and heat the water gradually, bit by bit, the frog will stay docile, floating happily, scarcely realizing it's being boiled alive until it's too late.

The desecration of my gender worked something like that. If my gender had been taken from me all at once, I would've fought for it. I would've screamed and shouted and stamped my feet. I would've hopped out of the boiling water. But it was taken from me so slowly, pried from my adolescent hands so gradually by so many different people that I didn't even notice the water around me becoming lethal.

One day I was swimming happily. The next, my identity was boiled alive.

It may surprise you completely, or it may not surprise you at all, but at the darkest time in my childhood, church was my saving grace. My church was the only institution that got me through it all; it was the only community where I continued to find affirmation in the darkness of my dysphoria. Other than my mother's arms, it was the only place where I felt unequivocally and unconditionally loved.

Chapter 2

Nerds and Wizards and Jesus, Oh My!

*T*oday, if you walked past a six-foot-tall cutie like me rocking five-inch-heeled black leather boots, dark purple lipstick, and a five o'clock shadow, your first reaction probably wouldn't be, "Well, *someone* loves Jesus!" Based on prevailing stereotypes about gender nonconforming people and Christianity, most folks probably wouldn't assume I'm a particularly "churchy" person.

Well, you're wrong. I am too a churchy person! Not, like, *too* churchy, but I get around. Like any good Christian, I go to church approximately two or three times a year: once on Christmas and any other time that I go home to North Carolina to visit my parents.

In my adult life, I'm a chilled-out, millennial-as-fuck Christian. You know the type: loosely believes in God, but tries not to use the label "agnostic" so they won't seem like an asshole; believes in the spiritual teachings of Jesus, but is unsure whether the whole "God impregnated Mary" thing makes sense; believes in the concept of the Holy Spirit, but believes equally strongly in the power of crystals. That type of millennial Christian.

I wasn't always mellowed out about it, though. My church was a primary community for me for the entirety of my young life, so much so that when I met queers in college who talked about their "chosen family" of people who were not biologically related to them, I was like, "Oh yeah, you mean your church family." St. Francis United Methodist Church was my first family of choice, filled with nonbiological aunties, awkward cousins, and adopted grandparents. They taught me important lessons about how to live in the world, how to love, who to be. Whether I like it or not, there are cute church songs, precious Bible stories, and little nuggets of good old-fashioned Christian shame scattered throughout the foundations of my life. And in my mid–elementary school years, when the rest of my world was filled with bullying, isolation, and damning silence, my church was one of the few places I could find affirmation.

St. Francis United Methodist Church is a midsize church in the burgeoning suburb of Cary, North Carolina. On a busy Sunday, there will be anywhere between two hundred and three hundred members gathered to worship, and on Christmas and Easter, double that number. The architecture says quite a bit about the progressive lilt of the church. The sanctuary is in the shape of a giant ring with an octagon in the center. Large, circular windows frame the North Carolina pines outside. Green carpeting and marble, golden brown oak, and interior courtyards give the sanctuary a warm, earthy vibe.

My earliest memories of church aren't of singing or preaching: They're of my butt falling asleep. Back when I was baptized, before we built the current sanctuary, we gathered for church service in what is now the church's multipurpose room. I don't remember too much about that space, other than the folding chairs. Back then, before Cary became the "it" suburb in North Carolina, we didn't have the luxury of pews.

Instead, we'd sit in metal folding chairs for the entire service. The chairs didn't have any padding, just a thin coat of white paint over cold metal.

After thirty minutes of sitting still on a metal folding chair, pins and needles were the only sensation I could feel. Everyone struggled with this. By the time the sermon was halfway done, our congregation was a sea of slowly shifting butts desperately attempting to avoid their fate. As a child, I thought this was just part of the whole Christianity deal: "We hurt our butts for Jesus." It was like we were trying to experience the pain of crucifixion or something. Our sore butts were part of our penance, part of atoning for our sins.

In those days, our church services ended not with a song, but with a chorus of loud clanging as each chair was folded and stored away. I also assumed this was a spiritual rite. Each week, we unfolded the chairs, we hurt our butts, we folded the chairs, and we put them back in the tomb. For a few days, they were dead to the world. But the next week, they were back again, Christ-like. A cycle of resurrection. A cycle of atonement. A cycle of cheap metal folding chairs.

When we built the new sanctuary and finally got pews, I was shocked. It wasn't the soaring, glorious wooden arches or gigantic circular windows that inspired me—it was the cushioned pews. Suddenly, I could worship Jesus without causing permanent nerve damage; suddenly, church was comfortable. It was a miracle. All glory to God in the highest. Hallelujah.

Church was my refuge, one of the few places where my sensitivity, my creativity, and my penchant for bigger questions and larger feelings were embraced. Those were all parts of myself that I had to silence at karate practice, in physical education class, and on the playground. But not at church. At church, my love of singing, my proclivity to ask too many questions, and my enthusiasm for arts and crafts were assets. Sure, I was being a little bit of a know-it-all in Sunday school, but I was a know-it-all for Jesus. Yes, I may have been queening out in the church musical, but I was queening out *for Jesus*, so it was fine.

I also really liked God, or at least the idea of God as he was presented to me, because God was a little bit of a queen, too.* I mean, think about it: He sits up in heaven on a gold-ass throne with a bunch of baroque naked babies flying around him and demands that you worship him and sing him lots of songs or else he will destroy your entire city and kill all your relatives. Talk about a diva. I mean, like, the Old Testament is pretty much just a litany of all the times God threw a diva tantrum in his dressing room because one of his fans coughed during his performance. He's like Naomi Campbell constantly throwing his phone at the paparazzi (by the way, I support you, Naomi).

And don't get me started on Jesus. I adored the idea of Jesus. If God is Beyoncé, then Jesus was Solange or Stevie Nicks or, perhaps, Bob Marley. He was a down-to-earth, gentle rebel who wore flowing robes and long, curly hair. He preached forgiveness and free love and hung out with prostitutes and hated the government and gave people free food and turned water into wine to liven up the party. He even had a weird stoner cousin, John the Baptist, who ate locusts and honey and lived in the woods, taking people on spiritual journeys in the local river. As a historical figure, Jesus was the best.

Despite how much I got along with God and Jesus, I had a complicated reputation in Sunday school. I haven't spoken to any of my former Sunday school teachers to verify this, but I'm fairly certain that I was a little shit. On one hand, I was the pompous teacher's pet. I knew all the answers, was skilled at reading aloud, and had a natural ability to bullshit when I wasn't quite sure what the teacher was asking. While my classmates were busy being sleepy and bored, convinced that Sunday school was a premonition of hell itself, I was perky, energized, and hungry for

---

* I know that I've already said that God is a trans woman, so I think it's worth clarifying: when God isn't busy being a woman, she can *also* take the form of a gay man, trans dude, or butch lesbian. God's genderfluid like that, praise be unto Her/Him/Them!

biblical knowledge that I could use to prove I was better than everyone else and gain favor with my parents.

On the other hand, I was a smart-ass with a budding intellect that I wholly dedicated to asking my Sunday school teachers very difficult questions. Questions like:

If God made everything in the whole world, why did He make people sin? Like, He could've just made us so that we'd be nice to each other, right?

On a related note, if God made the whole world and everything in it, then is God the one who set things up such that His only son had to die on the cross? That's kinda twisted. Why did God do that? I'm only seven and I still think Santa Claus is real, but that strikes me as kind of odd.

I've been praying for a new PlayStation for three solid weeks and it still hasn't happened yet. Are you sure God really answers our prayers?

God loves everyone and forgives everyone? Okay, then I don't understand why there's a use for hell. Hell must not exist.

Why did God make war? That wasn't very nice of Him. Also, why did God make homework? That wasn't nice of Him, either.

Mary was a virgin and God got her pregnant? What does virgin mean? How are babies made? Can God get ME pregnant?

Speaking of which, how do we know God is a Him? Does God have a pee-pee? Did one of the prophets see it or something?

I may have been a monster in Sunday school, but I was a star in choir—especially in my boy-soprano days. Like, I was good, okay? I was really good. I was so good that I had the starring role in an opera at my church when I was in fifth grade. The opera was called *Amahl and the Night Visitors* (which, it has only just occurred to me, sounds loosely like the title for a problematic Middle Eastern–themed porno. I can make that joke because my family on my dad's side is Lebanese). It's about a young boy named Amahl who used a crutch because he had a leg that didn't work. One night, the Three Kings show up unannounced at Amahl's house to crash for the night en route to visit the baby Jesus. They just show up. No letter. No call. No Airbnb reservation. They just knock on the door and are like, "Hey, we can sleep at your house, right?" to which Amahl's widowed mother just has to be like, "Okay, I guess, sure." The kings tell Amahl all about Jesus and how he loves everyone and is the king of the poor, and Amahl is so inspired that he offers to give the baby Jesus his most prized possession: his crutch. In the process of giving his crutch to the Three Kings, Amahl is (spoiler alert) magically healed by the love of Jesus and can walk again. So what do the Three Kings decide? They decide Amahl should go with them to meet the baby Jesus himself. And so the opera ends with Amahl's mother sending him off on a trip with three rich older men.

At the time, I didn't realize how good Amahl had it. Today, I would do anything—*anything*—to have three rich older men take me on a trip. Sigh.

Because being feminine as hell didn't set me up to endure enough bullying, I also joined my church's handbell choir. If there is one thing more homosexual than an opera about three older men taking a twinky guy on a vacation, it's a handbell choir. I played handbells through the entirety of my elementary, middle, and high school careers. To this day, handbell choir keeps me humble. Every time I go to a red carpet event in Los Angeles or a gallery opening in New York and start to feel arrogant about how cool I am, I simply remind myself that I played in a handbell choir and I'm cut right back down to size.

By third grade, that was pretty much it in terms of spaces where I could safely queen out: I had Sunday school, choir, and handbells. That comprised the entire dominion of my queenly reign. Pretty much everywhere else was hostile to my femininity.

There were a few exceptions to this rule, my grandmother's house being one of them. My grandmother on my mom's side was a classy, sweet, kind Southern woman who'd learned to live in a more open-minded way in the post–Jim Crow South. She wasn't perfect, but as far as old white Southern grandmas go, she was pretty dang sweet, and I loved her ceaselessly. Also, she wore geometric-print windbreakers from the 1980s well into the 2000s, which certainly didn't hurt. She held on to some of the pieces in her wardrobe long enough that they actually became *ahead of their time* again. I was always proud of her for that. If she were alive today, she would've *rocked* millennial pink.

Part of the love that I shared with my grandmother was based in the fact that she *adored* my sweetness, my kindness, my compassion, and my gentle manner. I don't know what exactly it was that enabled her to be so kind, affirming, and unrelenting in her support of my femininity, but I think it might have had something to do with being old enough not to give a fuck. Unlike many of the adults in my life, she never seemed worried about whether I was sufficiently manly. In fact, she would've been shocked and supremely disapproving if I'd ever lashed out in anger or been physically violent.

Where everyone else attempted to curtail or turn a blind eye to my femininity, my grandmother looked it in the face, unashamed and unintimidated. She never would've said it this way, but in my mind, I wasn't "Mom's little boy" or "Dad's little sport"—I was "Grandma's little sissy."

Weekends at Grandma's house consisted of all my favorite things. We'd run to the market to get fresh chicken salad and veggies, cook together, knit quietly, sip sweet tea, and play cards or Rummikub until about nine thirty p.m., which is when my grandma would fall asleep automatically, as if on autopilot, no matter where she was sitting. I would spend hours rifling through her jewelry collection and trying things on when she wasn't looking. When we got ready to go to church or to dinner, she'd let me help her pick out her earrings and brooches, and I'd always choose the ones with the sparkliest, biggest, gaudiest costume gems.

The most exciting trip I ever took to my grandmother's house was when I was seven, and we spent the whole weekend alone, just me and my grandma. No Dad or Mom to worry about, no annoying older brother to contend with, just us girls. I felt like I'd died and gone to heaven, or, more accurately, like I'd died and been transported into an episode of *The Golden Girls* (Note: Is there even a difference?). My grandma would play the character of Rose—sweet, funny, and warm, but oblivious to what was going on around her, notably the fact that her grandson was *obviously* a homosexual—and I would play Blanche, minus the sex but with Dorothy's wardrobe. No one would have to play Sophia because—call me a hypocrite or a blasphemer or edgy or whatever you like—she's my least favorite character.

During that trip, my grandmother and I had the best time. She taught me to memorize the Lord's Prayer, how to skip—which, shockingly, I'd never learned to do myself—and how to blow a bubble with gum. After that trip, I went from being an underinformed princess to being a fully equipped queen. I could now skip up to my enemies on the playground, blow a bubble in their face, insult them while smacking my gum, and, when they got angry at me, passive-aggressively remind them that "God forgives us our trespasses *as we forgive those who trespass against us, Susan.*" In reality, I probably couldn't have gotten away with that on the playground, but it was nice to know I could try.

My grandmother passed away before I had the opportunity to properly come out to her, but I find great reassurance when I think back on the time we spent together. *If she taught me how to skip and how to blow bubbles with chewing gum, she obviously wanted me to be a queen*, I tell myself. *There's no way she wouldn't be cool with this. She probably loves that I wear her earrings.* To this day, I still think of my grandmother whenever I skip through the streets of New York or through a parking lot in LA after a successful meeting with a producer. I also think of her every time I recite the Lord's Prayer, albeit my updated-for-the-feminist-matriarchal-twenty-first-century version:

Our MOTHER,
Who art in heaven,
Hallowed be thy name.
Thy QUEENdom come,
Thy will be done,
on Earth as it is in heaven.

While I appreciate my grandmother's unfazed support of my femininity as a child, I also blame her for some of my flaws. Namely, I blame her for my tacky fashion sense. To this day, many of my friends describe my fashion aesthetic as "Kinky 1980s Grandma," and I think a great deal of that has to do with the fact that my grandma was my fashion icon. Her chunky, brightly colored clip-on earrings, her love of sparkly brooches, her pastel-and-jewel-tone wardrobe, her windbreakers, the fact that she never bothered to cut out any of her shoulder pads, the way she effortlessly merged Jackie Kennedy class and early 1990s flair, all passed along to me. They're in my aesthetic DNA.

Some days, when I look in the mirror, I feel like I'm the spitting image of my grandmother; except that she was five foot three and I'm five foot thirteen, and I'm *significantly* hairier than she was. Also, my grandmother probably wouldn't have worn a leather dog collar as an accessory. But other than those things, we're basically the same person. If you think what I'm wearing on Instagram is tacky or outdated, you should think twice before leaving a mean comment. If you criticize my fashion sense, you're also making fun of *my grandma's* fashion sense. And honey, *you better not.*

After I gave up on expressing my femininity, my adolescent life became immeasurably easier. Once I'd accepted the rules, relinquished the idea that I deserved to express my gender in a way that felt authentic or natural to me, I was free to reemerge into the world of boys as a bona fide dude.

As a young dude at the dawn of the new millennium, the options were reassuringly limited. I had three: I could be a cool kid who played sports and wore preppy clothes, I could be a skater kid who drank Red Bull and wore baggy clothes, or I could go the classic route and just be a fucking nerd.

To me, the choice was obvious—organic, even. When I tried to learn how to skateboard, I hit an acorn, got thrown off, face-planted on the concrete, and started crying, so skater boy didn't seem particularly promising. And because I had glasses and braces and couldn't kick a football through a goalpost to save my life (in fact, I am *still* such a nerd, I just had to look up what a "goalpost" was called before I could write that last sentence—I Googled "big yellow football thing at the end of the field" to get the answer), neither jock nor prep seemed too promising, either.

In my eyes, nerds had it made. They proved themselves not with athletic prowess, but with knowledge about particle physics or the inner workings of trains or the capitals of obscure countries or the ability to recite pi to one hundred digits. Among the cool sports kids or the skater dudes, I would've been a B-rate member of the group, but among the nerds, I could be head of the pack.

Also, let's face it: What nerds lack in homoerotic locker room culture and late-night sexual experimentation, they make up for in the ability to be pretty queer on a daily basis. As a nerd, I could watch lots of gay-leaning stuff: shows about sparkly dragons, cartoons about fairies, anime with buff shirtless dudes screaming in ecstasy as they shot their giant laser beams at other dudes.

The Japanese cartoon *Dragon Ball Z* is a case in point. I'd venture to say it's the most homoerotic cartoon ever made, and I watched it *all the time* growing up. When Goku (the main character) would go "Super Saiyan" (his most powerful mode), he would grunt, scream, and moan as his muscles doubled in size—his veins throbbing across his *entire* body—and his hair slicked into a giant, electric, bleach-blond updo. Half the time, his muscles would get so *big* and *swollen* and *veiny* and *hard* that they would rip half his clothes off. Then, all blond and sweaty and powerful and rock-hard, Goku would fight with some other dude (or alien), who was *also* sweaty, powerful, rock-hard, bleach-blond, and throbbing. Honestly, *Dragon Ball Z* is so gay that even just *writing this paragraph* I got sorta turned on and had to suck on an ice cube to stop myself from going on Grindr. I could never have watched anything so homoerotic if I hadn't identified as a nerd.

Plus, nerds got *wizards*.

If Japanese homoerotic anime was the base of my queer nerd mountain, wizards were its zenith. All I ever wanted to be, all I *still* want to be, is a wizard. Not so much a wizard à la Harry Potter—though I'd take it—but more a wizard à la Merlin from Arthurian legend (y'know, the knights of the Round Table and whatnot) or Gandalf the Grey/White from the Lord of the Rings. I mean, can we take a second to talk about the impact that wizards had on my self-esteem and self-love? Or on my sexual fantasies? Because we're going to talk about both.

For whatever reason, we've decided as a Western culture that the only time a person assigned male at birth may dare to be effeminate is if they're magical. Gandalf the Grey is the best example. He is a weird outcast from most of society who runs around wearing flowy robes and recruiting his friends to help him destroy a *terrible, awful, simply atrocious* ring. He suspiciously has no sexual partners or desire to date women, loves crystals and sparkly magic, and carries around a long staff with a big ol' shiny rock on top.

So, being obviously feminine—and yet loved and adored and valued in the story—Gandalf already meant the world to me. Then he faced off with a Balrog (a giant fire monster) in Moria (this really evil part of Middle-earth), and fell into a fiery pit, never to be heard from again. *Sure, J. R. R. Tolkien, kill off the gay character, why don't you.*

But—surprise!—Gandalf comes back, and he's gayer than *ever*!!! Reborn through his struggle with the Balrog, he comes back as Gandalf the White. He now has shiny, flowing, gorgeous white silk robes in place of his tattered old gray ones, and a gorgeous platinum-blond hairstyle to boot. Not only that, but his staff is different, more powerful, elegant white metal replacing gnarled old wood. Literally, *he gets a makeover* to be *even more gay-slash-magical*, and it's one of the most dramatic and important parts of the whole book.

Growing up, wizards were the closest things I had to role models. Where other characters used the brute strength of their masculine bodies to vanquish their foes, wizards used their wit, their spirit, and their magic. They didn't need to be strong—they needed to be *dedicated*. They didn't need to be brutal—they needed to be *cunning*. Where others fought with their fists, wizards fought with their passion.

I started to realize that if being a nerd meant getting to read about wizards and talk about them with my friends, I could maybe make it through my childhood after all. When nowhere else in the world gave me positive messages about my femininity, Gandalf, Merlin, and, of course, Dumbledore, stepped in to save the day. They were my heroes. But more than that, they gave me a narrative of survival. All wizards were misunderstood as children. All wizards struggled to contend with their powers. All wizards had to go on a harrowing journey in order to find mentorship, support, and other people like them. And once they found that support, once they found a community that helped them learn to use their power for good, wizards were all-powerful.

If they could be unstoppable, I knew I could be, too.

Also, have you ever read any gay Harry Potter fan fiction? That stuff is sexy and *intense*.*

Unsurprisingly, my first successful friendship with another boy was with one just as nerdy as I was. His name was Nathaniel—he didn't go by Nathan, he went by *Nathaniel*—and we met as auspiciously as two nerds could expect to: at handbell practice. I recognized him from elementary school, but he was in a different class than me, so we'd never gotten to know each other until we bumped into each other at practice.

Nathaniel was a dream made in nerd heaven. He was the nerdiest boy I'd ever met. Some days, he even made *me* feel like the cool one. We would spend hours talking about the history of trains, and I learned very quickly that they were to be called *locomotives*, not *trains*. Apparently, the word *train* wasn't sophisticated enough for their sheer technical brilliance. If I ever tried to call them *trains*, Nathaniel would get angry with me and start yelling. Which is how I learned that, sometimes, the words we use to describe something can be really important to other people, even if the differences don't make that much sense to us, and that it's just easier to listen when people teach us how to talk about things that are important to them. (I'm assuming you get that this is a queer allegory by now, right?)

By the end of third grade, Nathaniel and I would spend our time together in nerd bliss. We'd build model locomotives, read books about science, and spend hours playing piano together. He'd play a song, I'd play a song, he'd play a piece that he was composing, I'd try to keep up.

---

* And my best friend Paige may or may not have written some herself in grade school/ throughout college.

He was a much better piano player than I was, but I was a much better singer, so we were even. He taught me how to play chess and lived to regret that decision, because I became a worthy adversary. He'd wanted a chess partner to beat, not a chess partner to legitimately compete against. Once, when I had him checked and was clearly going to win, he decided chess was no longer an interesting game.

"You know what? I'm bored. Chess is boring," he decreed. "Let's go play outside instead."

He considered it an incomplete game, but I recognized it for what it was: a forfeit. I was smug for the rest of the day.

We'd have sleepovers at his house or at my own, and because I didn't have a crush on him, they were just normal sleepovers. No sexual overtones, no romantic undertones, just the normal-ass tones of a great friendship. We'd stay up late at night talking about the theory of relativity and how if time was the fourth dimension, what could the fifth possibly be? We'd spend hours speculating on other universes, time travel, neutron stars, and the energy required to tear a hole in the space-time continuum.

Because of my friendship with Nathaniel, my nerdiness increased ten-fold and my queer escapism took on a more academic lilt. I was still into wizards, mind you, but *in addition* to wizards I became fixated on astronomy and Egyptology. Nathaniel thought both of these subjects were not only interesting, but cool.

Through focusing on ancient civilizations, I got a break from thinking about the present. Ancient Egyptians all seemed queer to me. Everyone, regardless of gender, got to wear gorgeous, thick, structured eyeliner and heavy lapis lazuli jewelry. Men and women alike were depicted in luxurious, flowing garments made of finely woven linen. Pharaohs were some of the original divas, demanding that they be buried with all their most beautiful possessions. I drank up every hieroglyph.

Astronomy provided a different comfort. Thinking about nebula that were millions of light-years away, I was able to get away from what was happening here on Earth. I loved looking at pictures of space. I'd spend hours reading through science books. I checked out every single book on space that my elementary school library had to offer.

Have you ever really taken a moment to look at photos of a nebula? The Hand of God, the Cat's Eye, the Ring? Each is captivating, each is stunningly beautiful. It brought me great comfort to know that floating above us in the night sky, far away from this planet, throughout the universe, there were shimmering clouds of glitter, rainbow constellations of gas, bursting with energy yet invisible to the naked eye. And that even if you can't *see* something, even if the sky appears to be black, there are infinite colors and shapes, beyond our wildest imagination, waiting to be discovered, waiting to reveal themselves to humankind.

At the end of fifth grade, Nathaniel's family moved to Austin, Texas. At one of the last sleepovers we had at his house, he went downstairs to work on something with his dad, and I was left alone upstairs for a few minutes. I looked to my left and noticed his sister Madeleine's Barbie collection sitting in a translucent plastic bin.

Listening carefully for any sign of Nathaniel, I cautiously took the lid off the bin to explore. In similar moments of surreptitious play, I would've reached immediately for the most ornate dress I could find and picked the most beautiful Barbie to put it on. But this time, when I opened the bin, something else caught my eye.

Sitting atop a mound of cheap sequined dresses and tiny plastic shoes was a totally naked Ken doll. I paused, captivated. Something deep within me churned; inexplicably, I was out of breath. I picked up the doll, slowly, carefully; I marveled at his complete nakedness, the muscularity of his arms, the gentle curvature of his butt. Ensconced in the safety of Nathaniel's playroom, I pried Ken's legs open, riveted by how his hips moved in their sockets. His chest was bare and muscular, his hair blond and coiffed.

There were feet on the stairs. Panicked, I threw Ken in the bin and put the lid back on, barely closing it in time before Nathaniel barged back into the room. Luckily for me, he was oblivious to what had just occurred. He sensed nothing of my sexual awakening.

I hadn't realized it yet, but my body was starting to change. Coursing in my veins, unannounced and unexplained, was a furious stream of hormones, an endless cascade of chemicals that would go on to alter almost every facet of how my body related to the world and, more important, how the world related to my body.

I spent the next three days puzzling over what my feelings meant. Overnight, I felt comparatively little interest in Barbie or her clothes. Where I'd spent so much of my childhood desperate to be able to dress Barbie up, a new desire had taken hold, one that supplanted my quest for sequins and tulle and ballerina skirts. My femininity and my gender issues took a back seat, because from there on out, it was about one thing and one thing only: *boys, boys, boys.*

Chapter 3

Inharmonious Hormones

*T*o say that I was an early bloomer is the understatement of the century. That metaphor just doesn't carry enough weight. I wasn't an early-blooming flower—I was a freak snowstorm in the middle of July. I was a twelve-day rainstorm in Los Angeles. I was so exceptional, so out of the ordinary, so singular in my ability to grow body hair, that I need a metaphor with more drama to describe myself.

It's almost as if my parents had set me up. First, my father is Arab American; my body's natural state is tan, fuzzy, and covered in olive oil. Second, because I had an August birthday, my parents started me in school a year later than normal. They knew I would either be one of the youngest in my class or one of the oldest, and they thought it was safer for me to be almost a full year older than many of my peers. I ask my mother about that decision to this day, convinced it had something to do with her knowing that I was super queer and wanting to be sure that if I was going to be so obviously homosexual, I could at least be older than the other kids as protection. She says that had nothing to do with it. When I ask her about it, she matter-of-factly says, "You were either going to be the oldest or the youngest, and we thought it'd be better for you to be oldest." I think there's more to the story. And if it wasn't my glaring queerness that inspired my parents to start me late, maybe it was because my mom loved having me around the house so much that she didn't want to let me go? That's probably it. That's what I'll tell myself.

Being older and having Middle Eastern roots was already a one-two puberty-punch. Add the fact that—surprise!—I'm trans, and the story becomes nothing short of comical. I have no choice but to have a sense of humor about the whole thing.

For many gender nonconforming and trans folks, puberty feels like a death sentence, the beginning of the end. Your body starts to change and everything suddenly feels *wrong* and your whole world is turned upside down. In retrospect, I hate my puberty. I loathe it. I wish I'd grown up ten years later than I did, after the Trans Tipping Point™, so I could've gotten on hormone blockers, thought through some things, and perhaps made a more informed decision about how my body was going to progress. I hate watching little-kid Jacob squandering their ability to slow down their biological process; I want to buy them a chance at transitioning physically. I want to put on a really cute skirt, hop in the DeLorean, go back to the past, slap my fifth-grade self in the face, and just be like, "Hey! You! Stop this puberty mess. You don't want it. Trust me." And then, just as my time machine is running out, cry out, "You'll have back hair by the age of twenty-siiiiiiiiiiiiiiiiiiiiiiiiix————save————yourself!"

But to say that I begrudged my puberty as it was happening just wouldn't be right. Honestly, I was way too busy being horny twenty-five hours a day, three-hundred-sixty-six days a year to even think about my gender identity.

When testosterone hit my system, it hit *hard*, if you, erm, get my drift. Like, just hard all the time. Like, hard for absolutely no reason. Like, the wind would blow and I would get an erection. I would be riding into school with my carpool and the car ride would get a little bit bumpy, and presto—I'd get a stiffy. I would take one look at my crush, and *kapow—accio, boner!* The only useful thing about the childhood bullying I endured was that it compelled me to switch from short shorts to baggy cargo shorts. The switch was fortunate because cargo shorts just had, well, more room to *move*, as it were, without being *seen*.

The worst part was that my voice started changing, and when it changed, it *dropped*. Over the course of a year or so, I went from a boy soprano (the highest women's vocal part) to a solid bass (the lowest men's vocal part). I went from being able to hit a high C two octaves above middle C to barely being able to hit middle C. I went from being a talented and skilled singer with an exceptional range to being a clumsy one who could no longer sing pop music. I pretty much had to give up the idea of being a diva. If my voice had changed and I'd landed as a tenor, I could've still been a front man. I could've still sung solos in church and praise band and school choir. But being a bass is being condemned to melodic obscurity. No pop music is written for basses. No lead parts in musicals are written for basses. In the choral world, basses get fuck all. Being used to getting any soprano solo I wanted, I cannot tell you how crushing this was for my fragile, fragile ego.

While my voice was the most emotionally devastating change, the leg hair was by far the most awkward. Not because it made me feel dysphoric, per se, but because it set me so far apart from the other kids my age. My shins and calves were pretty much covered in leg hair by about fifth grade. It felt shameful to be the only person in my grade with hair on their legs. I was scared to wear shorts for a full year before my friends began catching up body hair–wise, though many of my classmates didn't get real leg hair until well into eighth grade.

Looking back on my developmental advantage, I am split in two. On one hand, I wish puberty hadn't been so intense for me. I wish I was one of those blond, skinny, relatively hairless types who can actually pull off androgyny without immediately looking like a "man in a dress." I wish

I had one of those waifish, hairless, sleek bodies that look good in fashion magazines and on runways. Watching my puberty from afar, it's hard not to feel like my body was just getting uglier, less desirable, less conducive to my future safety, career, and romantic success.

By the same token, I can't help but be grateful for how my body changed. The fact of the matter is, throughout the entirety of middle and high school, my body was *always* more masculine than those of my peers. Even into college, I had the most masculine body in school. Because I had leg hair from fourth grade onward, because my voice changed in sixth, because I was six feet tall by seventh, because I started shaving in eighth, because I had chest hair by tenth and belly hair by eleventh— because of all those things, I was safer. I was less of a target for others.

My body provided protection and a stable identity, despite the fact that I was so obviously feminine. Many feminine-of-center boys and teens are bullied consistently throughout their entire adolescence, but for me, the bullying stopped as soon as I had body hair. Yes, it set me apart and made me feel a little bit like a yeti, but my physical body kept me safe where my gender identity was so uncertain. I'm sure my classmates looked at me with some frequency and thought, *Jacob is really feminine, huh?* But that thought was almost always countered with *But he's already shaving...*

The irony of this protection is not lost on me, because the thing that kept me safe as a teenager is exactly what puts me at the greatest risk today. Being gender nonconforming and existing in public is tricky for everyone. But it is especially tricky for male-bodied people whose bodies are very, well, *male*. For people who have more androgynous body types, less body hair, or less facial hair, you can sometimes wear a dress without eliciting too much unwanted attention. But for those of us who have full-on facial hair, semipermanent five o'clock shadow, fully furry legs, and a hairy chest to boot, there's never really any blending in. Even when I wear a dress and heels, no one looks at me and mistakes me for a female-bodied person. And that often makes walking in public an unsettling experience. People stare at me so much, I don't notice it anymore. People yell "faggot" or "tranny" or "What is *that*?" or "*What the fuck?*" at me so often, I don't even really hear them, a chorus of bigotry so constant and perpetual that it becomes background music.

So while the masculinity of my body would come back around to bite me in the ass, for the time being, I was safe. Safe, and *extremely* confused. I didn't know what was happening to my body. I didn't understand all the changes. And I didn't have the internet quite yet, so I couldn't just Google it or watch a "How to be trans and get through puberty and look *totally* cute" YouTube tutorial like kids do today. Instead, I got my information the old-fashioned way: My parents gave me a book.

The book was called *Puberty, Puberty, Puberty, Puberty: For Boys!**
On the cover, there was a picture of a dad and his son tossing around a baseball. The son had a bowl cut. The 1988 edition that we had in my house, acquired from a used bookstore at Raleigh-Durham International Airport, was special because it had a big orange sticker on the top right corner of the cover proclaiming that it "NOW COMES WITH IN-FORMATION ABOUT AIDS!"

It was the most scandalous book in our house. My brother had been given the book three years earlier, when he began his hormonal journey, but with strict instructions not to let me read it under any circumstances. Which of course meant that I wanted to read it immediately.

My parents didn't give me the book until two years later, but when they did, it was like uncovering the Holy Grail. All of a sudden, I had the power, the knowledge of good and evil, in my hands. I pored through the entire book in a day.

Most of it was pretty boring and medical, but neat enough. I thought it was interesting, for example, that my testicles hung at different heights

---

* Obviously, this was not the *actual* title of the book, but I'm not about to pay Harper-Collins $10,000 to use the real title. Besides, I think my fictional title is funnier.

so that they wouldn't smush up against each other so much. I also thought it was pretty cool that I could produce millions of sperm a day. But nothing excited me as much as the section about sex. It described, in detail, what (heterosexual) sex was, how (heterosexual) sex worked, and how to know if you were ready to have (heterosexual) sex. It even had a few diagrams, which I found thrilling, especially the one of an erect penis *inside* a vagina. But most important, it had an entire section about sexual orientation, and specifically, about *homosexuality* and *bisexuality*.

Homosexuality

When we talk about sexual desire and romantic attraction, there is one taboo topic that always seems to come up: homosexuality. The prefix "homo" means "the same." So being a homo-sexual means that you are attracted to other boys and men like you—that you fantasize about, crush on, or spend time daydreaming about people who are the same sex.

Go on . . .

Oftentimes, young boys are made fun of or taunted because they are perceived to be homosexual.

Uh-huh.

These insults and slang terms lead many adolescent boys who are experiencing homosexual feelings to be concerned that their feelings might not be natural or acceptable. You may have heard that many people believe homosexuality to be wrong, immoral, unnatural, or a sign of mental illness.

Wait, no one's said that to me. People say that? *What?*

> *Some religious and community leaders consider homosexual feelings to be a sin. Historically speaking, homosexuality has been classified as a mental disease that only a doctor or psychologist can treat.*

There you go talking about mental illness again. If it's *not* a mental illness or a sin, then do you *really* have to bring that up so often? I'm in fifth grade and reading this in 2002, so you can trust that I already have enough negative associations with gay people. Reading about this "mental illness" and "sin" stuff is not that helpful, to be honest.

> *But many of these views and opinions are now changing.*

Oh, okay. Phew. Wow, way to bury the lede.

> *These days, there are a lot of people who feel that homosexuals are natural, normal, and socially acceptable. Homosexuality is understood as a personal issue that should not be judged, mocked, or treated with disdain.*

Reading those last words, my brain was electric. It was like the first time someone shows you a diagram of the solar system and the earth's orbit. You've spent your whole life watching the sun go up and down in the sky, the moon mysteriously changing shape; you know, anecdotally, that celestial bodies *move*, that they *shift*, but until you see a diagram for the first time, until someone explains to you that these movements are called *orbits* and *revolutions* and *rotations*, the *how* eludes you.

Puberty, Puberty, Puberty, Puberty: For Boys! was my first blueprint of how human sexuality operated. Suddenly, the urges and feelings and *feelings* I'd been experiencing had scientific names. I was no longer jacking off, I was *masturbating*. I was no longer *gay* or *queer*, I was *homo-sexual* or *bisexual*. Everyone else (seemingly) was no longer straight, they were *heterosexual*. When you were as nerdy as I was growing up, having scientific words for the things you were observing mattered.

Which was what made the book's silence about queer sex and queer *lives* all the more conspicuous. In the present, the book strikes me as not only outdated, but alienating. Reading it now, as a queer/trans adult, the subtext of the whole thing makes me cringe. Other than that small section, queer people are hardly mentioned. While the book does mention homo-sexuality in a nonstigmatizing way, it is represented as the exception to the rule, a type of attraction that is not the norm and accordingly not worth spending much time on. While it talked a great deal about vaginal sex, it didn't discuss anal sex *even once*. It only referred to it ambiguously as a "very high-risk sexual act which results in large numbers of homosexual men contracting AIDS," and that was only in the introduction, which was written for parents. The entire book assumed that its reader was straight. While it told me that who I was sexually was natural and *perhaps* okay, it didn't really prepare me for what life was like as a gay person.

And where it only minimally served me as a young gay person, it com-pletely failed me as a young, gender nonconforming, trans kid: Like much of the world in 2003 (and certainly in 1988 when the book was written) it was completely silent about trans and gender nonconforming people.

None of this newfound knowledge could've prepared me for sixth grade. As every church kid knows, sixth grade is a big year. It's the year when you cross over from being in the "children's ministry" programs to being part of the "youth group" programming. The shift was important to me both socially and sexually: It meant I could hang out with high schoolers, young people who had grown beyond the gender-based insecurity of middle school to embrace coed friend groups.

It also meant I had an excuse to hang out with high school *boys*.

When I was twelve years old, high school boys simply *oozed* sexual confidence. You know, those *tenth-grade* boys. And oh my god, the *senior guys*. At the beginning of sixth grade, I still believed that a blow job had something to do with blowing air on or around a penis.* But those high school boys. They discussed making out and losing their virginity and *they actually knew what they were talking about* (or bluffed *very* convincingly). Those boys were music to my deeply confused ears.

The paradox of church youth group is exactly that: It is the space that is singularly accountable for introducing sexuality into young people's lives while simultaneously giving rise to sexual shame and insecurity. Church youth group is like that one aunt everyone has who bakes incredible cheesecakes, but spends the entire Thanksgiving dinner talking about her new diet. She sets you up with something delicious, conjures something rich and creamy and beautiful, only to shame you when you inevitably give in to the temptation to eat it. Each creamy bite feels wrong, each crumbly bit of graham cracker crust deviant, each calorie transgressive but seriously sexy.

Retreats were the nexus of this sexual torture chamber. Every spring and fall, we would pack our whole youth group onto charter buses and head off to a campground for the weekend, where we would spend 40 percent of our time talking about Jesus and the other 60 percent canoeing and speculating about the mechanics of hooking up. These were sexually charged weekends for everyone. Some of my friends even managed to sneak away for make-out sessions during free time. But they were literally and figuratively the hardest for me. At night, when everyone returned to the "safe space" of gendered sleeping cabins, I was plunged into scenes of sexual confusion and frustration that could last for hours, interrupting my sleep and ensuring that I was exhausted by the weekend's end.

There are two ways I can talk about those nights in the boys' cabin.

---

* I wish this were a clever joke, but sadly, it was something I and my friends believed.

On one hand, they were hilarious and fantastic. I got to watch my crushes walk around in towels, I got to sneak glances of people whom I adored in their underwear, and if I was lucky, I maybe even got to see a butt or two as people got in and out of the shower. Some of my fondest memories of eroticism as a young person occurred at church camp. The irony of church camp facilitating my adolescent sexual fantasies doesn't escape me.

But those weekends were also cruel and alienating. While I was closeted, I lived in fear that I would be found out. I lived in constant fear of my dick, terrified that it would give me away, that I would see someone I was attracted to, get a boner at an inconvenient moment, and have my secret, my deviancy, revealed to everyone.

Placing a young person in a sexual environment while simultaneously pretending it is totally devoid of sexuality reiterated the message, over and over again, that my sexuality did not matter, that my desires were irrelevant and abhorrent and should stay that way. So while the transgressiveness of being the peeping tom was sort of hot on the surface, it was psychologically destructive. I rarely felt more alone than I did in those cabins after the lights were turned off. As my friends drifted off to sleep, I spent countless nights staring at the ceiling, resisting both the urge to masturbate and the urge to cry. At the age of twenty-seven, I am still unlearning the shame and sexual erasure those retreats imposed on my adolescent body.

That being said, my church wasn't as bad as other churches could be. I have a ton of friends who grew up in churches that spent 90 percent of the early and mid-2000s talking about the precise circle of hell that was reserved for gay people. Something about George W. Bush's presidency really emboldened that conversation. I think, on some level, that a number of fundamentalist evangelicals actually believed that 9/11 was God punishing us for the scourge of butt sex and glitter that was sweeping the nation. Instead of helping them accept queer people, *Will & Grace* just seemed to make them *angrier*.

My friends who grew up in churches like that were delayed in their coming out process by easily four or five years. They generally came out in college. Also, a lot of them were frat boys. Go figure.

In the grand scheme of things, my church was just kind of undecided on the question of *homosexuals*. Given the political debate concerning queer people in the early and mid-2000s, this ambivalence was communicated through silence. No one ever really told me how I should feel about being gay. My pastor never said that homosexuality was wrong, but I also didn't know of anyone at my church who was out as queer.

This awkward approach to queer people was never more obvious than in the spring of my sixth-grade year, when our new youth pastor, Pat, decided we should spice things up by having a beauty pageant that featured exclusively guys. To this day, I can't say I understand Pat's motivations for staging such an event. What compelled him to have a drag beauty contest *in our sanctuary, in the room where we had weekly services each Sunday morning,* is beyond me. Maybe he was secretly trying to advance the queer feminist cause, empowering nascent homosexuals through the transformational power of ecumenical drag. That's certainly what *I* tell myself.

But the more likely explanation is that he probably didn't think too much about it at all. Or perhaps he thought about the beauty pageant in the same way that my grandfather would've thought about it.

In the 1950s and '60s, my grandfather actually participated in a few cross-dressing beauty pageants that were fund-raisers for his local Lions Club. At one point in time, my grandfather danced onstage with five other men wearing coconut bras and grass skirts. The way my mom talks about it, these cross-dressing pageants were *just for fun.* Which I guess means that in my grandfather's Southern mill town of Danville, Virginia, masculinity was so hegemonic and absolute, so *unquestioned* and *solid,* it never crossed anyone's mind that a grown man could *enjoy*

wearing women's clothes and dancing around onstage. There was no political or identitarian value in what was being done. It was just for fun.
Nothing serious to see here. Move along.

Pat must've been thinking about our youth group's beauty pageant
in a similar way. It was just fun and games, just boys hilariously running
around in dresses and their mom's shoes. Nowhere in his calculus did he
account for a ferocious, budding queen like me sashaying past the altar
and down the aisle.

The week before the pageant was to take place, Pat asked the guys in
our youth group to sign up if they wanted to participate. Of course, *no
one* signed up, because it would've been way too gay to volunteer to wear
women's clothes on a stage. So Pat spent the week reaching out to individual guys, eventually mobilizing enough contestants to make the
pageant a success. Why he asked me to participate is still beyond me. I
was close with him, and he knew I was a good actor, so perhaps he just
thought that pretending to be a woman would be a natural fit. Whatever
the reason, on Wednesday night between prayer group and Bible study,
he pulled me aside. I'm pretty sure this is how the conversation went:

> **PAT:** *Do you think you'd be able to be a contestant in the pageant on
> Sunday, Jacob?*
> **ME:** [screaming loudly inside] *Ummm . . . I don't know, maybe.
> Can I think about it?*
> **PAT:** [unaware of my internal screaming] *Sure—can you let me
> know by tomorrow what you think? It's going to be a lot of fun.*
> **ME:** [continuing to scream loudly inside, a twelve-year-old girl
> at an NSYNC concert] *Okay, sounds good. This is fine. I am
> relaxed about this.*

I went home and asked my mom whether she was okay with me bor-
rowing some of her clothes for the pageant. I think this set off some alarm

bells for her. It wasn't the first time I'd asked her if I could cross-dress or attempted to wear girls' clothes, but this was the first time I'd asked to wear women's clothes *at church* (little did she know that it wouldn't be the last). I don't think my mom was worried about me being queer—she already knew she had a sensitive, audaciously feminine son—but I'm sure she must've been worried that I would face bullying for participating in the pageant.

With some trepidation, my mom agreed. Her only condition was that we should probably keep this from my father for the moment. That made good sense to me.

It's not that my father is an asshole or a raging transphobic person. If anything, my dad is a reasonable, loving person who was completely unprepared to have a child like me.

My dad and I don't talk about his childhood a lot. My understanding is that it was pretty traumatic, due in large part to the loss of his sister Linda to pediatric cancer and the subsequent medical debt the family spent decades paying off.

The culture my father was raised in was blue collar, conservative, and full of machismo. I imagine that if my father had ever expressed any femininity as a child, it would've been swiftly coaxed out of him by his two older brothers, the kids from the neighborhood, someone at the Ford plant, or my grandfather. When you grow up in economic hardship in a masculine culture, like that of Ford's Cleveland plant in the 1960s, is it any wonder you might have some trouble accepting that your son plans to wear your wife's dress and shoes to strut around the church sanctuary for a beauty pageant?

At that point, neither my mom nor I was ready to start that conversation. At the age of twelve, I hardly understood my own identity. How could I have explained it to my father? Talking with my dad about my gender felt impossible.

Instead, that Sunday, my mom and I went up to her closet and picked out a long black dress and a pair of her shoes that loosely fit. To round out the outfit, we also grabbed a necklace, a pair of clip-on earrings, and a tube of lipstick. We put them in a big bag so I could leave the house sans paternal freak-out, and I headed off to church to compete.

When I got to youth group that night, I joined everyone for dinner and then went back to the vestry to change for the pageant. To my horror, I realized I was the only middle schooler who'd signed up. The only people who'd been convinced to compete were myself and three high school seniors. They had the social clout and cool points necessary to make it through the pageant unscathed. I, on the other hand, was a queenly little sixth grader who everyone had always thought was a bit too fruity anyway.

In the vestry, sandwiched between three eighteen-year-olds and a row of acolyte robes, I considered backing out. But by dragging me to choir rehearsal after choir rehearsal, my mom had taught me to always keep my commitments, especially when they pertained to church. So I pushed through. I donned my dress, slipped into my mom's shoes, put on a little lipstick, and took a deep breath.

I was horrifically nervous, but if I was going to do this, I was going to do it right. So when they introduced the four contestants in the First (and last) Annual Miss St. Francis United Methodist Church Beauty Pageant, I strode out like I owned the place. I sashayed like a professional, turning elegantly and perfectly, whisking up and down the aisles of my church in my mother's dress. Inside I was terrified, but on the outside, I *worked. it. the. fuck. out. honey.* RuPaul would've been proud.

The difference in attitude between me and the other contestants must've been apparent to everyone. Where the other contestants were grotesque in their gestures, I was elegant; where they were parodic, I was earnest; where they were clumsy, I was graceful. This was most notable during the talent portion of the contest. One of the contestants danced jokingly to a Britney Spears song, one juggled, and another blew bubbles.

I chose to sing. I can't remember exactly what song—it might've been a church song, but more likely it was something by Sheryl Crow or Shania Twain. Despite the clumsiness of my newly dropped voice, I did my best to sing earnestly. I sang truthfully. I sang beautifully, and in that moment, everyone in my church youth group must've realized that there was something profoundly different about me.

Afterward, the contestants all waited backstage while the judges deliberated. A few minutes later, the results were in and the contestants were brought back onstage.

"You've all competed beautifully," started Pat, "and each of you deserves recognition for your efforts here tonight, but there can only be one Miss Saint Francis."

I squirmed.

"Tonight's runner-up is none other than Praise Band's own James Benson! Give him a round of applause."

I could've vomited.

"And now, to crown Miss St. Francis. Ladies and gentlemen, this year's winner of the contest and Miss St. Francis 2004 is . . ."

Gulp.

"Jacob Tobia!"

The youth group applauded. Jamie, the assistant youth minister, brought up a surprisingly nice tiara and a sash made out of pink duct tape, adorned with beautiful cursive that read "Miss St. Francis." The sash was draped over my shoulder and the tiara was placed on my head. I faked a smile. I waved to the audience—elbow, elbow, wrist, wrist—in the queenly way I had learned from Julie Andrews in *The Princess Diaries*. I may have even made a small acceptance speech. But as I walked out of the sanctuary and back to the vestry to get changed, all I felt was fear. It was already weird enough that I was the only middle schooler who'd competed, but what did it mean that I'd *won*? As I changed out of my dress, I gathered myself, bracing for what I felt would be the inevitable taunts and bullying to come. I waited until most of the youth group had left before I went back to the sanctuary.

To my surprise, no one gave me a hard time. In fact, most of the kids in my grade actually *respected* me because, as a sixth grader, I'd beaten not one, not two, but *three* seniors. Strangely enough, there was real pride and street cred in being crowned Miss St. Francis. Contrary to what I'd thought, I wasn't seen by my peers as exceptionally flamboyant or "faggy"; instead, I was seen as the funniest kid in youth group, the courageous comedian who'd bested even the coolest, oldest members. At the time, I was relieved. For the moment, my peers had been thrown off my scent. In fact, it seemed that winning the Miss St. Francis pageant had paradoxically reaffirmed my masculinity by positioning me as bold and daring. After all, I was the only middle schooler who'd been *ballsy* enough to wear a dress, and surely I must've been deeply comfortable in my masculinity if I were willing to do *that*.

But looking back, I can see that participating in the pageant came at a cost. The pageant was not a celebration of femininity and gender nonconformity; in fact, it was the opposite. The pageant was a parody, a mockery, a public spectacle that created shame around femininity. Whether they realized what they were doing or not, there was something dehumanizing about watching three older guys, three cool guys, three *seniors*, mock feminine boys like me. With each laugh from the audience at a flamboyant gesture or swish of the hips, the shame I felt about my own femininity deepened. With each chuckle from my peers, I felt the possibilities for my gender expression narrowing, felt myself growing more and more distant from my body and my gender.

That I had to participate in this public ritual of shame was the greatest injury of all. That I had to strut onstage and mock myself, mock my own deepest desires, mock the generations of gender nonconforming people who came before me, mock the diversity of human expression, is one of the countless small tragedies I endured in my adolescence. That night, I learned a toxic lesson, one that would take years to undo: People like you are a laughingstock.

The transition to sixth grade wasn't just a big deal in terms of my church life. It also meant transitioning from elementary school to middle school. I went to a weird, hippie-leaning Montessori-style middle school called Exploris, attached to an eponymous global-themed museum in downtown Raleigh. There were only sixty kids in each class, so it was a small, intimate learning environment, the type of school where we didn't have lockers because lockers promoted being "closed off." Instead, we stored our stuff in milk crates, because they were open and communal. While we had janitorial staff, we took five minutes after lunch every day for "Blitz," where we would crawl around on the floor and clean up bits of trash and food. Oh, and there was no cafeteria. Or gym. It was in an old church building, so in place of a bona fide auditorium, we had a big room with a little stage at the end and stained-glass windows.

For me, it was paradise. I was an unconventional kid with too much curiosity, intellect, and sass for a standard North Carolina middle school curriculum. At Exploris, I got to write about my feelings to my teachers, who we called by their first names. My "Prime Group" teacher in sixth grade was Mary Beth. In seventh grade it was Shannon. Eighth grade was Frank. No "Mr." and "Ms." No hierarchy. We respected our teachers as people, and they respected us. While Exploris wasn't without issues, it was pretty damn utopian compared to most middle schools.*

By seventh grade, school had become kind of awesome for me, because of, ironically enough, the heterosexual awakenings of my peers.

I owe a lot to heterosexuality, actually. Under the aegis of heterosex-

---

* Shannon and I actually got dinner together recently. She is super proud that I'm writing a book, and is every bit as cool as I remember. She also loves the fact that I'm trans. She's the best.

uality, the gender divide started to fall. Okay, maybe that's a bit generous, but the gender divide certainly got mushier. *Mushy* is a gross word—like *moist* or *squelch* or *gush*—but it's accurate in this case.

The beautiful thing about girls wanting to kiss boys and boys wanting to kiss girls is that in order to accomplish such a feat, boys and girls have to actually spend time together. And more than spend time together, they have to *communicate*. All of a sudden, as my peers awakened to their sexual desires, as the fires in their respective loins were set ablaze, boys who hung out with girls were given incredible social standing. It took a certain grace, a certain sense of bravado, a certain je ne sais quoi, for a middle school boy to spend time one-on-one with a girl. It took class and elegance and endless amounts of cool for girls to grace you with their presence.

Seemingly overnight, hanging out with girls one-on-one had transformed from a damnable activity that condemned me to social isolation into something that only the coolest guys could pull off, the presumption being that if you were friends with a girl, you were that much closer to giving her a big ol' smooch. And while I wasn't smooching anyone, *boy oh boy*, was I good at hanging out with girls.

Not only that, but knowing how girls worked, knowing how to talk to them and get inside their heads, became a marketable social commodity. All the cishetero* boys I knew in middle and high school were desperate for my counsel. I always knew what to do. I always had the best advice, in part because I *sort of was* a girl. Being a gender-seer, one who can see beyond the two genders, the bridge builder between the "disparate" sexes, was an esteemed social position in the preteen and teenage pecking order. Who better than a budding trans weirdo like me to fill that role? I was more than qualified for the position.

I took this inch of mushiness, this iota of flexibility in the rigid gender

---

* cisgender + heterosexual = cishetero. It's an abbreviation that queer/trans folks use instead of having to type out "cisgender, heterosexual" a gazillion times on Twitter.

rules of my childhood, and spun it into a mile. I went from being the weird, nerdy sissy to being the glorified font of gender wisdom. Under the guise of wanting to have sex with girls, I was able to gain unfettered access to femininity. My straight friends wanted to get close to girls to know more about their boobs and vaginas. I wanted to get close to girls to know more about their shoe collections. I thought boobs and vaginas were awesome (I still think so), but they weren't my primary goal.

Nowhere was this shift more pronounced than in my relationship with my brother. We first learned to really *see* each other because of the girls my brother was trying to hook up with. The shift in our relationship started, predictably, at church, where my brother attended youth group with the sole purpose of flirting with his friends Karen and Tara.

When I started youth group in sixth grade, my brother was apprehensive. Having his nerdy little brother running around after him would surely cramp his style.

It couldn't have been more the opposite. Having a gay, feminine little brother is like walking around with a puppy. Girls are much more likely to talk to *you* if they want to hang out with *your cute dog*. As my brother soon discovered, there was *nothing* better for a straight man's romantic life than an effeminate little bro.

I was his youth group wingman, his matchmaker. I was Christian Mingle.com, bringing Christian singles together since 2001. Not only did I help the girls he was interested in feel comfortable around him, I also made him look *good*. By being gentle and sweet to me, by tolerating and being kind toward my *obvious*, *screaming* homosexuality, Matt looked sensitive, kind, sophisticated, and in touch with his feminine side. This put him, automatically, about three or four years ahead of basically all the other guys.

Through my prowess with women (again, because I was *basically* one of them), I earned my brother's favor, affirmation, and kindness for the first time in a very long time. And in return, my brother got some fairly risqué sexual experiences, including, but not limited to, a girl showing him her boobs behind the multipurpose room during the annual Mardi Gras celebration.* In exchange for beads, of course.

This gender mushiness also allowed me to again have friends who were girls. The most significant of these friendships was with my childhood best friend Paige. After being compelled to give up my friendship with Paige at the age of six, I was finally able to reconnect with her in seventh grade. Our rekindled connection was instant, affectionate, nurturing, and incredible. (She came out as queer many years later, something that I feel responsible for. You're welcome, world. She probably tells herself the same thing about me.)

My friendship with Paige was instrumental because she was by far the most open-minded person I knew. She thought gay and feminine guys were cool. She was *obsessed* with David Bowie and the entire glam rock movement. She was the first person to introduce me to *Labyrinth*, which by now she's watched at least three hundred times. I'm sure she meant this as a nudge in the right direction: *Look, Jacob, David Bowie is so cool and gender-fluid and incredible and sexy and you can be all those things!*

But I wasn't immediately a fan of Bowie, at least not Bowie circa *Labyrinth.* For one, I was legitimately perturbed by how much you could see his dick in that movie. You know how male ballet dancers always have those sculpted, beautiful, well-padded crotches? Apparently Bowie felt that was too much effort or something, because my biggest memory of *Labyrinth* was simply seeing David Bowie's flaccid, lumpy dick boppin' around inside those tights. I even remember that they were gray tights. That's how much the image stuck with me.

On a more general level, I wasn't really ready for Bowie. Sometimes, when you're queer or trans and you're in denial about it, when you aren't yet ready to recognize your truth and own it in public, when you feel

---

* We actually called it "Fat Tuesday," because "Mardi Gras" felt a bit too *scandalous* for a suburban Protestant church. It was an attempt to make the event seem more chaste. Lotta good that did . . .

trapped in a culture or a home situation where you don't think you can be open about who you are, seeing people who are liberated in their gender or sexuality can be too much to handle. It can be hard to watch. Looking at David Bowie, this gender-transgressive, suave musician oozing sex, I was simply overwhelmed.

As a teenager, I was hungry for queer affirmation and gender transgression *in my own life.* I was starving for it, but I didn't have faith that I'd get a meal anytime soon. I didn't have faith that I'd have space to safely express my femininity, let alone find a boy to kiss me, in the next few years. Watching Bowie gyrate, flounce, and throw glitter everywhere was the queer equivalent of watching the Food Network when you've forgotten to eat lunch and dinner is many, many hours away. What should be delicious, what should inspire hope, only inspires envy and insatiable, painful hunger. Sometimes, when you feel like that, it's best not to look.

While my newly socially permissible friendships with girls couldn't satiate my hunger or provide a real meal, they were identitarian snacks that helped tide me over: a scoop of hummus here, a few potato chips there, an Oreo or two. At school, my closest friends were Kate and Meredith, and they couldn't've been more different.

Where Meredith was girly, Kate was androgynous. Where Meredith was preppy, Kate was edgy. Meredith put bows in her hair when she had it up in a ponytail. Kate dyed her hair blue, then bleach blond. They were a good balance for me. Meredith and I could sing cute songs on guitar and talk about Disney Channel shows, and Kate and I could talk about the anime we were watching and the comic books we were buying and the Star Wars franchise.

Whenever I'd spend time with Kate or Meredith or Paige, my parents, especially my father, would give me an incredible amount of leeway. Before he went to bed each night, my father probably said a little prayer to Jesus that I would start dating one of them. When they came over, my dad would let us close the bedroom door, and no matter how much noise we made or how long we were silent, he wouldn't check in. When he wanted us to come down for dinner or when Meredith's parents came to pick her up, he would knock on the closed door, wait about five seconds (ostensibly for me to put away my dick or Meredith to roll off me or whatever he imagined was happening) and then ask, with the door *still closed*, "Can I come in?"

Meredith and I always thought this was hilarious. We'd joke about how badly my dad wanted us to date. On some level, I think Meredith always understood who I was and knew implicitly why that was never going to happen.

But while hanging out in coed groups became more normal and my friendships with girls started to feel effortless, hanging out with *just the guys* got worse. Despite going to a very open-minded middle school, there was only so much our teachers could do to rein in the budding masculinity. In middle school, masculinity became, for the first time, fairly violent. Being one of the "cool guys" in elementary school had only entailed playing gentle games of soccer and maybe throwing a football around every now and then, but being one of the "cool guys" in middle school entailed much, much more.

This pressure centered on Ty, my elementary school crush. Originally, we hadn't gone to the same middle school. He'd gone off to West Lake, the fairly normal school I was supposed to go to. Ty didn't last long at West Lake. He was too much of a middle school bad boy, too poorly behaved. He'd gotten in so much trouble that his parents thought it best for him to transfer schools. And where should he land but in my seventh grade class at Exploris.

In the beginning, it was awesome. The second he set foot in Exploris, Ty was *by far* the coolest boy in our class, and because we were already friends, that meant I got a serious boost in my social clout. In the video game of middle school, Ty's arrival meant I got to level up. I was a different person with him around, a person with more status and power. I liked that feeling a lot.

And he'd gotten *even cuter.* Unlike me, puberty had been good to him. Whereas I'd gotten lots of pimples and braces and tubby and giant, Ty had gotten taller, buffer, and more attractive than ever. His power over me was almost absolute. To stay in proximity to him, I would do anything, would try to fit in with any social norm. Which meant enduring some fairly ridiculous masculine bullshit.

At that age, boys try to become men much too quickly. They attempt to prove their masculinity to one another in the only way they know how, in the way they've been taught by popular culture over and over again: through normalizing and practicing violence. In middle school, hanging out with the boys meant enduring a gambit of violence and pain, a nonconsensual, biologically predetermined Tough Mudder.

This violence had many manifestations. All the cool guys got airsoft guns, the kind that shot plastic pellets, and then shot one another with them. All the cool guys got paintball guns and shot one another with those, too. I remember having welts on my body, bruises up and down my arms. I remember wincing at the pain, wondering why this was required to prove myself. I remember feeling ensnared. What had started as a desire to spend time with cute boys had become a trap, one in which I had to endure physical pain and humiliation in order to prove a manhood I didn't even want.

In my experience, the process of being masculinized, the process of becoming a man, was based on three practices: the practice of violence, the endurance of physical pain, and the violation of consent. As a preteen, you were supposed to punch each other at random. You were supposed to point your airsoft gun at someone else and ask, "Can I shoot you?"; when they said no, you were supposed to do it anyway. You were supposed to learn to never say no, and you were supposed to punish people when they *did* say no. You were supposed to stigmatize and victimize weakness.

What's most disappointing to me was that none of the adults in my life stepped in to stop any of this. In fact, they implicitly encouraged it.

We were "toughening up," "becoming men," or "just being boys." And this message was reinforced everywhere that I looked. On TV, in movies, in video games, men were supposed to enjoy violence. The more violence they could endure, the more violence they could do to others, the better. Is it any surprise that men are so violent in our culture, when we are raised this way?

The pinnacle of this, in my mind, was a game called Quarters. At lunch, all the cool guys would sit around a table and put their knuckles down on the table in front of them. Someone would place a quarter on the table, and we would then take turns flicking the quarter at one another's knuckles as hard as we could. It hurt. It hurt more than I can describe, and I'm someone who, as a consenting adult, takes it up the butt.* As the narrow edge of the quarter slammed past your skin and into your bones, it sent a sharp, stinging, relentless pain vibrating throughout your entire body. It was enough to make your eyes water. It was enough to make you bleed, and I often did.

More than the physical pain, what stuck with me was the collective psychology of the game. No one "won" the game really, but one person always lost. The first person who said, "I can't handle this," or "I'm out," or "I quit," the first person to opt out of the pain, was the loser. It was a game of mob mentality. The moment someone demonstrated weakness, the moment that someone winced too expressively or cried out, they became the immediate target of the group. You ganged up on the weakest person because it made the game end faster. Whoever appeared closest to breaking was attacked mercilessly until they did, all in the interest of "good fun."

The subtext of this game disturbed me then, and it horrifies me today:

You know how much it hurts when that quarter hits your knuckles? You

---

* Sorry Mom. I know you don't like this line, but I *just* couldn't help myself.

know how much it hurts, even though you're not the direct target? Well,
imagine if you were the direct target. That pain would be overwhelming. If
this is the pain you must endure in order to prove your manhood, if this is the
pain your friends do to you when you are one of the group, *imagine the pain*
they can inflict on you if you're no longer a member.

It is vile, acrid. It is a subtext that stays with us well into adulthood.
It governs the military and the prison system and the economy alike. In
order to maintain social standing as a "good man" or to be "man enough,"
you must participate in this perpetual ritual of violence. If you show
weakness, you will be attacked. If you opt out of this culture of violence,
you fail.

Though we did have legitimate moments of affection for and kindness
toward each other, my friendships with boys could be downright tyran-
nical; tempests of aggression and violence and sometimes cruelty. But I
put up with it. I put up with it all. This was the price of safety, and I endured it. This was the price of hanging out with cute boys, and I endured
it. But with each "boyhood game," with each "small" act of masculine
violence, I was pushed further and further away from recognizing my
gender, further and further away from my gentleness and sweetness and
sensitivity, further and further away from my feminine truth.

But even I had a breaking point. One day, Ty showed me a new trick
he'd learned. Apparently, if you sprayed a can of AXE body spray in
front of a lighter, you could create a massive, billowing flame—a flamethrower. He showed me this trick in his bedroom.

"That's neat," I commented, legitimately intrigued. I was, and am,
something of a pyromaniac. "But you really shouldn't do that inside."

"Really? You think that's a bad idea?" He smirked.

He then proceeded to *chase me around his house* with that makeshift
flamethrower, chortling with glee as I *very reasonably* freaked the fuck
out, visions of house fires and hospitals and skin grafts flashing in my
head.

Then, and only then, did I ever think, *Is spending time with this cute boy really worth it?*

If you're a cute boy and you're interested in bossing me around—something that, generally, I'm into—know that that's where I draw the line. You can get away with *a lot*, you can hurt me in a *myriad* of consensual and delicious ways, but you cannot, under any circumstances, chase me around your house with a flamethrower. I'll use the safe word every time on that one. Mkay?

In spite of growing masculine aggression, there were moments in middle school when my femininity was radically affirmed. Like, for example, when I went to the mall with Meredith for the first time.

In my adolescence, the mall was historically a place of restriction, a place where gender divides were pretty much absolute. It was an unspoken rule that when a girl was hanging out with a boy, she wouldn't make him go into women's clothing stores.

I'd spent a lot of time one-on-one with Kate and Paige at the mall, but because they weren't girly girls, we never really "went shopping." Kate and Paige were the type of friends who preferred band T-shirts to sequined tops or Lilly Pulitzer dresses, so hyper-feminine stores never really entered into the equation. We would look in a few stores that carried both men's and women's clothing (Hot Topic, Journeys, Aéropostale), and a few stores that weren't clothing stores at all (Brookstone, the Disney Store, the arcade), but our trips were never really "fashion excursions."

Not so with Meredith. In addition to being powerfully feminine, Meredith had the kind of gregarious, self-assured confidence that could knock down any barrier and open any door. She was both brilliant and audacious, with emotional intelligence and talent to boot. She knew that if you were confident enough, loud enough, and charming enough, you could break pretty much any rule. Meredith also knew what she wanted. She was a preppy, Southern girl who loved Jesus and wore ribbons in her hair and curated her wardrobe perfectly. And when we went to the mall, she wasn't messing around. She was going to get some cute new looks, and she was going to teach me to have some fashion sense if it killed her.

The first time we went shopping together, she forced me to enter my first American Eagle. I'd been too insecure to even walk into an American Eagle on my own. It was the hottest new club, and I wasn't on the guest list. I hadn't deemed myself worthy.

Meredith wouldn't stand for that. She'd been in that store easily twenty times. Meredith was a regular who could sneak me past my own mental bouncer and straight to the dance floor. By taking me into that store, she wasn't just giving me fashion advice, she was helping me re-define who I was, anointing me with newfound social and economic status. Before I walked into American Eagle, I was a nerd with braces and glasses who was struggling to figure out how to fit in. After Meredith took me shopping, I was an *American Eagle Kid*, transformed through the magic of capitalism.

Meredith also dragged me into every other store she liked.

That first shopping trip with Meredith was a dizzying thrill. It made my head spin off its axis. Not only did I have permission to *look* across stores to the women's section, I had permission to *walk over there and say hi to my friend.* I had permission to look at women's clothes, to judge them, to touch them, to weigh options and compare. The women's section was no longer forbidden terrain; it was somewhere I was welcomed. Without our peers there, without our parents, we were free to set our own rules.

And we did. Meredith dragged me into stores that were exclusively for women, into stores I'd never had the courage to set foot in on my own. We went to fabulous stores that weren't "classy" by any stretch of the imagination, that specialized in cheap sequins, towering heels, shiny polyester, and flashy costume jewelry that would turn your fingers green.

She took me to stores with names like Charlotte Russe and Wet Seal. She let me ogle the crystal necklaces and jewelry with her in Swarovski. Without shame, without apprehension, without any sense of anxiety whatsoever, she even took me into Victoria's Secret with her.

It was the first time in my entire life that I'd seen that type of femininity up close. It was mind-opening. I must've freaked some people out because I was obsessed with *touching* everything. It's like the first time you stay at a really fancy hotel. The sheets, the soaps, the lotions, the fancy chairs, the tile, the shower, the vanity, every single detail strikes you as incredible, as surreal, as something you've grown up seeing in movies but never had access to.

For those brief moments, I was over the moon. I was over the stars. I was beyond the universe and had ascended to a multiversal plane, somewhere beyond space-time, to a galactic layer where there were no more rules, no more despair, only hope. It was ecstasy. I was high, tripping on my newfound gender freedom, and perhaps some chemical fumes from the cheap dyes.

But like any good trip, it had to come to an end. The thrill faded because, as happy as I was in those women's stores, my existence there was still second-class. I was only granted unstigmatized access to those stores under the aegis of a female companion. My presence was only permissible if I understood that I was an accessory. *You can look, but you can't touch.* I could *see* the incredible hotel room, but I could never stay the night. I could stand in women's stores with Meredith, but I could *never, under any circumstances*, try on the clothes. They were not my stores. I could be her plus one, but I could never get my own name on the list.

Ultimately, however, these trips were transformative because Meredith took the time to care about my body and my look, too. She *styled* me. She pulled clothes (albeit men's clothes) for me to look at, encouraged me to take fashion risks (within the world of masculinity, but still), and took the time to help me ask questions that I couldn't bear to ask myself:

What do I want to look like? How do I want to dress?

Out of self-defense, I'd pretty much given up on clothing as a source of joy. I'd spent so much of my childhood longing to wear what was deemed women's clothing, longing to dress my body in frills and shimmer and fluff. I'd taken so many risks trying to obtain and wear these clothes, only to be shot down, bullied, or isolated every time. By the age of seven or eight, I learned to give up; to stop caring about what I looked like *at all*. It was easier to shut down that side of myself than to address the pain, hurt, and frustration it entailed.

Looking back, it's almost comedic. As someone who has *so many* aesthetic preferences now; for whom clothing is perhaps the most important signifier of individuality, self-worth, self-love, and affirmation; for whom *distinctive* (albeit not necessarily *expensive*) clothing is imperative—as someone who recently went to a fitting at a major designer and got in a fight because all they had for me was a simple black dress, I have to look back on that period of my life with wistful mirth.

My "fashion sense" in middle school was nothing short of tragic. It was a tragedy that I didn't get to wear clothing that expressed my identity. It was a tragedy that, for many years of my life, I gave up wearing clothes that brought me joy. It was a tragedy that wearing button-down polyester dragon shirts and Hawaiian shirts was the closest I could get to wearing bright colors without scorn. No offense to any butches out there, but it was a tragedy that I ever thought cargo shorts were a look. It was a tragedy that, out of a desperate need to cover up my femininity, to shield my femme from the world, I compelled myself to wear cargo shorts nonetheless.

Meredith opened me back up. While she may not have known the reason I'd stopped caring about what I wore or understood the coping strategy behind my aesthetic complacency, she knew that it had to change. She knew it was important for human beings to feel happy with how they looked, that dressing as you want—not necessarily expensively or even "well," but *of your own volition and according to your heart's desires*—was an important part of expressing your agency and identity in the world. It was a way to tell the world you valued yourself and knew who you were.

Meredith taught me basic tenets of fashion that I'd never known. She taught me to button up an oxford shirt, but to leave the top (or even the top two) buttons undone. She taught me how to cuff my sleeves so that I looked casual but put together. She also taught me that it was okay to wear clothing that simply *fit well*. That I could wear shirts and pants that fit my body; that everything didn't need to sag all the time. To a kid like me, who had been taunted mercilessly, publicly shamed for wearing shorts that were too short and too tight, the idea that I could wear clothing that fit me as I desired, that hugged my body in ways I liked, was revolutionary.

In the end, Meredith compelled me to buy two shirts from American Eagle that I will never forget. Together, they probably cost me $30, but they felt like a million bucks. Up until that point, I'd only worn dragon-print button-downs and plain T-shirts from Kohl's. She made me buy a pink button-down with blue and white stripes, as well as a brown form-fitting T-shirt emblazoned in teal with the phrase *Almost Handsome*.

Looking back, it probably should've read *Seven Years from Fabulous* or *I'm Trying, Okay?* or *This Gender Stuff Is HARD*, but for the time being, *Almost Handsome* would have to do.

We can never underestimate the power of naming something, the power language has to transform our consciousness.

Take, for example, the color blue. Did you know that for millennia of human history, in languages across a significant portion of the ancient world, there was no word for the color blue?

Most of us can't begin to imagine a world without "blue." For our modern imagination, a world without blue seems inconceivable. Blue is a color most of us consider to be foundational, the color of the sky on a gorgeous day, the color of the water that covers 70 percent of our planet, the color of fire at its hottest, of sorrow at its deepest.

No matter how strange it may seem, for thousands of years of human history, the color blue was never paid any attention to: It isn't mentioned once in *The Odyssey*, in the entirety of the ancient Greek canon, or in thousands of other ancient texts. Homer was famous for writing not about the deep *blue* sea but about the *wine-dark* sea. Without a word for "blue," the color of wine was the closest Homer could come to describe the brooding, tumultuous ocean.

When I look back on my early childhood and adolescence, I feel like a Greek poet: staring at the sky, marveling at the Mediterranean Sea, gazing deeply into a piece of lapis lazuli, confounded. Blue was right in front of me. Blue was everywhere. It was searing into my eyes from all directions, informing everything I saw, but its name evaded me.

As a child, I understood that my difference was beautiful, was natural, was fundamental. I knew just how special my gender was. But without a *name*, without language to put to what I was seeing and feeling, I had no way of sharing the importance of my difference with others. To them, gender could only be painted in bright red, deep green, or electric yellow. But floating at the edge of my consciousness, perched on the tip of my tongue, I knew there was more.

In the absence of the words *trans*, *genderqueer*, *gender nonconforming*, *nonbinary*, or *gender-fluid*, in the absence of the modern language we have created to name the natural, beautiful diversity of human gender, I used the best language I had at the time to describe myself.

I chose the word *gay*.

Looking back, that word feels foolish, primitive, and imprecise. Looking back, I see how lacking the word *gay* was, how unprepared "gay" was to hold the depths of my gender exploration. I could see that my ocean was something more, was something *different*. But I didn't have a word for it yet.

Choosing the word *gay*, seating "gay" at the head of my identity, set in motion dual arcs of self-discovery and self-loathing. Over the next five years, understanding myself as gay would fill my heart with dichotomous feelings of power and shame, beauty and repugnance, community and isolation, peace and despair. As a gay teen, I had a long, arduous journey ahead of me, one that would ultimately undo my idea of myself as a man.

At the time, I didn't have a clear road map of what that journey would entail. Back then, in the paucity of my queer adolescence, I knew only two steps.

Step 1: Come out.

Step 2: Buy some glitter, probably.

With trepidation in my right hand and gay identity in my left, I got started.

PART II

Teenage Dreams

Chapter 4

A Very Dramatic (First) Coming Out

*F*or queer and trans people, life in "The Closet" can be nasty business. It's not just the experience of withholding your identity from people you love, living a half-truth while you navigate the world as someone else, that is traumatic. It's also the way we *talk about* that period of our lives, the limiting metaphors we use to structure our self-knowledge. As a kid, I didn't pause for a moment to think about whether the metaphor of "The Closet" *worked* for me. I took The Closet as a shameful, for-granted part of my epistemological reality.

But what's obvious to me now, as an adult, is that this metaphor doesn't allow young queer people to have empathy for ourselves when we aren't yet ready to proclaim our identities to the world. I've come to loathe the idea of "coming out of the closet." There's something about its black-or-white, in-or-out nature that rubs me the wrong way. Thanks to many queer theory classes in college and the brilliant work of writers like Eve Sedgwick, I'm starting to imagine other narrative possibilities.

Instead of The Closet, I'd like to propose a more humane metaphor. What if we talk about queer/trans people "coming out of our shells"?

When you think about it, us queers are a lot like garden snails anyway. We love flowers. We have beautiful, curly shells. We are slimy and understand the power of proper lubrication. We leave a shiny, glittering trail wherever we go. And did you know that most snails are gender-neutral and play both "male" and "female" roles in procreation? That many snails change gender multiple times throughout the course of their lives?

More important, when you fuck with a snail, when you make it feel like it's in danger, it'll go right back into its shell. It will protect itself. You'll no longer be able to see its gorgeous, glistening, alien-like body—only a hard shell of its former self.

When a person hides in The Closet, we act as if it is their responsibility to come out. But when a snail hides in its shell, we don't delegate responsibility the same way. A snail only hides in its shell because the world outside feels hostile. If a snail recoils at the sight of you, it's not because the snail is cowardly or lying or deviant or withholding, it's because you've scared it. When queer people hide our identities, it's not because we are cowardly or lying or deviant or withholding, it's because the world and people around us *felt* predatory; because someone scared us—intentionally or unintentionally—and we were trying to protect ourselves. Like snails, we too are defensive.

All this is to say that the metaphors we use to talk about queer and trans experience matter. The Closet is a metaphor that sets queer and trans people up to feel that we are somehow dishonest or immoral for concealing our identities; that it is somehow our *lack of courage* that is to blame.

The Closet spent over a decade controlling my life and how I thought about myself, making me feel ashamed for hiding my identity from the world and the people around me. The pressure to come out weighed on me constantly. According to what I'd been taught on TV and in books, coming out of the closet was *my* responsibility. It was my responsibility to open up that door and step bravely into the light. It was my responsibility to correct what the world had assumed about me—that I was straight, that I was a boy, that I was cisgender. I owed it to *them* to be honest, not the other way around.

The closet led me to blame myself for *my own* lack of courage, *my own* inability to be honest, *my own* inability to "just open the door," rather than blaming the people around me who'd built a world where everyone was presumed to be straight and cis in the first place, where queerness was an inconceivable other.

Add to that the fact that I was raised in the church, that I had a fairly rigid moral compass—one that clearly and sometimes crudely delineated right from wrong—and you've got a recipe for disaster. According to my moral compass, being in the closet was immoral because being in the closet *was lying.* My silence about my identity became an indictment: indicating that I was untruthful, a bad person. I felt wrong, sinful, even, for deceiving those around me.

When I wasn't busy *blaming myself,* another emotion found me: the feeling of being deeply, seriously alone. I was facing this Goliath, this golem, all by myself. And because I am a hopeless extrovert, I knew I wouldn't last long if I kept it to myself.

As with most complicated questions in my life at that time, I turned to the church for answers. Despite its setbacks, church youth group was where I first learned what it meant to embrace the more complicated facets of my identity. In fact, youth group was the first place in my life where I came out as gay. In sixth grade, I reached out to Jamie, our assistant youth pastor, and told her I had something I wanted to talk about. The following Sunday after church service, we walked to Java Blu, a coffeehouse in the shopping center on Kildaire Farm Road, just across the street.

I'm still not quite sure why I told Jamie before anyone else. I think, on some level, I knew she would keep what I told her private, that she wouldn't share my secret before I was ready. But it was a big risk. Because we never talked about queer desire or *homosexuality* at church, I didn't actually know what anyone thought about it. Would she be understanding and nurturing toward me? Or would she try to tell me I was a sinner and attempt to "fix" me? Would she turn around and call my parents? It was a gamble, but for my own sanity, it felt like a risk that I had to take.

I asked her to a coffeehouse because, in every TV show I'd seen where two people had a serious conversation, it was always in either a coffeehouse or a restaurant. I knew my allowance wouldn't cover a restaurant, so I thought a coffeehouse was best. Jamie ordered a cup of coffee and I ordered a hot chocolate with extra whipped cream. She paid for both.

As we sat down to talk, I remember feeling at odds with myself. Coming out to her was simultaneously the most rational and irrational thing I could do. It made no sense. It made perfect sense. I had to get out with it. Sitting on a couch in the coffeehouse, I told her I knew I was gay, that no one else knew, and that I just needed to tell someone.

Looking back on that moment, I can't begin to imagine how hard this was for her. I can't imagine what I would've done if, as an adult, in Cary, North Carolina, in 2004, I'd had a twelve-year-old come out to me. But somehow, Jamie knew what to do.

I saw her demeanor soften. I watched as her face shifted from anxiety to confusion to pity and ultimately settled on a quiet look of love.

"Have you told your parents yet?"

"I'm not ready to tell them. I don't think I'll tell them for a while. I just don't think they'd be ready to hear it. They'd probably think it was a phase or something."

"That's okay, Jacob. You don't have to tell them until you're ready. You don't have to tell anyone until you're ready."

A pause.

"I'm not quite sure what to tell you. I can tell you that you're not alone. I can tell you that you're going to be okay, okay?"

Another beat. It felt like hours.

"Have I ever told you about my friend Pete? We met in college and are still in touch every now and then, and he's gay. From what I know, he's happy. There are other people like you out there."

I thought I would start crying, that this would feel like catharsis, but instead I just felt blank. It was more like shock. It seemed that, at least for a while, things were going to be okay. I tried to respond to her, to say something back, but I just sat there, stunned.

"Why don't we pray on it? It's what God calls us to do in times of trouble."

Jamie took my hands in hers.

"Dear Lord, I thank you for the light that Jacob brings into this world, for all that he is and for all that he will become. We ask that you bless him and guide him along his journey, that you comfort him and walk beside him down this road. We also ask that you give Jacob the wisdom and love to be courageous, that, through him, others may learn of your love for them. Amen."

"Amen."

I sat there, gently shaking, eyes dry, hugging myself. Jamie scooted closer and hugged me, too.

"Why don't we head back to church?"

"Okay."

And then:

"Thank you, Jamie."

When people ask me about when I first came out, I generally tell them about coming out to my parents. I often overlook this experience, overlook my time with Jamie. Perhaps that's because it feels like it doesn't count, because I didn't tell the rest of the world until four years later.

But I don't think that's really why. I think it's because this story, my first coming out story, doesn't match the template of what coming out is "supposed to be." It's too quiet, too devoid of drama, filled not with rejection or chaos—or with glitter or rainbow streamers—but with a quiet, trepidatious sort of love.

Or perhaps it's deeper than that. Perhaps, in my heart of hearts, I know that some moments are too sacred to be recounted without context.

Following this talk, I wish I could say that I had everything figured out. I wish I'd internalized what Jamie had said and ended the self-hatred, the self-loathing. In fact, it took years for me to process, to digest what she'd said, to take the love she'd given me and make it my own.

What coming out to Jamie really did was give me permission to be patient with myself. I'd done it once. I'd popped my head out of the closet and said, to someone who was very important to me, "Hey, I'm in here, just wanted to letcha know," then immediately ran back inside and shut the door. I'd poked my head out of my shell just long enough for my weird snail-y eyes to see the garden around me.

If Jamie had told me being gay was sinful, that I was doomed to hell, I likely would've been galvanized to come out to everyone right then and there, just to prove her wrong. If she'd told me that I *needed* to talk to my parents about this right away, I would've panicked and cried and felt trapped in my secrets.

But her gentle love—her affirmation that I was on a journey and had to give it time—allowed me to give *myself* the permission I needed to take things slowly. Her imperative, to practice kindness and be gentle with myself, was very different than what I'd heard about the closet. I didn't have to figure it out just yet. I didn't have to have all the answers. I wasn't on a deadline to throw a Pride parade or make a Coming Out YouTube Video™ within the next two weeks. I didn't need to tell everybody right away. And I didn't have to leave my church family while I figured out who I was.

I'd grown up being told that secrets were *dirty*, were *mean*, and I thought I must be dirty and mean for keeping my identity secret. I thought that being in the closet meant I was necessarily a skeleton. From Jamie, I learned that secrets aren't always closets; sometimes, secrets are cocoons, and we are butterflies. Sometimes, secrets are shells, and we are snails. We have to take our time, grow in our secrets, make a home in them, build our wings cell by cell. Sometimes, our secrets are precisely what keep us safe. It's okay to go back into our shells when we're frightened. It's okay to draw into ourselves when our safety feels impossible. There is no need to come out of our cocoons before we are ready. It's okay—in fact, it is *most natural*—to let our metamorphoses happen at their own pace.

With the understanding that my secret didn't make me dirty and that I was simply mid-metamorphosis, my relationship to God and to my church grew deeper, more fervent. I doubled down on my commitments, spending anywhere from ten to fifteen hours a week at church, between handbell choir, youth group, Sunday services, Sunday school, and choir practice.

During that time, my queerness, my difference, still weighed heavily on my mind. It wasn't that I thought I was a sinner or anything. On television and in the newspaper, I'd heard lots of people say that "homosexuals" were destroying the moral fabric of our society and were sinners who were gonna burn in hellfire. Or whatever. But I knew none of that was true. First off, I knew that global warming, wage disparity, war, racism, patriarchy, and corporate greed—not homosexuality—were to blame for the fraying moral fabric of our society. Second, I knew that all those dudes on TV who spent so much energy talking about how nasty homosexuals were either secretly wanted to get it on with other dudes or were just jealous of our innate ability to match fabrics.

In my own head, I was crystal clear that Jesus didn't hate me because I was gay. Jesus was *wayyyyyy* too chill of a dude for that, and also Jesus hung out with hella prostitutes and weirdos, so he'd be like, "Sure, homos, come hang out too! We can all walk on water! Have some wine!"

I knew God didn't hate me for being queer. But that didn't mean I didn't hate *myself* for being queer.

I was just so mad about it. I hated that I was different. I hated that my life didn't make sense and that I couldn't just want what other people wanted. I hated that I had to bother with this whole coming out business. I hated that I couldn't just ask a girl to the dance like all my other friends. I hated that I felt constantly uncomfortable around groups of guys. I hated that I had to deal with other people's bullshit about my identity.

God didn't hate me for being gay, but I sure as hell hated God for *making me gay*. And hating God imposed something of a barrier on my spiritual journey. It would take four years for that barrier to eventually fall. But don't worry, you don't have to wait four years. You only have to wait until later in this chapter.

Thank Goddess for Jamie. She saved me years of agony. She made it so that coming out was no longer some moral crucible. Instead, I could appreciate it for what it was: a logistical and public relations nightmare. I was able to approach this whole "how do I tell the world that I'm a faggot goddess?" thing with a clear, strategic, neon pink mind.

The first decision I made was that I didn't need to hurry. I'd heard from a lot of different sources (the internet, which by sixth grade I had) that a lot of times, when kids came out as gay *too* early, people were liable to just sorta dismiss it. Moms would say things like, "Little Timmy, you're not gay! How could you know something like that? You're only twelve! It's probably just a phase. Oh, Timmy, stop pouting about the fact that I dismissed the entirety of your identity. If you keep pouting like this, you're going to be late for gymnastics practice. Oh gosh, now you're all upset. You know what? We can listen to the *High School Musical* soundtrack in the car while you put on your tights—would that cheer you up?"

From my research (what I read on the internet), I determined that the best age to come out was sixteen. When you're sixteen, you're probably old enough to be taken seriously as a proto-adult, and according to my sources (what I read on the internet), you're definitely old enough to start dating and messing around with other guys. So sixteen felt like the perfect age to do this thing. I was like Hillary Clinton *circa* 2011. All I had to do was wait four years and bide my time before I could announce my candidacy for president. How hard could it be?

As it turned out, waiting was excruciating. Not so much in the "I feel alone in the world and no one understands me" sort of way. Mostly just in the "oh my god I want to kiss boys so bad and I can't" sort of way. For those four years, my sexual frustration was profound. I masturbated eight thousand times a day.

But luckily, that *always* gets better when you come out, right? That's why you never hear about sexually frustrated gay men, and you certainly don't hear about sexually frustrated gender nonconforming or trans people. Once you come out, you just like, get a sex life handed to you, right?

Right?

Anyway, at a certain point, the pressure became too much. Two years into my four-year probationary period, I got tired of waiting. I had to tell *someone* that I was, for sure, 100 percent running for Gay President. I had to declare my intentions. And I had to hire a campaign manager before they committed to another candidate.

For my campaign manager, I chose my best friend Paige, the one who loved art and glam rock and David Bowie and cool gender nonconforming drag queens on Myspace. Paige was functionally gayer than I was—she was pretty much *my* gay best friend—so coming out to her wasn't scary, per se. I knew she wouldn't reject me. I knew she would likely be *thrilled*.

I was only hesitant because coming out to her represented a security risk, a gap in my firewall. I was not worried in the slightest about what she would say when I confirmed her suspicions. I was only worried that she would accidentally tell someone else, that it would spread like wildfire and might make it back around to my parents or my friends at school or the old ladies at church before I could tell them myself. In campaign terms, Paige could be a leak in my public relations plan. I wanted to tell Paige and a few other people that, yes, I was running for president. But I wanted it to be off the record. I wanted to give my parents the exclusive when the timing was right.

What was remarkable about coming out to Paige was just how un-remarkable it was. She *doesn't even remember* exactly when it happened. I, of course, remember it clear as day. We were walking around in the woods behind my house, and we sat down to take a breather on the trunk of a giant fallen tree. This was one of my favorite trees on the entire planet. It's almost completely rotted by now, absolutely covered in ter-mites, but it was my favorite place to spend time as a kid, so it was special that Paige and I went there.

Seated on the tree, legs akimbo, I took a deep breath.

"Paige, I want to tell you something. There's not really a way to preface this without giving it away, so . . ."

She stared deeply into my eyes, knowing something juicy was coming.

"I'm gay."

She sat quietly for a moment as a smile spread across her lips, cresting to a full-on toothy grin. She was *thrilled*. Her eyes shimmered.

"Jacob, this is *the best*. Does anyone else know? I'm so excited for you! Oh, you're so awesome!"

She threw her arms around me in a bear hug. We hugged for what must've been a minute, not crying, not shaking, but giggling. We couldn't stop laughing. It had been so obvious to both of us, and now it was out there. And it was fun. It was electric. It was exciting. We had a secret—and the fact that I'd told her *first* meant our friendship was that much more riveting, that much more complex, that much more iri-descent.

It was the fairy-tale, indie-movie-style coming out that every queer or trans person deserves, but not everyone gets. As far as popping my coming-out-to-friends-cherry goes, this was a slam dunk.

Paige honored her word. She kept my secret off the record. And now, whenever I was frustrated or upset or boiling over, I had a pressure-release valve, a way to blow off steam. I knew I could last the two more years until my sixteenth birthday.

Well, there was *one* other time I came out before I turned sixteen. As I waited to make the big announcement, I found myself breaking the silence in a letter. To, of all people, Jon Stewart.

On June 6, 2006, Jon Stewart did an interview on *The Daily Show* with conservative pundit Bill Bennett about his new book, *America: The Last Best Hope, Volume I.* During the interview, they got into a big argument about gay marriage, where Jon eviscerated right-wing opponents of same-sex marriage, disemboweling their arguments in the way only Jon Stewart could.

I remember how formative this interview was for me. Back in 2006, when most public figures and politicians alike were still reticent to endorse same-sex marriage or stand up for the LGBTQ community, watching Jon Stewart—a straight dude—defend people like me felt earth-shattering.

Let's be clear, though. Today, I couldn't give two shits about marriage as a political issue. Part of that is because, in my adult life, I am perpetually single, so weddings make me grumpy and I am bitter. Especially cute gay weddings. *We get it, Charles and Ian, YOU'RE MADLY IN LOVE AND YOU BOTH HAVE GREAT PECS. That doesn't mean you have to rub your perfect love in our faces, okay? (Though you're welcome to rub other things in my face, just sayin'.)*

But it's also about the principle of the thing. Ask any feminist scholar and they will tell you that marriage's history has always been, at best, sketchy. It literally used to be a *property arrangement*, a *contract*, wherein *women were the property.* And today, even at its most meaningful, it's often just an excuse to spend ungodly amounts of money on flowers and to force all your femme friends to buy dresses they'll never wear again. I don't need a wedding to do either of those things. I will spend too much money on flowers any day I want, thankyouverymuch. I will spend half a month's salary on a vintage flapper dress if I damn well please.

Personally, I think the government shouldn't sanction marriage for anyone, that the government should only provide civil unions—for straight and queer couples alike*—and that you should go to a mosque or a synagogue or a church or whatever if you want to get married in front of God. I don't like the idea that government names any relationship that it sanctions *a marriage*. Feels to me like a violation of the whole "church and state" thing. And on a movement level, I feel like marriage was a distraction from bigger queer and trans issues like employment discrimination, access to public facilities and services, gender-identity-related healthcare, and hate violence, to name a few.

All that being said, I'll probably still get married to someone someday, even though I'm sorta *meh* about the whole institution. But I'll only do it to make my mom happy. She doesn't say it out loud, but I have a sneaking suspicion that she *super* wants me to get married and, like, *do the whole wedding thing*. I figure staging a solid wedding is the least I can do after she literally *3D-printed my body*.

But back in 2006, marriage mattered to me greatly. Not because the institution was important to me—I was still years away from having a serious romantic partner[†]—but because marriage was the vehicle through which the world debated the worth and humanity of queer people. People who were "opposed to same-sex marriage" were not overly concerned with marriage. Their distaste for same-sex marriage was only a derivative symptom of their primary condition: the cold, hard fact that

---

* If we're being completely honest, I don't even think you should have to be "a couple" in the classical sense to get married. I want people to be able to marry as many of their platonic friends as they want. If I'm Phoebe (and I am), why *shouldn't* I be able to marry both Monica *and* Rachel? I mean we all (basically) live together, we're functionally codependent, and we all find Ross obnoxious. Sounds like marriage material to me . . .

† Still am, apparently.

they disliked queer people and did not believe we deserved happiness, community, family, or respect.

Marriage was a mirage, an illusion that clouded the minds of so many, obscuring the *real* question we were debating as a country, a question that continues to be debated today: Are queer and trans people worthwhile?

According to Jon Stewart, who was basically *the face* of the resistance circa 2006 and who I may or may not have had something of a crush on, the answer was a categorical *"of course* queer people are worthwhile." Not only was I worthwhile, I was "part of the human condition." In my impatience to come out, my impatience to start fighting back against all the idiots on television who said that people like me were immoral or bad or villainous, hearing Jon Stewart stand up for me was pivotal. It made the waiting easier. Advil in the face of a searing identitarian migraine—it couldn't fix it per se, but it certainly helped dull the ache.

So, the summer after eighth grade, I wrote this letter to thank him. And to let him know that I'd be more than happy to be a guest on his show. (Jon, if you're reading this, that offer still stands, by the way.)

June 7th, 2006

Dear Jon Stewart,

I know you will probably never read this, but I would really like to thank you for your defense of gay rights during your interview on June 6th. It is really nice to have someone advocating gay rights who isn't wearing a thong and dancing around in the street.* As an in-the-closet teen of 14, the world is already difficult enough for gay people, and we don't need closed-minded s***heads making it worse.

---

* The irony of my disdain here does not escape me. In eighth grade, I thought that flamboyant, sex-positive gay men made "the rest of us" look bad. In the present day, I have *become* a flamboyant, sex-positive activist who dances in the street, scantily clad, while demanding my rights. Whoops.

As an aspiring actor or politician* you are definitely a role model for me, changing the world through comedy, what a great way to do it. Man, you SERVED that guy. Did he not see what you did on Hardball? I wouldn't show up if I had to debate you!

By the way, I think you should have me as a special guest, because people under 18 can't get into The Daily Show! :'(((

Or, I could write a book! Then I could be a guest. YAY! Or, I'd be more than happy to just randomly come out of the closet on your show, "And now we have a special message from Jacob Tobia to anyone it may concern" "I'm GAY!!!" the end.

You want to know what sucks? You can't write to a celebrity you want to compliment without sounding like "I WANNA BE ON UR SHOW I LOVE YOU ETC. ETC. ETC." Because I started writing some other complimentary stuff, and I realized how desperate and stupid it sounded. So I guess I'll just keep my letter short (Especially because you probably won't even read it), and wrap up with another thank you. I really appreciate you standing up for me; it really made me happy, because most of what gay people get are weird glances and awkward conversations. Being gay sucks enough without people discriminating against you, I mean I REALLY want to have kids, but if I ever did I would always feel guilty because I might've screwed them up for life. It really sucks, I wish like hell I wasn't gay, but I am, shit.

Thanks,

Jacob Tobia

P.S. If you get this could you send me an autographed picture or a little note saying "I got your letter!" It'd be cool to know if you actually read this. By the way, if you actually write back (which isn't

---

* It's cute that I used to think that these were two distinct careers.

going to happen) don't say anything about me being gay, I'm still in the closet over here. Thanks!

P.P.S. The world didn't end!

P.P.P.S. If you could actually arrange for me to be in the audience or on the show or something, I WOULD LOVE YOU FOREVER! (I can act)

P.P.P.P.S. Reading over this letter, it's a really bad letter, and I sound like a desperate loser . . . OH WELL, I'll send it anyways

I sneakily saved the letter in a secret folder on my computer, printed it out, shoved it in an envelope, and sent it off to New York, with my parents none the wiser. As I suspected, I never heard anything back from *The Daily Show* or from Jon Stewart. Which is fair. As someone who now receives some fan mail, I would've seen a letter like that and solidly filed it under "Basketcase, Do Not Write Back."

That being said . . . Jon, it's never too late to write back to an adoring fan. Especially one with a book deal. Or you could slip into my DMs if you want. Whatever works for you works for me. It's chill.

When my sixteenth birthday finally arrived, the pressure was on like Donkey Kong. My self-imposed coming out deadline was upon me, and I was officially late turning in the assignment—something that my over-achieving ass has never stood for. I was *never* late with homework.

Ultimately, the courage and confidence to pull the trigger came from the least (and, knowing myself, most) likely source possible: a church retreat.

That September, following my August birthday, I went on a retreat called Chrysalis, a weekend retreat that brought together kids from Methodist churches all across the Raleigh-Durham area. It was just what it sounds like: You came into the retreat as a lil' caterpillar, cocooned yourself up, went through your metamorphosis, and emerged from the retreat a spiritual butterfly. The whole thing was low-key gay as hell. Also, it was a boys-only retreat, so it was just a weekend where a buncha dudes got together, cried a bunch, hugged a ton, and became butterflies. No big deal.

Perhaps you're thinking this is going to be a story about falling in love for the first time on an all-boys church retreat. On that front, I'm terribly sorry to disappoint you. Despite my most sincere efforts, I never managed to hook up with a guy at church camp. I have many friends who did manage such a feat, but I have no game at all, and spontaneously start farting and burping any time I try to hit on boys.

That being said, the retreat was an incredible time of personal growth for me. At Chrysalis, I continued my long tradition of using evangelical Christian methodologies and principles to come to the wrong conclusion. I'd been doing it for years, and this retreat was no exception.

On the last night of the retreat, we were surprised with a ritual—the full cultiness of which I have only recently come to appreciate. Have you ever seen that documentary *Jesus Camp*? It was sorta like that.

After an evening activity, they walked us from the dining hall to an undisclosed location. They'd taken away our cell phones and watches and any time-telling devices for the weekend, so I didn't even know what time it was. I just knew the sun was down and that I was walking in the dark with a group of twenty teenage guys and twenty adult leaders.

They told us to be silent, to pray, on our walk. I whisper-asked one of the retreat leaders what we were doing, where we were going. He said he couldn't tell me. That I had to trust in the process and in God's love. I realized we were heading back to the campground's chapel.

When we walked in, the chapel was completely dark except for a cluster of tea lights. In the center of the flames was a life-size wooden cross, big enough to actually crucify a person, with hammers and nails scattered across the floor. Each of us was given a red construction paper heart and told to pray over what had been keeping us from growing closer to God. We were then instructed to write this on the red paper heart, take it to the front of the chapel, and physically nail it onto the cross.

Now, at the age of twenty-seven, this whole thing feels creepy to me. Why couldn't they tell us where we were going? Why did the lights have to be off? Why did they have to have a life-size cross? Why did we have to physically nail the paper to the cross? Why did our parents think this was chill? (Come to think of it, I'm not sure if my mom ever knew about me doing this.) The only thing they could've done to make it *more* creepy and culty would've been for us to have actually nailed our *own hands* to the cross.

But the thing that's most striking to me about this ritual is that, at the time, I was really into it.

It makes sense on some level. I was desperate for love. I was scared of who I was. I was vulnerable and wanted to grow closer to God, to understand myself better. I wanted to be in deeper community with my church and to feel more at home in my body and my life. If that meant I had to participate in a culty ritual in a dark room surrounded by candles in which I had to pretend I was crucifying a piece of paper, I was game.

As creepy as the ritual was, it was transformational. It worked wonders. I sat in the chapel, praying in candlelight. What was keeping me from God? What was stopping me from walking with Her and having a deeper relationship with Her? In classic Jacob form, I came to the opposite conclusion than intended.

Yes, I hated God for making me gay. I hated God for making me queer. But instead of trying not to be queer anymore, I decided that night that the only way to move forward in my faith journey was to forgive God for making me gay and finally embrace that the thing that made me different was the thing that made me beautiful.

I stared down at the pen and the red paper heart and, after what felt like an hour, finally mustered the courage to write, *I hate that God made me gay.*

I stood up from the wooden pew, walked slowly forward and fell to my knees. With tears in my eyes, I picked up a hammer and a nail, and I nailed that motherfucker into that cross so hard you'd think I was a butch lesbian.

As the name "Chrysalis" would suggest, I emerged from that night a big gay butterfly with rainbow sequined wings. Through the power of an evangelical ritual, I'd been transformed from a commoner into a goddess, my faggotry ordained. After that night, I never looked back. I never allowed myself to hate who I was again. As strange as it may sound, the foundations of my pride, my identity, my ferocious queer self-love, were born in a ritual likely intended to make me hate myself.

I left that night knowing a truth that I hold dear to this day: *God didn't just make me queer—God made me motherfucking fabulous. It is my God-ordained duty to share every ounce of that glitter with the world.*

With my newfound divine queer confidence, I finally started telling other people my truth: that I was as gay as the day is long.

I thought of the first few people I came out to as open dress rehearsals in the lead-up to my parents. I made the strategic decision to come out to three people: my friends Kate and Meredith, and my brother.

My brother was first. I don't remember the exact evening I decided to tell him or what compelled me to do so. Though I can't remember the context, I remember the conversation vividly. We were sitting in his room, watching TV or playing video games or something, and I started the conversation with what would go on to become my signature line:

"There's not really a way to preface this, but I want to tell you something."

The reason that was my signature line is because time was of the essence. Let's be very clear: I knew that many, many people in my life already suspected I was gay. I knew there was suspicion out there about why I hadn't ever had a girlfriend or hooked up with anyone, speculation about why I seemed to be so at home with femininity onstage. I wasn't one of those queers who spent tons of time proactively covering their queerness. I didn't have fake girlfriends. I didn't try to make out with a bunch of girls. I didn't adopt a more butch persona in order to cover things up. I just never named my queerness.

So I knew that when coming out to people, I faced the very serious risk of them beating me to the punch. And I never let *anyone* beat me to the punch.

If I took forever to just say the damn thing, people might get ahead of me and blurt it out before I could. Here's the scenario I was trying to avoid:

ME: *Hello, dear friend/mentor/person from my community. I want to speak with you about something very important to me. I want to share something with you that is a vital part of how I understand myself, but something that I hope, once I share it with you, will not change the way that you think about me or compromise our relationship. It is something I have known about myself for many years, since I was very young, and it's very important to me that—*

THEM: *Oh my god, you're gay!*

ME: *DAMMIT YOU'RE SUPPOSED TO LET ME SAY IT FIRST WHAT THE FUCK COME ONNNN*

THEM: *Oh . . . erm . . . sorry?*

uncomfortable pause

THEM: *. . . but also it's fine!*

ME: *Whatever, you ruined this. You ruined this whole thing. God, you're such an asshole, Elaine.*

In order to avoid that scenario, I adopted the swift one-two punch of:

1. *"There's no way to really preface this, but I want to tell you something"; and*

2. *"I'm gay."*

With my brother, the line worked like a charm. He didn't beat me to it, though I could tell that if I'd gone on for five more seconds, he probably would've. He'd been waiting for this.

"Oh thank god." He sighed, relieved. "I'm glad you finally said something so I didn't have to."

"Uh . . ."

"So have you ever done anything with a guy?" he inquired, swiftly moving the conversation forward to the things that really mattered.

And like that, I knew we were back to normal. In true bro fashion, my brother and I recounted almost every detail of our sexploits to each other while we were growing up. Because I didn't ever have anything to report, it was mostly just my brother recounting *his* sexploits—vivid details of make-out sessions in movie theaters or heavy petting on the living room couch—to me, but it was a hallmark of our improved relationship as brothers.

Which made the fact that he was inquiring about my nonexistent sexplorations with other guys a serious gesture of affirmation. By asking if I'd ever done anything with a guy, he was implicitly saying that who I was was fine, that we could still have every bit of the relationship we'd had up until that point, and that he remained sincerely interested in hearing about my sexual experiments and journey. In an early 2000s culture that taught straight dudes to be *totally revolted* by any mention of intimacy between two guys, I cannot emphasize strongly enough how radical this was.

"I haven't yet," I informed him, realizing that the tables had completely turned. My brother wasn't disappointed that I was gay, but he *was* disappointed that I wasn't getting any. We were "The Tobia Boys," and he wanted me to uphold the family reputation for being cool, romantically successful, and sexually active, even if it was with other dudes.

He pushed further. "So what's that *like*?"

I didn't really know how to answer that. What *was* being gay like? I hardly knew myself.

"It's like . . ." I stumbled. "I guess it's like—you know what you feel for girls? I just feel that for guys, I guess."

"Oh, cool. Can I tell Jill?" Jill was his serious girlfriend at the time, who was at that point basically a member of our extended family.

"Please don't. I don't want a lot of people to know yet."

"Okay, I won't tell her. Your secret's safe with me."

A few hours later, I got a call from Jill congratulating me for coming out.

I imagine that my brother waited approximately five minutes after I'd left the room before calling her. She was so excited, and my brother was so sweet to me about everything, that I couldn't even bother to be mad.

My plans to come out to my parents after my sixteenth birthday were stymied every step of the way. Like most of my life, it was a comedy of errors. The timing was never right, or too much else was happening.

Later that August, after I'd turned sixteen, my brother went off to college. The separation was a huge transition for my parents, and I realized I needed to give them some time before dropping the gay bomb.

Then, a month later, my brother was busted for smoking weed outside his freshman dorm. My parents were (un/reasonably) upset by this, their perfect image of their firstborn child shattered. Once again, I gave them a minute to adjust.

Then in October, my dad lost his job. And it was like, *Fuck. I'm never gonna get to do this thing, am I?* In terms of our family life, things went downhill pretty fast. Have you ever had an unemployed parent in your house? Most people have at one point or another. It's the pits, and it certainly isn't the best environment in which to be like, "Oh, by the way, I'm a fag!"

So, my self-imposed deadline a solid four months behind me, I tried my best to maintain the facade. I tried to keep quiet, but every day became excruciating. When you're ready, you're ready. And I'd been ready for months. If I didn't say something soon, I worried that it would just erupt out of me, unprompted, a cascade of fury and glitter and unicorn farts.

The final straw came that December, at my best friend Paige's sweet sixteen. She had a big dinner with a bunch of her friends at Carrabba's Italian Grill, and one of the guests was her friend from school, Chris.

Chris. Chris Chris Chris. Oh my God, *Chris.*

At that point, Chris was my tormentor. He had many severe faults, so many that they were hard to rank. First, he was gorgeous. Second, he was charismatic. Third, he was artistic. Fourth, he was funny. Fifth, he was gay and open about it.

A veritable monster, the idea of him clawed at my heart and pawed at my loins, running around in my fantasies, disrupting my focus in class, corrupting my oh-so-pure mind. And I'd never even met him in person. He was just an *idea.*

Up until that dinner at Carrabba's, I only knew about Chris secondhand. Paige had told me about him and I'd spent hours looking at pictures of him on Myspace and Facebook, but we'd never actually met. This was intentional on my part. Chris was too tempting. If I started hanging out with Chris, I knew I would try to kiss him, that we would start dating, and that my parents would wonder why I was spending so much time with this Chris fellow. If I started hanging out with him, my whole system would be compromised.

So I kept my distance until that unavoidable dinner. It was a torture chamber, because while most of Paige's friends ran in completely different circles than mine, Paige happened to be friends with one girl from my church youth group, and she was there. So I was face-to-face with my crush for the first time, but unable to say anything without risking being outed to my entire church. It was the most unique of purgatories.

As I twirled my pasta, Chris sat across the table from me, smiling, giggling, effortlessly gay. Tantalizing dimples in full view, unrelenting in his sweetness, his charm was radioactive, penetrating my heart from miles away, turning me slowly loopy.

It took everything within me not to flirt with him, not to reach across the table and brush his arm, not to make too much eye contact or laugh too loudly when he made a joke. I ended up changing seats at the table so that I could get farther away from him, hoping that physical distance would make things a little easier, a little less obvious. In actuality, the distance only made things worse and more conspicuous. I must've spent half the dinner staring down at the other end of the table. I couldn't stop looking.

When the dinner was finally over, I drove home, my feelings oscillating wildly between despair and rage. I was furious that I couldn't just flirt with him, angry at myself that I may have sabotaged one of the only chances I'd get to charm him and make him mine. I'd finally been around a real-life gay boy, one that I could ostensibly *date*, and I'd totally messed it up. I made myself so invisible that I don't know if he even *remembered meeting me* after that dinner. My anger spiraled outward, at the world around me, at Paige for (unknowingly) setting me up, at my dad's company for laying him off and making me wait so long to come out, at my brother for getting busted for smoking weed and putting my parents on edge, at the world for this entire mess.

I'd had it.

She was done.

I had to end this.

Sometimes queer people come out of our snail shells because we feel safe, because we know that the garden outside is friendly. Other times we come out of our shells because we haven't nibbled any leaves in weeks, and if we don't come out to forage for food, we'll eat ourselves alive. I'd felt the pangs of hunger for so many years: the hunger to live openly, the hunger to be honest, the hunger to smooch some cute boys, the hunger to *get on with my life.* If I didn't make a move soon, I knew I'd starve.

Two weeks later, on December 15, 2007, I was sitting alone upstairs in our bonus room watching reruns of R. L. Stine's *Goosebumps*. It's a silly children's horror show that originally ran from the time I was four to the time I was seven. I'd always watched the newest episodes with my brother. Watching the reruns now, with their crappy, late-nineties special effects and cheesy music, I experienced something powerful for the first time: I experienced nostalgia.

I started to have a sense of just how long I'd been alive already, which, in turn, made me think about just how long I'd been hiding this whole gay thing from my parents. I'd been hiding it from them for five years. Five years out of sixteen and a half. Essentially, a third of my life.

A third of my life.

One-third.

That fraction tumbled around in my mind for a while. And suddenly, out of thin air, I was resolved.

Tonight is the night.

I am going to do this.

This secret ends now.

This snail is coming the fuck out of her shell.

I picked up the phone and called Paige.

"Paige, I'm going to do it. I'm going to come out to my parents tonight."

"Oh, wow! Are you scared? You got this, okay? Just call me after and let me know how it goes."

I called my brother, told him the same thing.

And like a robot who'd been reactivated, I got to work.

The first task was finding a way to organically get my parents in the same room. It had to be organic, we all just had to sort of *end up there.*

Otherwise, I'd have to do the whole "Mom, Dad, can you come downstairs? I need to talk to you about something" line, and they'd be like "Oh God, is Jacob on drugs or did he get some girl pregnant or crash his car or get chlamydia or something?" If I could, I wanted to avoid starting the conversation on those terms.

Turns out, I couldn't. My parents would not get in the same damn room. My dad was upstairs watching TV. My mom was downstairs reading. My dad went downstairs to get a snack, but then my mom was in the bathroom. My mom went upstairs to brush her teeth, but then my dad was back downstairs putting up his plate. They played musical chairs for over an hour as I attempted to ghost around the house, seeing where they were without attracting too much attention.

At a certain point, I'd had it. We were going to have to do this the old-fashioned way.

"Hey, Dad, when you get to a stopping point in your show, can you come downstairs? I want to talk to you and Mom about something."

"Okay. Be right down."

"Mom, are you at a stopping point in your book? I want to talk to you and Dad about something."

Three minutes later, I had them around the kitchen island. This was it. *Give 'em the performance of your life, kid.*

"Well, there's not really a way to preface this, but . . ."

The rest goes by double-time in my mind, less "Disney Channel Original Movie" and more "contender at Sundance." In my memory it is understated, matter-of-fact, almost clerical.

My mother asks sweet, kind, empathetic questions, trying to make sure she understands. I answer. My father stays silent. My mother asks more questions. I answer. My father stays silent. My mother asks her last question. I answer. My father stays silent.

A pause.

My mom turns the questions on my dad.

"So, Abe, what are *you* thinking?"

His silence smolders a moment longer, burning with heat and pressure and intensity.

He finally speaks. Processors whirring, I listen.

"You'll always be my son, but if you choose this lifestyle, I want no part of it."

Processing. Processing . . .

"If you choose to be with a man, he will never be my son-in-law."

Processing . . .

"If you choose to adopt children, they will never be my grandchildren."

Processing . . .

"This is not a choice I agree with. This is not a choice I will ever approve."

Overwhelmed, my processor shut down. Rainbow wheel of death. Spinning, spinning, spinning. Survival mode enabled.

"Okay, Dad. It's good to know that's how you feel. We can keep checking in about it."

Panic mode operational.

"I'm gonna—"

Engage force field, Captain.

"I'm gonna go."

I head for the garage, get in my car, and turn the engine on. My father comes to the garage door.

"You can't leave," he proclaims.

Watch me, I think.

When I turn around, I realize his car is parked behind mine in the driveway. I can't go anywhere. At least, not in my car.

I black out.

It wasn't my father's rejection that started it. It was the overwhelming totality of emotion. It was the rejection, the revelation, the honesty, the five years of boiling up and over unleashed all at once. I wasn't running away from home. I just needed some space and, in panic mode, didn't know how else to get it but to put one foot in front of the other as fast as I could.

Suddenly, I'm running running running through the December rain. I'm sobbing sobbing sobbing through the December rain. *Why did I have to pick a rainy December night to do this? Why didn't I grab an umbrella out of my car? Why am I even running? This is so dramatic. This is so stupid.*

A few minutes and half a mile later, I'm on the swing set by the neighborhood pool, sitting in the rain, shivering. I call my brother.

"Dude, you have to stop crying, I can't understand what you're saying. You have to calm down."

I hang up on him.

I call Paige. I tell her that things were okay, but I am overwhelmed and need to get away for a while. Like a best friend does, she doesn't ask any questions or hesitate for a second. She marches immediately downstairs, fearlessly telling her parents, "Look, Jacob is gay and he just came out to his parents and he's upset and crying in the rain, can we go pick him up?"

Without missing a beat, Paige and her dad hop in the car. They pick me up at the pool. Paige holds me in the rain for a moment, then beckons me inside the vehicle. The car ride back to her house is silent. Not because it is awkward, but because it is human: because she wants me to focus on breathing, on slowing down.

When we get to Paige's house, her mom digs out some old sweatshirts, gets me out of my wet clothes, makes us hot chocolate, and leaves us alone to talk. Out of all possible nerdy things to do next, Paige and I make a list of pros and cons. At the top of the list is:

You can date boys now!

As if.

Half an hour later, I call my mom. She pleads with me to come home. I tell her I never planned to run away, that I wasn't running away forever or anything, that I was sorry for being dramatic, that I wasn't mad at her. Paige and I turn on some Food Network while we wait for my mom to come pick me up. *Barefoot Contessa*, I think.

Back at my house, my dad has shut himself in my parents' room. Now *he's* the one who won't come out. My mom and I are both grateful for the space, grateful that he's left us the rest of the house. We sit on the couch and begin unpacking years of baggage, unfurling scarves and socks and underwear and pants. T-shirts and beanies, hoodies and metaphorical belts. It feels good to have it out in the open. Now my mom is the one who's crying.

"When you were born sixteen and something years ago, you know what I said to the doctor?"

She cradles me against her chest, running her fingers through my hair.

"I told him it was like an angel had fallen down from heaven and landed in my arms. You were so beautiful and perfect."

I breathe in and out. She breathes in and out. The universe breathes in and out. Our Christmas tree twinkles on the hearth.

"I'm just worried that life is going to be harder for you. I don't want life to be hard for you. The world can be so mean. I want you to have everything you want without having to deal with people being cruel to you. I love you."

We sit on the couch for hours, until two a.m. I can't remember the last time my mother stayed up until two a.m. At the end, before I head up for bed, she makes me pinky-promise her that I won't get AIDS. I tell her I will always use a condom. She says okay. I say good chat.

My father and I don't speak a word to each other for a week. The next weekend, I tell him I want to talk.

Like the little shit that I am, I start our conversation by turning the tables. I tell my father that I have chosen to accept him *as he is.*

"Look, you are my dad and I love you and accept who you are no matter what. If you choose not to affirm my sexuality, I will still love and accept you. There's nothing you can do to shake me, to make me stop loving you."

He is taken aback, unsure of what to say. This was not the conversation he was expecting.

Scrambling, he tells me that homosexuality is a sin. I tell him I don't care what the pope says, that I'm not even Catholic—I'm Methodist—and that I choose to interpret the Bible differently. He reiterates that he believes gay people go to hell. I tell him he should go to church more than two times a year if he plans on condemning anyone to hell. Checkmate. He drops the religious argument forever. He never really meant it in the first place, he was just panicking and saying whatever popped into his head.

We agree to disagree. We agree to passive aggression. We agree to not really talk about it. We agree to a fraught truce, an imperfect armistice, a Cold War. Neither of us is truly okay—it'll be a long time before we'll be okay, and to this day, we still work hard at it—but for the next few years, we'll do our best to pretend.

So there you have it. There's your drama. There's your classic teenage angst. There's your glorious, Jacob-erupts-from-the-closet-in-a-burning-fire-of-self-actualization showdown. There's your delicious courage-in-the-face-of-adversity sandwich.

But that's the last one you're going to get in this book. That's the last great coming out story I have. From this point onward, coming out becomes more complicated, becomes messier and more nuanced alongside my burgeoning identity.

For years after I came out as gay, when people would ask, "So what was coming out to your parents like?" I would recount this entire story to them word for word, even adding a few embellishments to make it more grandiose. I relished every dramatic detail. The fact that it was December. The fact that it was raining. The fact that I ran. People like you better when you give them a show.

When I was younger, this story held real weight. This was my war story, the proof that I was a veteran of this struggle. I held it close, hopeful to tell it to anyone who'd listen.

As I've grown older and my identity has become more complex, this story has hollowed out. Not all at once, but bit by bit. Each time I made a new discovery about my gender, each time I reconnected with my femininity in a more powerful or significant way, each time I brushed polish across my nails, another piece of this story would fall away. It's not that the story was bad or incorrect or too traumatic, it's just that with each passing day, as I got further and further from feeling simply like a gay man, the story of coming out to my parents *as gay* mattered to me less.

These days, my answer has changed pretty substantially. When people ask me when I "came out to my parents," I just sorta scratch my head, because which coming out story do you want? Which identity interests you most? Some days, when I'm feeling generous, I may tell you the partial answer, which is that I came out to my parents as gay and then never really came out to them again. If you're *really* lucky, I may still recount the sordid emotional details of that rainy December night.

But most of the time, I brush the question off. I give some half-assed answer like, "Well, my mom was great with it, and my dad took his time. But he's mostly come around," and then I move on.

No one ever gets the full answer. The full answer, the one I wish I could give my sixteen-year-old self, is that I will never be done coming out to my parents, because I will never be done coming out to *anyone*. The reality about gender is that we are all morphing all the time. We are all growing and evolving, excavating and renovating. I will be discovering new facets of my gender until my last breath. And so my coming out is never complete. My parents (along with everyone else in my life) will be learning new things about my gender and my sexuality well into their retirement, well after they've sold my childhood home, well after they've moved into an assisted living community (though hopefully they'll never have to), because *I* am still discovering new things.

For me, coming out is less like a closet and more like a software update. I go off, further developing and tweaking my code, changing my algorithm to be better, stronger, faster; and every few months, the people in my life get an update to their operating system. Sometimes, the upgrades are so substantial that you can hardly recognize the computer in front of you anymore. You have to learn how to use the system all over again. Start from scratch. Sometimes, the upgrades are cosmetic but profound, like when emojis were first added to the default iPhone keyboard. Sometimes, the upgrade is so minuscule or behind the scenes that you don't notice it. But no matter how old you get, there will always be another upgrade. I will always be tweaking my OS.

Looking back at my sixteen-year-old self, what I hate most for myself is the fact that on that night in December, I thought I was done. I thought that with that one software upgrade, I'd fixed the bug and could move on. After all, I'd come out of the closet and I was in the room now—so we were good, right?

Right?

I also lament the weight I put on honesty. I was told I owed it to my parents to be honest with them about who I was. But did I really owe them that? Do queer people really *owe honesty* to people who have spent their entire lives precluding the possibility that we are anything but straight, anything but the gender we were assigned at birth?

I feel this most acutely in regards to my relationship with Chris. I did not have to wait until after I'd come out to my parents to start dating him. I could've started dating him without disclosing my sexuality to my parents. I could've sucked a dick or two before having the big talk with my folks. My straight friends never had to have a conversation with their parents about their heterosexual desire before slurping on a D or munchin' on a muff, so why was I held to that standard? It strikes me as ridiculous that I should have to declare my sexual consciousness to the world around me before I could even explore it, before I really even knew what it was. No one should have to come out before they get the chance to (consensually!) put their mouth on genitals of some sort, just to be sure.

After I came out as gay, I never officially came out as genderqueer or as nonbinary or as trans or as feminine. I never, not once, sat anyone, much less my parents, down and said, "My gender is different than what you think it is." "Coming out" stopped being a useful or productive way to think about my journey.

I couldn't have properly "come out as trans" if I'd wanted to, because I never closeted my gender identity in the first place; instead, I buried it. As a teenager and young adult, the fullness of my gender was unknown, even to myself. It was buried underneath layers upon layers of shame, two decades of gender policing and self-alienation. As I began to excavate, I did so in the light of day, an open-air dig for everyone to see.

My queerness and transness were a gradual unfurling, a slow blossom. I expressed my gender in real time as I discovered it. I didn't say, "Mom, Dad, I'm questioning my gender," I just showed up at the dinner table in lipstick one day. I didn't say, "I'm genderqueer," I just started shopping for different kinds of clothes. I never said, "I, Jacob Tobia, am now a member of the trans community," I just started hanging out with more and more trans folks until it became an afterthought.

What I'm saying is this: From now on, you're going to have to work a little harder. There is still drama. There is still angst (trust me). There are still funny stories about how clumsy and awkward I am. And there are still lots of bad dick jokes. But from this point onward, my identity stopped being something I withheld and withheld and withheld and then finally released. It became something I chipped away at bit by bit, that I unearthed in real time.

After coming out to my parents as gay, I was done building reservoirs in my heart. I was done storing up water behind a dam, praying that it wouldn't burst as the pressure mounted. I was done hiding. From here on out, I vowed to myself that I'd be a free-flowing river. That I'd do my best to try.

The Christmas following my little announcement was awkward. If you want to seriously ruin a family holiday, all you really have to do is tell your parents that you're into pounding—and, more important, getting *pounded by*—other men.

Chapter 5

In My Own Two Shoes, On My Own Two Feet

*T*he summer of 2008, just before my seventeenth birthday, my grand-mother passed away. Her death itself wasn't a tragedy: four days away from her eighty-eighth birthday, she'd lived a long, robust life. She'd built a family, traveled internationally a few times, and even gone back to school at the age of fifty-eight to complete her college education. She'd done a lot and been places. Once she brought me back a soapstone owl from Greece.

Her death was sudden, but in the right way. One month, she was living alone at her apartment in the small town of Danville, Virginia. Mostly independent, happy, in fairly good health, taking walks up and down the hill outside her apartment complex each day, going to the beauty school every two weeks to get her hair done. The next month, she was in the hospital. Nothing was particularly wrong, she was just feeling weak and in a bit of pain. No cancer, no debilitating injury, some dementia but no Alzheimer's. Then quietly, suddenly, a week later, she died.

I was on a church retreat, in the middle of a small prayer group, when I heard the news. I left the room to take the phone call from my mom. She told me that my grandmother had died. I walked back in and fell to the floor—my prayer group huddled around me as I let the feelings wash over me. I shed a lot of tears that day. It wasn't because my grandmother's death was untimely or unjust; it wasn't that her death felt unfair. As far as deaths in the family went, her death was peaceful and sweet; which, paradoxically enough, made it easier to connect to my sense of loss.

When someone is taken before their time, when someone is taken in political violence or brutality, when someone dies in pain, the feelings of rage can stand in the way of properly grieving. In those instances, we must split our heart between feeling anger and feeling loss. Like when another trans woman of color is murdered in hate violence. Or a person we love dies in prison. Or cancer takes a twelve-year-old. In those instances, our grief and anger are grueling.

In the case of my grandma, I was given the grace that comes with a painless, peaceful death. I didn't cry because I was mad at the world for taking her. I cried simply because I loved her. I cried because I adored spending time with her, playing cards and Rummikub. I cried because I am a nostalgic person who feels and feels and then feels some more.

After the funeral, we began the long process of going through my grandparents' possessions. The decisions about what to keep and what to give away were exhaustive and relentless, and my mom was mainly the one who had to make them. My father and brother and I were just there for moral support. I spent most of my time digging through an old crate of letters my grandmother and grandfather had written to each other during World War II, when my grandfather was deployed to the Pacific only a few months after they'd been married. They were engrossing and romantic, filled with *"I love you, my darling"* and *"You are the most cherished part of my heart."* Scrawled in a deeply slanted cursive, half of them written at sea, they took forever to read. I sat in the guest bedroom of my grandmother's apartment, wading through each word, reading about the time my grandfather had spent in Hawaii before deployment and then the time his ship almost sank, finding photos of him on a rock in Central Park before he shipped out, feeling awed by my grandmother's courage in the face of economic hardship at home. I marinated in their deep, abiding longing for each other in the face of war.

Before I knew it, hours had passed. My parents, who'd been slowly working their way through the living room, had arrived at my grandmother's bedroom. I recognized the sound of her wooden dresser sliding open and closed. I recognized the clanking of costume earrings, the snaking *clink* of necklaces, the *pop* of her jewelry box lids. I could recognize those sounds anywhere. It was the same jewelry I'd spent hours and hours of my childhood trying on.

As far as I was concerned, that was *my* jewelry collection, but my mom—who'd never particularly cared for my grandmother's classically Southern, feminine taste—was deciding its fate. I had to save it, but how could I without giving away the fact that I *wanted it*? And what did I want it *for*?

The beauty of a crisis is that it compels us to act out of instinct. When the stakes are high and the decisions imminent, we don't have the chance to question our motivations or doubt our intentions. We must simply *do something*. So I didn't have time to think about what it meant that I wanted my grandmother's jewelry. I didn't have time to question whether it would be risky for me to seem too interested. I didn't have time to agonize over whether I had the courage to say I wanted to inherit my grandmother's clip-on earrings. And I certainly didn't have time to debate whether wearing my grandmother's chunky clip-ons from the 1980s would be a solid fashion choice when I finally got the courage to take them out in public. I just knew that if I didn't save her costume pearls and Christmas-themed brooches, I would spend the rest of my life—and every subsequent holiday party—regretting it.

Without a plan, I put down the letter I was reading and attempted to casually float into the room to see what my mom was doing, immediately giving away that something was up. I am not the type of person who casually enters a room. Like a true Leo, I only know one way to enter rooms—loudly and with fanfare. Which is why, within three seconds, my mom knew something was going on. And if she didn't know it then, she definitely knew it when I *casually* sat on the bed and said,

"So . . . um . . . whatcha doin', Mom? What are you . . . erm . . . looking at?"

She sighed and wiped her nose. I like to think her nose was running because she was emotional, but it also could've been the fact that we'd stirred up literally all the dust in the entire apartment over the course of ten hours.

"I'm going through your grandmother's jewelry. Remember how much you used to love these earrings? You'd spend hours in here playing with them."

Wait, she knew? I was taken aback. Like with all parts of my childhood faggotry, I held fast to the delusion that I'd been subtle. That I'd *sneakily* loved my grandmother's jewelry, or that I'd played with my neighbors' Barbies *unnoticed*. Memory is fickle like that. You give yourself the delusion that you need at the time, and back then, I needed to believe I was actually hiding, when I was always sort of just hiding *in plain sight*. I wanted to believe my identity was in a closet or a chest or a bank vault. At best, it was a china cabinet with glass doors. The contents were fragile—precious, delicate, beautiful porcelain swirled with gold and blue, wisps of floral detail, shimmers of crystal—but they were on display for pretty much all the world to see, including my mom.

I was uncomfortable that she'd clocked me and only mustered this response:

"Yeah, haha, I remember that. I would spend a lot of, um, yeah, a lot of time playing with that when I was a kid."

My discomfort grew. I crawled in my skin.

Dammit, Jacob, this is a crisis, so you have to keep making the words with your mouth, okay? Just ask. Just ask the question.

"So . . . uh . . . what are you thinking about . . . I dunno . . . doing with her jewelry?"

"I'm not sure. I mean, most of it's costume, and I certainly wouldn't wear it, so I'm thinking that it might be best to give the lion's share to Goodwill."

Oh no oh no oh no oh no oh no. Oh god OH GOD NO. You gotta do something, kiddo, because this shit is about to be gone forever.

Then, a flash of brilliance.

You have cousins who are girls and they aren't here! You can say that we should keep it for them! Aha! A scapegoat!

I was suddenly flooded with confidence. "I mean, we could give it to Goodwill, but don't you think that we should hold on to it so that Kaitlin and Lindsay and Courtney can look through it when they're next in town and see if there's anything that they want? I'd hate to get rid of it if there's anything that they'd like to keep."

My mom mulled this over, then smiled, pleased with the empathetic child she'd raised. Little did she know that I never intended on giving any of that jewelry to my cousins. I was just using them as an excuse to get it back to our house, where I could squirrel it away.

"Look at you, being so considerate of them. I suppose we can hang on to it until they have the chance to look through it."

Oh my God, that plan worked. Jacob, don't act too excited. You can smile, but, like, not too big, okay?

"Why don't you hold on to it until then? Can you put it in the pile of stuff that we're keeping?"

Keep it chill, Jacob.

"Sure. Sounds good, Mom."

Okay, stop talking now and leave the room. Definitely don't turn around and say something else.

I reached the door, then turned back to my mom. "Okay. Great. I think it's wonderful that we're keeping this for the cousins."

Why are you still talking? Just go put it in the pile.

"Because, y'know, so much of grandma's jewelry is just really beautiful and I'm certain that they'd like some of it."

Jacob. You have to shut up. You're giving yourself away.

I backed out of the room awkwardly. "And I love a lot of it, too. Especially the brooches, because they're so sparkly . . . so . . . yeah . . . anyway, I'll go put it in the pile now. I might look through some of it before I put it away."

Jesus, kid, way to be subtle.

I took the four boxes, placed them in a brown paper grocery bag for safekeeping, and, with great aplomb, placed the bag in the pile of items we were taking home with us. On the car ride home, I was smug. My cousins were never going to get any of it. I didn't completely understand why yet, but that jewelry was for me.

A few months later, when my cousins *did* end up coming to visit, I knew just what to do. As a freshly out homosexual, I combined my newfound gay fashion powers with my catty teenage powers of manipulation to dissuade them from taking anything whatsoever. Putting on my best Tim Gunn, I passive-aggressively introduced the jewelry to my cousins:

"Here's some of Grandma's tacky costume jewelry if you want to dress up like her or something, lol."

My strategy was a great success. I managed to persuade my cousins that our grandmother's jewelry was undesirable. Other than a locket or two, they didn't take a thing.

Grandma's jewelry was mine. Now I just had to figure out what *the fact that I wanted it* meant.

News of my budding identity as a queer weirdo (queerdo?) spread slowly, in hushed tones, through my home church. During this period of time, the adult leaders in the church knew what was going on, but were ambivalent about how to respond. For the most part, the approach was always one of "live and let live." Jacob can be gay and be a leader in youth group, as long as they don't like, *talk about it all the time.* As long as everyone was nice to me and I was nice to everyone, they could let it stand. Some of the adult leaders even went so far as to let me know that they supported me. Overall, it was an atmosphere of love, but the limitations of that love were tested sooner than I'd anticipated.

The major test came a year after I came out, when I was asked to give my first testimony. I was ecstatic. For church kids, this was the closest you'd ever feel to a rock star.

Testimony was when shit got real. During your testimony, you took the stage in front of the entire youth group and told your deepest, darkest secrets. You confessed that you were struggling with an eating disorder or with self-harming; you shared that you'd been abused by a relative or lost a family member to addiction; you recounted the story about the terrible illness you fought or the horrific car accident you were in and told everyone how God's love was the only thing that got you through it. You cried. You confessed. You found catharsis. You found absolution in front of the collective. For a queen like me, testimony was the best part of church, the closest I could get to a bona fide diva moment, sans sequins. It was dramatic, it was performative, it was emotional, it was indulgent, and I loved it.

I spent years thinking about what my testimony would be. I fantasized about the soaring rhetoric I would use, about the way I would make people cry, about the adoration I would receive when I reached my triumphant conclusion and claimed it for God. But for years, I had to wait, because it was an unspoken rule that testimonies were only done by juniors or seniors in high school.

Finally, my time had come.

I was asked to give my testimony for a retreat called Discovery, which the high schoolers planned for the middle schoolers. For the middle schoolers, it was a chance to grow spiritually. For the high schoolers, it was an opportunity to hang out and flirt and get free food while also learning leadership skills. That year, I was asked to give the "God Created You" talk.

I mean, what did they *think* I was going to talk about? The struggles of wearing glasses in middle school? Having a lot of body hair? Not being good at sports? Of *course* I was going to talk about being a big ol' queen.

By this time, most of the high schoolers at church knew I was gay, but no one really told the middle schoolers what was going on. I was allowed to be gay at church, but they probably weren't ready for me to say, "Jesus made me gay and maybe he made you gay, too" in front of a bunch of sixth graders. I knew it was risky to write a testimony about being queer, but I couldn't let my church's reticence to publicly embrace my identity stop me from trying. So I sat down at my computer, and I started writing.

The week before the retreat, each person who'd been selected had to first give their talk to a committee of adult leaders. This mechanism wasn't usually used to censor talks; it was mostly in place so that young people didn't procrastinate and put off writing their talk until the night before. One Sunday after church, I went downstairs to the prayer room, sat in front of the committee, and gave the following talk:

As is the custom, I'd like to start out by reading a Bible verse for you guys, a Psalm that I picked out.

Psalm 139:13–18 (NIV)
"For you created my inmost being;
you knit me together in my mother's womb.
I praise you because I am fearfully and wonderfully made;
your works are wonderful,
I know that full well.
My frame was not hidden from you

when I was made in the secret place.
When I was woven together in the depths of the earth,
Your eyes saw my unformed body;
all the days ordained for me
were written in your book
before one of them came to be.
How precious to me are your thoughts, O God!
How vast is the sum of them!
Were I to count them,
they would outnumber the grains of sand."

When I read that verse, all I can say is wow . . . It honestly and completely blows my mind that God created me, created all of us, with such love and such thought. My favorite part of that verse, and the words that resonate with me so deeply, is the part right in verse 14 where it says, "I praise you because I am fearfully and wonderfully made."

I guess I never realized it until I was writing this talk, but that verse speaks so strongly to who I am, and what my experience in life has been. You see, I'm not sure if you guys know this, I don't know if someone has told you, if you've heard it from a friend, from Facebook, or if you just had a sneaking suspicion, but I'm gay. It's funny, no matter how many times I say it, or how many times I come out to people, it's always hard for me just to say those words, "I'm gay." Being gay has made life pretty interesting for me. Sometimes it's been okay, sometimes it's been kind of fun, sometimes it's been pretty lonely, sometimes it's been downright traumatic, and more often than not, it's been a challenge.

When I finally came around to that realization, it was terrifying, straight-up terrifying. It was like this wall had been drawn between me and everyone else in the world. I sort of began to panic, I didn't know where to turn, I didn't know who to talk to. So

I talked to no one. I didn't tell a soul. I clammed up, and didn't really let anyone in. I pretended that this whole sexuality thing simply didn't exist. I became an actor.

I pretended to like girls. I pretended to have crushes, I pretended to be this person that I clearly wasn't, and retained this fear that if I ever slipped up, if anyone ever understood who I truly was, if anyone ever saw through my disguise, my whole life would be ruined. I became pretty depressed, because when you hide who you are like that, you lose a lot of your ability to connect with people. You live in this constant all-pervasive fear that someone will find out how much of a freak you are. You can't connect with people because you can't connect with yourself. You lose a fundamental part of your humanity. In that capacity, I was an incomplete, destitute person. That's right about when the questioning started. I began to ask, "Why me? Why do I have to be the gay kid, why do I have to bear this burden?"

As I got older, the question of why became more and more important. The only conclusion that I came to was that God had made me gay, and I wasn't okay with that. Why would God want me to be miserable? Why would he put me through all of this, why would he put this burden on me for seemingly no reason? I couldn't even begin to understand. I just got angry.

Honestly, I began to hate God. I hated him for making me this way, I hated him for making me flawed, I hated him for not making me normal, I hated him for forcing me to be this person, I hated him for putting this thing in my life, I hated him for SO many reasons and I didn't know how to change that. So I began to withdraw from Him. I began to hate God and consequently, I began to hate myself. I was reduced to a closeted, scared, dishonest, miserable person. And it was that way for the span of around 4 or 5 years.

I began coming out to my closest friends the summer before sophomore year. The first time I came out to anyone, it was a nerve-racking, scary thing. I had become so used to putting up this facade, that breaking it down was hard. I felt so vulnerable, and vulnerability can be horrifying. Yet by making myself vulnerable to others, I began to make myself vulnerable to God, and he slowly began to make his way back into my heart. I began to open up my heart to the love that God has to transform us all.

A little over a year ago I went on a retreat called Chrysalis. While on Chrysalis, we had a nighttime candlelight service devoted to recognizing our sins and giving them to God. What I realized that night is that for so long, I had been trying to hide a fundamental part of who I was from God. It's a funny idea really, I was trying to hide a part of me that God had shaped, that God had formed. I had forgotten that God loves me no matter what, and not only that God had made me, but that God had made me in his image, and that because of that love and that creation, who was I to question why I was made this way? Who was I to hate who I am? It was at that point, at that service that night, that I said to myself, "This stops now." So I approached the altar, taking slow, careful steps. I kneeled in front of the cross, and I began to pray, and I said, "Hey God, it's Jacob, and I think I have something to tell you." And I paused for a second, I took a deep breath, and I told God, "I'm gay."

Now, I'm not one to claim that I've heard God very often. I'm not the kind of guy who says that God talks to me—Lord knows I'm not a prophet—but at that moment, I swore I heard God say, "I know. I'm here, I love you." And that was the moment I knew. I knew that who I was, that who I am is beautiful. I knew that God loved me no matter what. I had spent SO long hating who I was, and all in a moment, in two simple words, that hatred disappeared, and I knew that I was a child of God and that no matter what the rest of the world told me, I could always be confident in myself and my life because God loves me regardless. That God's love is so complete that nothing can get in the way of it.

That's when I got it. I am fearfully and wonderfully made.

I guess that what I'm trying to tell you tonight is that God made you for a reason. He made you just the way you are. You are fearfully and wonderfully made. Sometimes that word fearfully *seems out of place, but through my life, I've learned that it's not just something to disregard. It's a reality. Sometimes who we really are is scary. Sometimes who we are isn't easy. Sometimes we can hate who we are. We hate fundamental parts of our personalities, of our bodies, of many things. But the promise we have in God is that all of those things are not only wonderful, they are intentional, they are beautiful. And sometimes that is a scary idea, sometimes that is hard to accept.*

We all have parts of ourselves that we hate, we all have insecurities, whether we think we're too fat, or too skinny, or too smart, or too goofy, or not pretty enough, or not good enough at sports, or not cool enough, or whether we think our nose is too big or our feet are too small, or we have too much acne. If we think that we've done something that God could never love us for, or if we are a certain way that God could never be okay with, or if we simply cannot accept ourselves. Tonight, I invite you to take whatever it is that you hate about yourself, whatever it is that you think God could never love, whatever it is you think is disgusting or wrong or ugly, and give it to God. I invite you to know that you are fearfully and wonderfully made, that you are a child of God and consequently, every single part of you is perfect in his eyes. You are created by God and you are beautiful. Never forget that.

Let us pray. Dear God, I thank you for all of the beautiful people in this room. I thank you that we are created in your image, that we are all perfect in your eyes, and that we are fearfully and wonderfully made. I pray that you will guide us, and lead us in a direction of love and of self-acceptance. I pray for everyone sitting around me, I pray that whenever they feel ugly, whenever they feel downtrodden, and whenever they feel that who they are isn't good enough, I pray that you will be with them and that they will see the beautiful creation that they are. I thank you that you love us not in spite of our "flaws," but because of them. Please watch over us and be with us tonight. In your name we pray, Amen.

By the time I'd finished the talk, each person was in tears, myself included. I'd known that God loved me just the way I was, but it was the first time in my life I'd proclaimed that truth in public. I hugged the adult leader who I was closest to on the committee, and we prayed over the talk, prayed that God would guide me and help me get through it.

A day later, I got a call from Michael, our youth pastor, who I adored. He wanted to know whether I had time to meet him after handbell practice that week.

Uh oh.

The next day, we walked to the Wendy's across the street and Michael bought us both Frostys. If *anyone* buys you a *Frosty* before a meeting, odds are they don't have something nice to say. They're just hoping that the sweet, cold, chocolaty goodness will lull you into accepting bad news with grace.

In this case, the Frosty strategy proved ineffective. Michael told me that after speaking with a few adult leaders, he didn't think they could let me give my talk at the retreat. It wasn't that people had a problem with my talk per se—it was that he wasn't sure some of the adult leaders could handle the conversations that would follow. He was worried—and in retrospect, rightfully so—that a number of adult leaders would respond negatively to the talk, say bad things about homosexuality, or freeze up completely when they broke into their small groups. He wondered if I might keep my message, but change my topic. I told him I'd think about it.

I was heartbroken and furious. But I wasn't angry at Michael. He'd supported me steadfastly after I came out, and besides, it wasn't even *really* his decision. He was simply the messenger who'd been tasked with delivering the unfortunate news.

Instead, I was mad at my church family. The whole community. The collective that had let me down heinously and cut me to the bone. I felt like Jesus, forced by the Pharisees to deny his own divinity. I felt like Galileo, forced by the Inquisition to recant his suggestion that the earth revolves around the sun. I felt like Oscar Wilde, compelled to deny his love when put on trial.

How could they do this to me? It was *my* spiritual journey, it was *my* testimony. Who were they to tell me that my path with God wasn't good enough? Who were they to tell me that the love I knew wasn't real? Who were they to tell me that God didn't love me just as I was? *How dare they.*

As I drove home from church that night, something broke inside me that in some ways I'm still mending. It was the first time in my life that I felt not just redirected or ignored, but *silenced*—literally, figuratively, emotionally, all of it.

All I could think about was the impact this decision would have on the middle schoolers. I thought about who I was in sixth grade, just how scared I was of my difference, of my identity, and how much it would've meant to me to hear someone a few years my senior speak in such a positive, healing way. A talk like that could've saved me. A talk like that could've cut through five years of shame, loneliness, and self-hatred. At the tender age of eleven or twelve, a talk like that would've changed my whole world.

That was, and still is, my deepest lamentation about what happened. We had the chance to circumvent so much hurt. By opening up a conversation and allowing queer people at my church to own God's love for them, we could've healed.

I stormed into the house to tell my mom what'd happened. I was screaming. I was furious—not at her, but at the world. And, as anyone who has raised teenagers knows, my mother did exactly the thing that she shouldn't have—she tried to help me understand where the church leaders were coming from. That sent me over the edge. I stormed out.

I blazed through the woods behind my house, walking until my legs couldn't carry me anymore. I collapsed in sobs, the gravel digging into my knees. I knew God still loved me, but why couldn't the rest of the world?

While my sorrow that night was acute, the real tragedy was that it was only the beginning of the silencing I've endured, the silencing that I often endure, each time my identity or political consciousness takes a step forward.

In the end, I still gave a talk. But I did exactly what they asked of me: I edited it, keeping the message and changing the topic. It made me feel dirty, stained, dishonest.

Later in the evening, they let me give the talk as I first wrote it, but only to a group of high schoolers at a separate event. By that point, it felt empty. Hollow. It's hard to tell people that you embrace who you are, after you've heeded their command to be silent about it.

Following the incident with my testimony, my relationship to my church became strained. It was difficult to listen to the sermon without feeling cynical. It was difficult to feel God's love in that place. So I grew distant. I went to church less frequently.

In terms of being a functioning member of heterosexual society, the freedom that came with my distance from church was lethal. In terms of being a queer person with self-esteem and the ability to own their identity, that freedom was a blessing. I had the space I needed to experiment, to explore my queerness to its fullest extent. This exploration reached a fever pitch the spring of my junior year, at the mall (because *of course*).

That spring, I was hanging out with my friends Katie and Davis, a straight couple who were totally badass and super active in the Gay

Straight Alliance at school. Collectively, the two of them comprised *the entire* straight side of the group. And as far as they were concerned, I was their official third wheel. We weren't a throuple, per se, because they would only kiss each other, not me; but I'd like to think we were emotionally polyamorous. I'm not sure if Katie or Davis would agree with that assertion, but it's my memoir, so I'm entitled to my delusions.

On a mundane Saturday in late February, Katie, Davis, and I were hanging out at Katie's house when she decided that she wanted to go to the salon. Neither Davis nor I were interested in going with her, but we didn't want to just hang out at the house. Katie agreed to drop us off at the mall on the way to her appointment.

Davis and I spent an hour or so wandering around before we got bored of the whole place. In high school, the mall wasn't nearly as entertaining as it had been when we were younger. What once felt like an incredible place to explore now felt stale, a place you came to get generic Christmas presents for people you didn't care about that much.

Unamused and underwhelmed, Davis and I sat down on a bench. We texted Katie to see when she would be done, but she was going to be another hour or so. I should note that this was before you could check Facebook on your phone. I'm not sure Instagram even *existed* back in 2009. This was the old-school type of boredom. There were no cat videos to entertain us.

An idle mind is the devil's workshop, and in this case, the devil had some serious fun. After about five minutes of doing nothing, Davis looked me in the eye, dead serious, and uttered the nine words that would change my life forever:

"Dude, do you wanna go buy some high heels?"

I stared at him blankly, unable to compute. One of my best straight friends was proposing that we purchase high heels for ourselves. Shouldn't it be the other way around? Wasn't I supposed to be the one proposing this to him? Wasn't I the one who was supposed to drag him, kicking and screaming, into a women's store to buy girly things? Mind whirring, I said nothing.

Undeterred, Davis continued.

"Wouldn't that be awesome? You know how we were talking about gender being a spectrum in GSA? Well, let's go buy some heels. Katie will flip."

The truth of what I was being asked finally landed, and it hit me square in the solar plexus. I knew what I was supposed to say. I knew the safe answer. The safe answer was, *Nah, I'm okay. I mean, I'm gay and all, but just because I'm gay doesn't mean that I like to wear high heels. Besides, won't it be awkward to go into a women's store to get them? And what will our parents say if they find them? I don't think that's such a good idea. And I don't really want high heels anyway, I mean, aren't they uncomfortable?*

But that's not what came out of my mouth. What came out of my mouth was:

"Oh my God, *totally.*"

The rest, they say, is herstory.

A few moments later, we were standing outside Charlotte Russe, which carried the flashiest, tallest, most fabulous heels Crabtree Valley Mall had to offer for twenty-five dollars or less.

I took a deep breath. For Davis, it seemed like this was just a fun experiment, but for me, it was much, much more. I thought back to all the times I'd walked past this very store, uncertain why it entranced me so much, wishing I could walk in. I thought back to the first time I'd gone into Charlotte Russe with Meredith, how transgressive it had felt, how I'd had to feign disinterest in the garments and shoes. I thought back to the moments when I'd been caught red-handed experimenting with gender as a child, nails sloppily covered in polish, lips messily adorned with color.

I couldn't let those memories hold me back forever. I refused. So I summoned all of my queer courage, feigned some confidence, and put one foot in front of the other.

As I tramped along the tiled mall floor toward the store entrance, I felt myself on the brink of something massive. I was no longer entering the store under the aegis of disinterest or female companionship. For the first time, I was walking in of my own accord, in full (well, maybe partial) ownership of my desires and dreams.

When we crossed the threshold, I felt like an insurgent, like a spy, like I was in a James Bond movie. Davis was Daniel Craig, I was the Bond girl (or perhaps Dame Judi Dench), and we were running into a cocktail party, guns blazing, to assassinate the Russian ambassador. We stormed (well, walked swiftly) past the racks of clothes and headed straight to the back, to the sale section.

Though I played it cool, I was frantic. It was abundantly clear that we didn't belong. Would we be asked to leave? Would they refuse to sell us something? Would someone call mall security? Would they call my parents or fine me for disorderly conduct or something? *Was the sky going to fall? Y'all, it feels like the sky is going to fall. I'm not out freaking out, you're freaking out! Omg, stop telling me not to freak out, it's only making me freak out more!*

The emotional weight was gargantuan, but the reality was tepid. Yes, one or two of the women in the store shot glares of contempt in our direction, and a few others stared disapprovingly. But for every woman who was nasty (and not in the cool, Nasty Woman, fuck-you-Donald-Trump way), there were a few gorgeous souls who gave us knowing glances. In some cases, we even got smiles.

As we looked over the sales rack, clearly overwhelmed and disoriented, a store clerk approached us to ask if we needed any help.

"Yeah, um, yes, so, we are, uh—" I choked.

"Where can we find your cheapest high heels in the biggest sizes?" Davis interjected. Efficient.

The sales rep was lovely, albeit taken aback by how hard I was wigging out. She focused on talking to Davis because he wasn't hyperventilating and crazy-eyed and sweating.

"Well, our sales rack is over here, and we have the largest sizes grouped in this section. There are some size tens, and there might even be an eleven or two in there, but that's the biggest they run. Let me know if you need any help!"

She floated away and we started searching. I looked as fast as I could, desperate to get out of the store. Insular in my quest, I found a pair of size 10, black faux-leather pumps with a four-inch stiletto heel and a one-inch platform. Why I thought that was an appropriate "starter heel" for someone who'd never walked in high heels before, I will never know. Go big or go home, I guess? For expediency, I tried on only one shoe. My foot *barely* crammed inside, but I figured that was good enough.

I threw the shoes back in the box and turned around to find Davis confidently, albeit clumsily, strutting around in a pair of purple velvet heels with cheap metal buckles. He was beaming. "Look how great these are!" he exclaimed.

His courage was both inspiring and off-putting. How could he be so unafraid of what this meant? How could he be so bold? How could he just stand there in high heels in a women's store like it wasn't a massive deal?

I word-vomited, trying to hustle him along. "Haha yeah that's great are you gonna buy them awesome love it can you take them off now so we can go? youlookgreatpleasegetmeoutofhere."

Before I could rethink the decision or what it meant, I hurried both of us to the register. Davis's heels were seventeen dollars. Mine were a whopping twenty-three.

As we walked out of the store, I could finally begin to breathe, and my nerves gave way to giddiness. I was overcome. It was the kind of giddiness that comes from getting away with something, with pool hopping and not getting caught, with crashing a wedding reception and getting free champagne, with beating the final level of a video game, with a first kiss. It was a breathlessness, a high. A feeling of complete and utter joy.

Unstoppable waves of satisfaction and freedom and power and self-actualization. Not quite an orgasm, but still pretty *whoa*. All that over a shitty pair of twenty-three-dollar high heels that were a size too small.

"Davis, can you *believe* what we just did? That was so, so—"

"Awesome?" he interjected. I nodded in agreement.

An hour later, Katie picked us up outside the Chick-fil-A. Davis rode shotgun and I hopped in the back.

"Katie, you'll never guess what Jacob and I did," Davis exclaimed, opening his shoebox to show off his new acquisition. "We bought high heels!"

"You did *what*?" Katie was a font of pure, unadulterated excitement.

"It was Davis's idea!" I interjected jocularly (and perhaps a bit defensively). "I swear to God."

"Hon, I am thrilled that you have your own pair of heels; it's about damn time. Do you know how to walk in them yet?"

I took a moment to think about it.

"Not really."

"Well, we can fix that. Also, is anyone else hungry? Actually, it's my car so I don't care. I want a McFlurry. *We're going to McDonald's!*"

We drove to McDonald's and got some McFlurries and French fries, and Katie proceeded to give Davis and me a runway coaching session, Miss J. Alexander style, in the parking lot. Now that I was out of the mall and away from the prying eyes of other shoppers, I could put on my shoes and really give it my all. The anonymity of the empty parking lot was exactly what I needed to really shine. Despite the shoes being too small and very high, I was something of a natural. In my mind's eye, I'd like to think that I looked glamorous. Or at least as glamorous as one could expect to look while strutting around in a McDonald's parking lot in North Raleigh.

On the ride back to Katie's house, I looked at the open shoebox, high heels standing at attention on the seat next to me. Though the box read

"*Charlotte Russe*" in swirly letters on the side, I could've sworn it read "*Property of Pandora: DO NOT OPEN.*"

When I opened that shoebox, I'd experienced my first adult taste of emancipation from the gender binary. I think Davis experienced something similar. And though we didn't realize it at the time, neither of us would ever be able to close it again. There was no turning back.

When I got home that night, I ghosted swiftly through the front door and immediately up the stairs. Fortunately, my parents were asleep, so I was spared an awkward conversation about my purchase. I gingerly avoided the places I knew creaked, discouraging my plastic shopping bag from crinkling too loudly.

Once in my bedroom, I took the shoes out of their box, buried them in the bottom drawer of my dresser underneath some papers and T-shirts, and made quick work of disassembling the shoebox and discarding it at the bottom of the large trash bin in the garage. This would've been damning evidence if it'd been discovered, so I needed to be thorough.

Because I didn't have the courage to wear my high heels in public yet, I found any opportunity I could to wear them in private. I'd started staying up late to finish homework, which meant my parents went to sleep before I did. After they'd been asleep for half an hour or so, I would scurry up to my room, grab my high heels, and put on a little runway show for myself in the kitchen. I'd sit on what we'd affectionately deemed my "homework couch," bobbing my ankle in five-inch stilettos while casually studying French adverbs, reading about the temperance movement, or solving differential equations.

These late-night study sessions were responsible for some of my greatest personal discoveries. One night, I sat down to write an assignment about which of my identities were most important to me.

Eyes bleary from a long day, my feet clad in black pleather, I listed the following:

1. *High-Achieving and Intelligent person*
2. *Gay Advocate*
3. *Volunteer*
4. *Neither a man nor a woman: Genderless*
5. *Privileged*
6. *Non-smoker and non-drinker: non-partier in general*
7. *White? Maybe . . . Arab, too.*
8. *Christian?*

I looked at what I'd written, fixating on the fourth bullet; the others fell away. It was the first time I'd written that down. There was overwhelming power in seeing it on the page.

On another evening, I was perched on my homework couch—reading *Walden* by Thoreau and studying the transcendentalist movement—when I found myself brainstorming in the margins of my book:

Gender Transcendentalism?

I chewed on those words. Wasn't that what I wanted? To go into the woods, into a world of my own, build a gender of my own design, and set my own rules, free from the influence of the outside world? Didn't I want to transcend the binary? Float above the idea of manhood and womanhood, float above and beyond the idea of gender altogether, transcend to a higher spiritual plane?

I twirled my hair with my finger, and after another moment's thought, scrawled:

I'm a gender transcendentalist!

The words radiated back at me from the page, as if emblazoned in gold.

Some nights, when I was feeling my friskiest, I'd give up on studying altogether and put on a show instead. I'd choreograph little dance routines in my heels. Using the reflection in the kitchen bay window as my mirror and the breakfast nook as my studio, I would dance as softly as I could, almost in slow motion, so that my parents wouldn't hear the *clip-clop* of my heels on the hard tile floor. One time, I even choreographed a little routine to Lady Gaga's "LoveGame," using a brass fire poker in place of a proper disco stick.

Just past midnight, out of my parents' sight, I carved out a precious slice of femininity just for myself. It was mine to enjoy privately, in the dark, a textbook in hand. I was Cinderella in reverse. When the clock struck midnight, my fairy godmother returned, my pumpkin turned back into a carriage, my ball gown unfurled, and I could dance in my glass slippers once again.

But also like Cinderella, I knew my fantasy was on the clock. It would always come to an end. My dream was ephemeral and kept on a strict timer. Even in my happiest moments, as I twirled across the kitchen floor, I was haunted by the specter of impossibility. Claiming my truth in the quiet of the night was one thing. Claiming my femininity in the light of day, for the world to see, would be something else entirely.

The summer after my junior year, I was lucky enough to attend a North Carolina program called Governor's School. Many states have something similar, but in case you aren't familiar, it's a state-funded program for high schoolers who love school so much that they want to do *more* of it over the summer. Over six weeks, nerds, geeks, and artsy freaks from across the state live together on a small college campus, exploring their minds, the world, and one another's bodies. It's got all the debauchery, drama, and scandal of normal summer camp, but unlike summer camp, the jocks and the cheerleaders aren't there. Which meant that yours truly, who was usually just "the overachiever," finally got a shot at being "the cool kid," or at the very least, "sort of edgy."

Given how methodical and strategic I was about the process of coming out as gay, it should be no surprise that I took the same approach to sharing my nascent femininity with the world. In my trademark coming out style—obsessive, slightly maniacal, and overplanned—I'd determined that Governor's School was the perfect place to publicly experiment with my gender and push some boundaries free from penalty. I had six weeks and six weeks only with kids who I didn't go to school with from across the entire state. If I took a risk and it proved disastrous, it was fine, because I never had to see any of those nerds again. So when packing, I made the rash and ultimately beautiful decision to throw my high heels in my suitcase, wrapped up in a sweater so my parents couldn't see them.

I hadn't anticipated just how perfect Governor's School would be. To this day, it was still six of the best weeks of my entire life. It was the freedom of college, without the pressure to keep up your GPA. It was the freedom of Burning Man, without the sunburn and the dust. It was the freedom of adulthood, without the bills or the landlords or the choice between taking a corporate job in order to get healthcare or pursuing your dream of being a writer/actor in LA with no healthcare.*

The release of pressure was so vital for me. For six beautiful weeks, I didn't have to accomplish *anything.* I didn't have to worry about managing thirteen extracurriculars in order to "fully round out" my college applications or about taking just one more AP class on top of the four I was already enrolled in. For the first time in my anxious, stressed-out, college-preparatory life, I had six weeks to just fuck around, chill out, explore my gender, take a few ungraded classes, and try to seduce boys on the quad. I had the freedom, space, and time necessary to care for

---

* Sorry, Mom and Dad, but I made the less responsible choice on that one. God bless Obamacare and the LGBT Center of Los Angeles's health clinic. Oh, and it should go without saying, but *fuck* capitalism.

myself, to ask myself hard questions, to write bad poetry while sitting on a picnic blanket. I could think about who I was and, college be damned, who I wanted to be.

The heels sat unnoticed under my bed for the first four weeks, but by the fifth, the pressure was on. As each day ticked by, my window of opportunity was diminishing. One day, I decided that enough was enough. I was going to wear those fuckers out and about, and I was going to look great, goddamn it.

That day forever changed my life and altered the very shape of my shiny, too-trans-to-function consciousness. Just the process of putting on the shoes, of stepping out of my room and into the hallway, impacted me so much that I ended up making it the subject of my college application essay, and it is through that lens that I'd like to share it with you.

While the essay I submitted to colleges was adjusted somewhat, tamed and sanitized to be more *appropriate*, more *palatable*, more *focused* and *intellectual*, I feel that the first draft shines the brightest. The first draft is the crystal in its true form: a gorgeous chunk of rock hewn from inside the earth, rough edges and imperfections unpolished. To me, the crude theory and unfiltered moments of minor incoherence are everything. They are what bring out the full rawness, the disorienting, visceral, messy quality of what I was exploring at that stage of my life. Also, I wrote this essay at the beginning of my senior year of high school, so please take a moment to appreciate that I was a goddamned prodigy, thanks.

I knew I could do it; I had done it before.

My foot contorted, I pointed my toes, I wiggled my foot, straightened my ankle, and tried again. And after a minute or two of somewhat exasperated effort, there was a moment when my ligaments were aligned in just such a way that my foot managed to make it into the shoe. It was a very tight fit, and I had to readjust my toes manually, but the shoe was on my foot nonetheless. It felt strange, wearing a size 10 in women's when I was used to wearing a size 11 in men's.

I stood up, and immediately thereafter, I sat back down. I did not know how to walk in high heels. My body just couldn't quite get the mechanics right. I couldn't keep my calves constantly engaged and I didn't understand how to swing my hips in the manner requisite for being mobile while wearing such contraptions around my ankles.

It was an experiment really. I had heard some of my friends complaining about the blisters on their feet, the aching of their toes, and the pain in their backs as they strutted about daintily in three-inch pumps; I'd had numerous conversations with one of my friends about why she felt the need to wear high-heeled boots every day, in spite of her severe back problems; I could hear the "click-clack" of my teachers walking on the hardwood floors in the upstairs hall of my school—the sound evoking images of patent leather. I'd been observing silently, intrigued by why a woman would ever make the choice to wear a pair of heels and by what that choice indicated about the world around us. I wanted to understand the reasoning behind it all, because while the sex appeal in wearing heels was evident, I couldn't seem to grasp any sort of logical reasoning that really seemed to justify it all.

So I bought a pair at Charlotte Russe, a women's clothing store. They were a pair of four-inch stiletto pumps that were encased in synthetic black leather—the kind that would make many women cringe. But they were exactly what I wanted, subtle enough in color as to not be apparent on first glance, but tall enough that I could gain a real perspective into American womanhood.

I stood back up and strode over toward the full-body mirror that hung on the door of my dorm room. The silhouette of my foot was somewhat alarming—it was overtly sexualized in a way that I had not quite expected. It was still a hairy foot, but aside from that it was much more feminine than I would have expected—a sort of anachronism of the body. As my initial state of alarm faded, I was pulled back into the reality of the situation. I was about to leave my male dorm room, into a guys' hallway, in the men's dormitory, all of which while astride four-inch stilettos. Thus, my sense of amazement with my feet faded into fear of them. I sat back down on my bed in order to regroup, in order to reanalyze the situation.

Outside of my room, I could hear rowdy teenage guys throwing a football back and forth down the hallway. I could hear their exclamations of disapproval at someone dropping the ball, or throwing it incorrectly. Their words obliterated whatever sense of courage I had and conjured within me a recollection of the ever-pervasive presence of masculine expectation. The word "faggot" kept ringing in my ears and, before I quite knew what was going on, I realized that my room had shrunk to the size of a closet.

With each successive "thump" of the football hitting a wall and with each verbal expression of masculine dominion, a multitude of closet doors were slammed in my face. Some of these doors were ones I had never seen before, some led to rooms I had never known existed, and some were doors that I thought I had opened long ago. They were the doors of fluid sexuality, of ominous white privilege, of pervasive masculinity, of continual and sustained affluence, of reformed gender identity, of under-the-rug misogyny, of flawed moral principle. By opening the door of my dorm room and crossing the threshold of private life into a public forum, I would be opening so many other doors simultaneously, obliterating every preconceived notion of my identity and self-definition, chipping away at the supposedly infallible obelisk of societal expectation. I took a deep breath, hoping that maybe with more oxygen I would be able to gain the courage, the audacity, to step outside.

After a moment or two had passed, I turned the door handle, heard the latches click, and pushed open my door ever so gingerly. I stepped outside of the room, locked my door, and proceeded to walk down the hall and into the stairwell. The boys in the hall said nothing, although an absence of words in many cases can be indicative of something much more terrible than approval. I carefully continued down the three flights of stairs, all the while holding on to the railing for stability and praying I wouldn't break my ankle. I walked through the lobby and toward the dining hall for breakfast.

I could hear the *click clack* of my heels on the brick walkway.

click

A boy starts a ballet class and doesn't worry about what his friends will say.

clack

A college student reads Judith Butler.

click

A transgender person understands that, while they have a difficult life to face, they will not be alone.

clack

A sex worker reclaims her dignity and autonomy from a world that says she's worthless.

click

A woman finds freedom from her abusive husband.

clack

A friend, struggling with bulimia, realizes that she is beautiful.

click

All people, man and woman, realize that in some small way,
they have not been true to themselves, and the bonds of gender
stereotypes and heterosexism dissolve into truth.

clack

It was eight a.m. and I was feeling the foreshocks of morning
hunger. But that hunger never seemed to be able to take a firm
grasp, because somewhere in my soul, I was satisfied beyond
explanation.

Upon rereading my first draft of this essay, the roughness is obvious: At the age of seventeen, I had to come up with a justification for wearing high heels, something other than the full truth. I told the world, told myself, that I was trying to gain some kind of empathy with women, that it was all an intellectual experiment and nothing more. I still didn't know how to claim to anyone else—or, for that matter, to myself—that I wanted to wear high heels simply because *I wanted to wear them*. I didn't know how to say that I wanted to wear high heels because I thought *they were great*, because I thought *I looked good in them*, because *I was a motherfucking goddess and you're just going to have to deal with that*.

I also know that in the part where I wrote about "a transgender person," I didn't yet realize I was talking about my own heart. Back then, I had such a narrow definition of what transness could be. I thought you were only trans if you wanted to change your body in a serious way. I thought being trans was a cookie-cutter, one-size-fits-all identity, one that certainly didn't seem to fit me. Along with not knowing how to claim that my desire for femininity was *mine*, I was also years away from claiming my proper place as part of the trans community.

But for everything I got wrong in the essay, there is so much more that I got right; in some cases, without even realizing it. I understood intersectionality—the way that white supremacy props up patriarchy props up poverty props up environmental destruction props up white supremacy again—on a gut level, even if I didn't know to call it "inter-sectionality" yet. I understood that sex workers are often stigmatized, barred from claiming their full humanity, by sexist culture and feminist movements alike. I understood that the idea of "The Closet" applied to so much more than just queer people, that we are all in a closet of one kind or another. And, contrary to all of my actions since, I understood that high heels and back problems were, in fact, related.

What stands out to me most is that, at the age of seventeen, I seem to have understood the full stakes of what I was doing. I understood that by challenging gender norms and conventional masculinity, I was chal-lenging, well, *everything*. Through challenging the idea of manhood, of being "a good man," of "manning up," I was burrowing deep into the core of power, privilege, and hierarchy. On a gut level, I understood that my freedom and liberation were wrapped up with those of so many others who were facing oppression.

Ironically, it might've been helpful if I were a bit, well, *dumber* about the whole gender thing. It might've been a lot easier to strut out in a pair of heels if I didn't already perceive the weight of the world on my shoulders, if I hadn't already begun to calculate it. It might've been easier to don stilettos in public if I were just another stereotypically ditzy queen. But I'm not a ditzy queen. Most people who are perceived to be "ditzy queens" aren't even ditzy queens. We're all pretty damn brilliant. It's just that we aren't understood as such because we love glitter and se-quins and vintage dresses from the 1980s and our grandmother's clip-on earrings, and patriarchy deems all things feminine to be less intelligent.

The rest of the day, which I spent running around campus in heels, was earth-shattering in that it was *almost* uneventful. After leaving my dorm, I headed to the dining hall to meet my friends for breakfast and got pretty much nothing but praise. I wasn't just *daring* for wearing high heels; it seemed that I was downright *inspirational* and, in the context of nerd camp, *kind of cool*. It went by like a dream. Friend after friend stopped to take pictures with me and my shoes. People exclaimed at my ability to walk in heels that were so high without falling. And apparently, when I had high heels on, my scrawny legs (that had been less-than-affectionately called "chicken legs" on many occasions) were suddenly *great* legs. In heels, I wasn't scrawny—I was waifish and flowing and gorgeous and glamorous. Go figure.

The affirmation I received radically shifted my consciousness. Up until that point in my life, the script had always gone like this:

ACT I: *Jacob attempts to be feminine*
ACT II: *Jacob is chastised for being feminine*
ACT III: *Jacob gives up on being feminine*

For the first time in my life, I realized this script wasn't the only possible version. I started rewriting, going through drafts like:

ACT I: *Jacob attempts to be feminine*
ACT II: *Jacob is praised for being feminine, and people realize it's actually pretty great/interesting*
ACT III: *Jacob gets a book deal and a TV show*

Or:

ACT I: *Jacob attempts to be feminine*
ACT II: *Jacob is praised for being feminine and everyone is fine with it*
ACT III: *Jacob runs for Senate, helps pass universal healthcare and a living wage, and gets to wear one of Madeleine Albright's brooches—on loan from the Smithsonian—to the inauguration of their sexy, handsome husband as president.*
ACT IV: *While maintaining their public criticality of the military-industrial complex and calling for the abolition of the American*

prison system as we know it, Jacob manages to be the most
fabulous First Lady since Michelle Obama.

After going out on a limb and falling so many times, I was convinced that branches were designed to break. That day, the branch finally held. I didn't fall. It didn't break. And from my new vantage point, I saw infinite possibility.

Also, it's worth mentioning that the day I chose to wear heels for the first time just *happened* to be the day that the supervisors from the North Carolina Department of Education came to assess how the program was going. Without realizing who they were, I sashayed past their table with my tray of eggs like I owned the place. What they thought, I can never be sure, but I will say this: The year after I attended, Governor's School started getting its funding cut by the North Carolina General Assembly. The unspoken consensus of conservative legislators was that the program was basically a queer socialist liberal recruitment camp for homosexuals. I can't know for sure whether that stereotype was *wholly* based on me, but if I ever found out that it was, I'd be honored.

As compelling as the essay was, many people in my life were apprehensive. An essay like that, an essay about wearing high heels and being the gayest thing on the planet, was seen as a big risk back in 2009. After all, Lady Gaga hadn't come out with *Born This Way*, Barack Obama was still "undecided" on the question of same-sex marriage, and streaming TV basically didn't even exist, so no one knew who Laverne Cox was yet (can you imagine?). It was a darker time, exempting the fact that Donald wasn't smashing stuff in the White House yet.

My parents, more than anyone else, were hesitant—and, on a few occasions, outright angry—about my essay. They were terrified that I was destroying my life (and sabotaging any chance I had of getting into a good school) by writing about high heels. In their eyes, I was likely throwing away all my hard work over a pair of shoes.

Thankfully, my teachers were hesitantly optimistic, and they helped me tweak the essay to make it more palatable to colleges. We honed the essay so it would more adequately address the diversity prompt on the Common Application, and added paragraphs like this one:

> *The pain in my feet was more than simply a physical pain; it was a pain that mirrored some part of what women are subjected to each day, and each step seemed to teach me something new. With each step, I began to more seriously question what this pain meant about masculine privilege. Was this why women are often expected to be subservient? Was this why there is a glass ceiling? Was this what Susan B. Anthony was referring to when she said, "The fact is, women are in chains, and their servitude is all the more debasing because they do not realize it"? With each step, I began to envision a world where women and men would not be confined by their gender, but liberated by it.*

I think my teachers and college counselors were probably thinking, *Jacob, you can write about wearing high heels for your college essays, but for the love of God, please don't say you* liked *it! High heels are uncomfortable and awful and* real *feminism is trying to get away from high heels, okay?*

And in my head I was probably like, *But high heels are so cute and powerful, and yes, I may have a colonized aesthetic sensibility, but so do you, and ugh fine okay, I'll take out the part where I write about loving how my legs looked.*

So instead of writing about how sexy my legs looked in heels, I did what any self-respecting college administrator would want and added some boring neoliberal stuff about diversity, doubling down on my gay manhood in the process:

As a gay man, I understand diversity through the lens of privilege; because, in essence, diversity and privilege are diametrically opposed to one another. The presence of privilege is the absence of diversity, and conversely, true diversity can only exist after all systems of privilege have broken down. I have come to understand this through the process of coming out and through various advocacy efforts in my church, school, and larger community. I have learned that the walls of "the closet" are not composed of ignorance as much as they are built by the reality of heterosexual privilege. Thus, the closet door is the threshold between the world of privilege and the world of diversity.

(I mean, it's good, but it's kind of a snoozefest, right? I was eighteen years old and I sound like a forty-three-year-old VP of Student Affairs.)

Through this understanding of privilege as antithetical to diversity, I constantly strive to understand my own privilege in the name of furthering diversity. That is what I sought to do by wearing a pair of high heels for a day. Because high heels are such an emphatic symbol of feminine oppression, I sought to break down some of my own privilege as a male through wearing them. In turn, through breaking down my masculine privilege, I was able to further diversity in the community around me.

(The fact that I had to double down on my "male privilege" in order to make this essay make sense fucking sucks. Sure, there are ways in which I have had greater access to privilege because I was legally designated male at birth, but I think the whole having-to-silence-my-gender-identity-for-two-decades-of-my-life-then-being-a-gender-freak-for-the-rest-of-it thing more than accounts for that. What's interesting, though, is that if you just replace the word *privilege* with *identity*, this part of the essay still reads true. I sought to break down not "my own privilege as a male," but "my own *identity* as a male." Through "breaking down my masculine *identity*," I was in fact able to further diversity in the community around me.)

> *That is how I understand diversity. Diversity is not a statistic or a static state of being; rather, it is a way to approach the world around you. It constitutes the ability to deeply empathize with those around you, and the propensity to consider experiences that are not your own. It requires you to not only reconsider your preconceived notions of normality, but to truly immerse yourself in the world of another person. Diversity is an action, not a state of being, and that action is the action of sacrifice. In order to truly understand another perspective of the world, you must be willing to sacrifice the way that you are used to experiencing it. You must put aside your privilege and step into the role of someone else. You must give up what you have in order to understand who you are. That is the kind of challenging and exciting diversity that I try to practice in my everyday life, and that is the kind of diversity that I will bring to a college campus.*

(Okay so maybe some of that was insightful, but I was super bored by it at the time.)

As it turned out, my parents' anxiety was completely unfounded, because *girl, that essay got me into Harvard.* I wrote about wearing high heels and being a total goddess and Harvard was like, "Yeah we *def* want this cutie in our freshman class next year!" My admissions officer at Harvard even sent me a handwritten note saying that it was one of the *best college essays she'd ever read in her entire career as an admissions counselor.*

It also got me into Princeton and Columbia. And a full ride at Duke.

Oh, and a full ride at UNC, too. Interestingly enough, it did *not* get me into either Yale or Brown, Ivy League schools that are notoriously queerer than the others. Go figure. They probably had too many queens already.

Based on some bad advice and knowing nothing about how elite culture works in New York City, I ended up choosing to go to Duke on a full ride, even though Harvard would've been fairly affordable with financial aid. And since I am a petty and insecure person, I've always been grumpy about that decision because

1. **Duke was kind of awful in a way that Harvard may not have been.**

I mean don't get me wrong, Harvard is atrocious, too. It can be a cutthroat, cruel place and as an institution it is singularly responsible for incredible inequality throughout the world. I am not endorsing Harvard here. But when choosing between fancy private schools, it's not a question of *if* you're going to go to school with assholes, it's a question of *what type* of assholes you'll go to school with. And the truth is that I find the average Harvard asshole a fraction more tolerable than the average Duke asshole: Duke assholes love money and basketball; Harvard assholes love money and *books*. Also, as an *actual* Southerner, there was something uniquely insufferable about a kid from New Jersey coming to Duke, learning to play banjo, and *pretending* to understand barbecue.

2. **No one tells you that if you don't actually *go* to Harvard, you don't get to tell people that you *got in*.**

Like, if you *actually graduated* from Harvard, you get to walk around with your crimson-colored, Harvard-branded dick out all day being like, "I graduated from Haaaaaaaahvahhhhd. Look at me!" even though *everyone* knows that graduating from Harvard doesn't mean shit. Everyone who goes to Harvard pretty much graduates. Graduating isn't the hard part. It's the *getting in* that counts.*

But if you're dumb like me and get in and then *don't go like a provincial queer idiot*, then you *don't* get to walk around parties with your dick out being like, "I went to Harvard!" You actually have to move to New York City *without a job at the* New Yorker *already lined up*, keep your dick *in your pants* while attending a fancy party at the Harvard Club, and then get drunk enough to start blurting out, like some insecure asshole, "Oh, I totally *got into* Harvard but didn't go" in order for people to fully understand your intellectual pedigree.

Then people are always like, "Well, why didn't you *go*?" and you have to be like, "Because I *wasn't a personal-brand-obsessed monster* when I was eighteen so I thought I could pass the whole 'went to Harvard' thing up? Also I guess I didn't realize that it might be cool to go to a school that is basically a feeder for (*hiccup*) *SNL* writers? Who even cares about Lorne fuggin Michaels (*hiccup*) anyway? Fuck you, Kristen Wiig, I love you (*gag*) so goddamn much. Alsoo I'm durnk rightnow so pease don't makeme essplain m'self. HEY. hey. *hey*. y'know Kate McKinnonm isLESbian rihgt? I wann'be (*retch*) lebbian too—" before you run to the bathroom to avoid throwing up on the floor.

Anyway, the point is, I wrote an essay about wearing high heels and got into Harvard because of it but didn't go because I didn't understand elite culture. For the love of God, can someone *please* go update my Wikipedia page? I'm really tired of drunkenly telling people I got in. I'd rather drunkenly tell people to read my Wikipedia page and let Wikipedia do the heavy lifting.

At the time, getting into Harvard *specifically because* I was both super

---

* Or, conversely, you get to be the sheepish asshole who just tells everyone at a cocktail party that you went to school "in Boston" and then people have to go on your LinkedIn page when they're hungover at work the next morning to double check that you were, in fact, one of those sheepish assholes who says "Boston" but means "Harvard."

smart and super queer felt like just the validation I needed. As a queer high schooler, I was often denied the same types of validation that were afforded to my peers. I never had a boyfriend or a girlfriend. I never asked a crush to prom or was asked to prom by someone who had a crush on me. I didn't have the unequivocal support of my church or my faith community. I didn't see lots of people like me all over TV or in the movies. I didn't even have the validation of being able to shop in the stores I wanted to shop in or wear the clothing I felt most comfortable in. Validations were few and far between. "Achievement" was often *all that I had*. I clung to it with all of my traumatized, emotionally neglected might.

That's why affirmation from Harvard hit the spot, albeit acidly. Harvard felt like my *consolation prize*, granted to me in exchange for rarely feeling at home in my body or my community growing up. It was a lonely, selfish affirmation—one that few of my peers could share—but it made all the difference to me at the time.

My senior year, I didn't go to my prom. I was spared having to hide in plain sight amid my mostly straight, mostly cis classmates while they celebrated their gender and sexuality openly. I didn't have to spend an evening standing around in a tux that I hated, constantly being reminded of the fact that feeling sexually isolated and sexually unattractive go hand in hand. I didn't have to spend an evening longing to be touched while I watched my friends touch one another freely.

While the rest of my friends were dancing at senior prom, I was at Harvard's "for admitted students" weekend, watching a student fashion show and hearing a speech from Vera Wang.

That weekend, for the first time in my life, I tasted a new flavor. Wrapped in the validation of the ivory tower, protected for the first time by its toxic mantle of privilege, I finally gave myself permission to feel bitter and vindictive toward all the straight and cisgender people I grew up with. Sitting in Harvard's Memorial Hall, listening to Vera Wang talk about her journey as an Asian American woman in the fashion world, a brooding thought flashed through my head, directed at all the people who hadn't created space for me throughout my life, at all the people who never had to feel uncertain in their gender or isolated in their sexuality:

I made it. Take that, motherfuckers.

As complicated as it was, this affirmation emboldened me to start claiming my truth differently. There *was* a world out there that could affirm me, that could hold the full complexity of my queerness. Or so I thought.

From that emboldened, vindictive place, I was able to begin the long process of holding my church accountable for abandoning me in my time of need.

Graduation Sunday is an annual celebration for church members who are completing their education, from high school diplomas to PhDs. Each senior wears their graduation robes to the service and stands before the congregation to be celebrated. The usual sermon is replaced by senior sermons, where chosen high school seniors ascend to the pulpit to preach. It is a special moment in any young person's church life, a send-off as you begin your journey into the adult world.

Normally, senior sermons are beautiful, indulgent, sentimental, and tearful. Or they're poorly written, uncomfortable, and awkwardly de-livered. Either way, they are the time when you say thank you to the church for everything.

But by the time I sat down to write my senior sermon, I felt hollowed out. I tried to write a sentimental sermon with soaring prose that would shine above the others. I tried to write a sermon replete with love, grat-itude, and adoration. But it simply wouldn't come. By that point, I'd been too hurt, too dismissed, too scarred by my church to leave on good terms or to let them off the hook.

When I sat down to write, the words that flowed from my fingers scared me. Among the requisite reflections on how St. Francis United Methodist Church had helped me grow, on how much the church had taught me about myself, I wrote this:

> *Things haven't always been so wonderful for me at St. Francis. As one of the very few openly gay members of this congregation, there have been times when I have needed support and have not been supported, and there have been times when I have needed to be nurtured, and not been. In many ways, as a gay Christian, I have been alone in struggling to reconcile my gay identity with my faith. Thus, it is my sincerest hope for St. Francis that I will be leaving behind a changed church. It is my sincerest hope that, when I'm gone, St. Francis will continue to grow and continue to thrive, and it is my sincerest hope that I am leaving behind a St. Francis that will actively support and nurture all the diverse and wonderful members of its congregation.*

After I finished writing, it struck me: My senior sermon wasn't me saying thank you—it was me saying good-bye. It was my breakup letter. It was the only way I knew to tell people I had to go, that this relationship was no longer working, was, in fact, abusive. When I read the sermon to my mother, she begged me not to give it. She knew I was injured, that I was hurting, but this just wasn't what senior sermons were for.

"Can't you just say thank you for the good parts? Can't you just thank people for the ways they've helped you and supported you? Can't you just focus on the positive? I know that being gay at church hasn't been the easiest, but can't you keep this upbeat? It's probably the last time you're going to address the congregation like this, and I'd hate for people to take it the wrong way," she pleaded.

I understood where my mom was coming from. I think that, on

some level, she didn't want to admit that the church had been anything but loving for me; on some level, she felt accountable for the pain the church had caused me. She'd invested so much time and love in ensuring that I had a faith community and a spiritual practice. She'd woken me up on countless Sunday mornings and gotten me into the car. She'd driven me to and from church thousands of times. Church was our special thing. My dad didn't really go, and neither did my brother, so losing me at church must've been painful for my mom. She didn't know how to let that part of our relationship go.

In the end, I didn't listen to her—I couldn't. I had to speak my piece, so I gave the sermon I'd written. I held back my tears as I broke up with my congregation, as I said what I thought would be a final farewell, leaving a relationship I thought was over. I had never wanted things to come to this, but despite my best efforts, it seemed they had.

When I went off to college, I didn't look back. I didn't try to join the Methodist group on campus, I didn't find a new church to attend in Durham, and I didn't make a point of telling people in my life about my faith journey. As far as anyone who went to college with me knew, I wasn't a spiritual person, and I certainly wasn't a Christian.

The distance was healing. I hadn't realized just how badly I needed to be emancipated from the church for a while. I had damage that needed time to mend. In high school, I hadn't given myself the space or time I needed; I kept picking at the scab over and over, desperate for healing. College allowed me the time to properly treat my wounds, to wrap them up in gauze and wait out the stitches. As I grew more distant, I also grew stronger in my sense of self and knowledge of my own power. Even though I went to college forty minutes away from home, I never went home on Sundays to go to church.

Instead, I would spend my Sundays like most college students: sleeping in late, recovering from the night before, and—in my case— trying to figure out why there was so much glitter in my bed.

PART III

Big Queen on Campus

Chapter 6

A Gothic Wonderland, a Major Letdown

*I*f my intentions were to write a book after I graduated college, I couldn't have chosen a more perfect place to go to school than Duke University. Duke is infamous. The only Ivy League(ish) school that also excels in athletics, with a basketball program that has won five NCAA Championships since I was born in 1991, Duke is pretty much considered a bully by everyone. The Ivy League schools hate Duke because we have that effortless sense of "State School Cool," and the state schools hate Duke because we are pretentious sons-of-bitches from the tri-state area. Feminists (rightfully) hate Duke because they/we/I still haven't forgotten about the Duke Lacrosse scandal, but feminists also love Duke because queer theory pretty much started with Duke University Press (or, at the very least, Eve Kosofsky Sedgwick wrote *Epistemology of the Closet* while she was there). People from North Carolina hate Duke because we're a bunch of terrible kids from The City whose parents singlehandedly destroyed the economy in 2008, but they also love Duke because it is the number two employer in the state, second only to Walmart.

This tension is baked into the school's very architecture, into its stones and mortar. Looking up at the Duke Chapel, a neogothic masterpiece that soars to a height of twenty stories, it can be breathtakingly gorgeous, recalling the spires of Oxford and Canterbury, mystical tales of castles and knights and damsels in distress. But it can also seem menacing. At the right angle, it looks kinda like Sauron's tower from the Lord of the Rings—the one with the big red flaming eyeball that looks out across all of Middle-earth. So it's hard to say. Is Duke beautiful? Yes. Does the architecture suggest that some kind of medieval torture occurs in the chapel crypt? Also yes.

Incidentally, Duke is a memoirist's dream. It is the perfect antagonist: complicated, multifaceted, dynamic, awful-yet-desirable. Like the Grinch in *How the Grinch Stole Christmas!* or Meryl Streep in *The Devil Wears Prada*, Duke is a villain you love to hate. And *oh boy, did I ever.*

You, my dear reader, are in for a convoluted treat. This is the point where my problems start wildly oscillating between real-people problems and fancy-queer-lady-who-doesn't-actually-have-all-that-much-money problems. This is the point where I get to dish about what goes on *inside* the country club—about the sexism and misogyny and transphobia and racism of the protected upper echelons of society—while still feeling like a sellout for joining in the first place. So pop some champagne, stuff your mouth with complimentary hot nuts, and enjoy your trip on Bougie Trans Weirdo Airlines. Apologies in advance, but the captain has turned on the fasten seatbelt sign for the duration of the flight: It's gonna be a bumpy, turbulent, gut-punching ride.*

My college experience didn't begin with a keg stand or a visit to an austere library: it began with a twelve-day romp through the Appala-

---

* And if you stick with me for the journey, you might even get to hear about the time I bumped into Bruce Springsteen at a bar on graduation weekend. So there's that.

chian Mountains. The program, called Project WILD, was one of the most popular among Duke's pre-orientation offerings. Incoming first years would pack up all their things for their college dorm rooms, bring them to campus, leave them, and immediately hop on a bus to the mountains.

The Appalachian Mountains are some of the oldest in the entire world, predating the Atlantic Ocean itself. They originated when the world was but one continent, soaring to Himalayan heights at the center of Pangea. Over 480 million years, they have been carved, slowly and beautifully, to their present-day shape. Standing in the shadow of that much geologic history, among mountains that have seen the birth of entire oceans, it is easy, and indeed proper, to feel minuscule and irrelevant.

With nothing but an endless vista of mountains in front of you, flecked with outcroppings of rock, the deep green of pine and the dusty green of late-summer maple and oak cascading down their sides, you lose track of yourself. You lose sense of each other. Your identity becomes a tabula rasa, a blank slate upon which to draw.

To treat nature as wholly idyllic is to oversimplify a harrowing force, but to disregard its transformative qualities is an equally grave oversight. The twelve days I spent hiking around Pisgah National Forest in the most temperate part of an Appalachian summer were sublime. I felt at peace with the world around me, my worries about what "typical Duke students" would be like placed on the back burner. The nine people on my hiking crew were kind, empathetic, sweet, and motivated. We did long days of hiking, using only old-school topographical maps. In the era of smartphones and GPS, the experience was novel—and replete with all the campiness you'd hope for from a pre-orientation camping excursion.

It was everything you'd expect. Like a bad sitcom version of a collegiate backpacking trip, there were songs by the campfire, silly nicknames, collective nudity, and *way too much* group bonding time. As someone who adores both nature and overly sentimental traditions, these are some of the happiest memories from my freshman year.

What pleased me most was that, in nature, our normal approach to gender melted away. It melted so effortlessly that most people hardly noticed. Like an ice cube on a summer sidewalk, suddenly, it's gone. Presto. Poof. Alakazam.

It's hard to say exactly why this happens, but it's a fairly universal phenomenon in outdoor programs. Part of it has to do with the radical change in architecture. Without rigid physical barriers, without corners or walls, without doors or locks, structures that are designed to keep us all separate, the metaphorical structures between us tend to disappear as well.

And it's baked into the psychology of backpacking. Backpacking demands a profound kind of acceptance. If it is raining, it is raining. If you stink, you stink. If your boots are wet, they will simply be wet. No matter how tired you are of going uphill, the topography of the mountain can only ever be what it is. It may change over thousands of millennia, but you will not see those changes in your lifetime.

Without societal structure, in the shadow of the oldest mountains on Earth, you just sort of lose track. Gender evaporates. What is our modern concept of gender to a 480-million-year-old outcropping of rock?

Overnight, gender-as-division was gone, replaced only by the imperative to be good to one another, care for one another, and treat one another with dignity. For those two weeks, my gender could not have mattered less. No one cared about whether my behavior was "appropriate," because they were too busy caring for my body and heart just as they were. When you're alone in the woods in a group of nine people, no one is disposable. You help one another, you respect one another, and you value one another, because you can't afford not to. Any sense of hierarchy or stereotype suddenly feels not just irrelevant, but counterproductive.

Gender no longer dictated responsibility, either. If you were stronger, you would carry a bit more weight on a voluntary basis. If you weren't as strong, that was okay, too. The group was not calibrated to the strongest performer, but rather to the weakest. It wasn't just that no one was left behind; it was that the slowest person *went first*. The person who was struggling the most set the pace, and everyone else followed. Because I was spritely and lanky and my back problems hadn't started in earnest yet, that person was not me. I was one of the fast hikers. But my speed wasn't connected to a sense of masculinity or femininity. It was simply connected to my body's structure, to my vital signs.

One of the greatest shifts also came from the fact that, in the woods, bodily functions immediately stopped being gendered. Everyone talked in depth about bowel movements. Everyone peed outside. Everyone used leaves for toilet paper. And we were unapologetically gross. We washed our bowls with saliva, licking everything clean because, without sanitary drinking water, that's the best way to do it.

Each time we wanted to relieve ourselves, we had to tell each other with specificity exactly what type of movement we were having, because it determined how far we'd stray from the group. If I just had to pee, I would go one "see-far" from the trail, a distance still just barely in sight of the group. And if I had to poop, I would take the communal trowel, go two "see-fars," and take however long I needed, using a hole that I dug myself.

We monitored one another's bowel movements as a community. Sometimes it could take a few days for someone to become comfortable pooping in the woods. But if it took *too* long for your body to acclimate, it could become a health problem, and thus a concern of the entire group. Having explosive diarrhea is never desirable, but having explosive diarrhea thirty hiking miles from civilization can be medically dangerous. By the third night, it is the responsibility of every group leader to ensure that each person in their group has had a bowel movement, and if someone is still holding out, you prompt a bowel movement by making the most infamous meal of the trip: veggie chili.

After the fifth day, our inhibitions about potty talk were completely gone, and on the sixth—after we'd stumbled upon a wild blueberry patch and eaten so many berries our mouths turned purple—three of us were thrilled to report that the berries were potent enough to turn our poop green. By day seven, pooping wasn't even a big deal.

On day eight, my group stopped for a break and I left on a two-see-far trip, trowel in hand. At one see-far, I noticed that the tree line was breaking. At two see-fars, the whole valley opened in front of me, Cold Mountain (yes, the one from the movie) looming ahead. It was a few hours before sunset, and with the valley bathed in gold, I began digging into the rocky earth. Birds soared over the ridge, a poetic silence surrounding their cries. The leaves rustled beside me, wind gliding up the mountainside. As I gazed out, contemplating the beauty of our natural world and every creation in it, I knew that no gender-neutral bathroom on Earth had ever been so opulent.

At the time, I didn't realize the significance of what was happening; I just knew I was happy. I could sport whatever color bandana or shirt I wanted to. I could wear any clothes that felt good, or I could wear no clothes at all. I could sleep wherever I wanted, provided it was dry. I could cuddle with whoever wanted physical affection. I could touch and be touched without imminent sexual pressure. I could cradle any person of any body against my bosom after a long day on the trail. I could speak as much or as little as I desired, with as faggy a voice as I pleased. I could adorn my body with flowers however I chose, and those around me could, too. Bodies no longer signified behavior or character traits; breasts were breasts, nipples were nipples, genitals were genitals, hair was hair, none of them bearing ideological weight.

Without external walls to hold them up, my internal walls broke down day by day, bit by bit. It is a freedom I would yearn for throughout the rest of my time in college, a freedom I continue to yearn for, a freedom I haven't quite tasted since.

Nothing epitomized this more than the trip's penultimate day, when all two hundred of us were gathered back into an unshowered, grimy, fabulous group. The final ritual, other than a campfire and songs on the last night, is the Big Naked Slide—a ritual so fabulous and scandalous that the program was briefly suspended because of it.

Near the final campsite, there is a creek with a thirty-yard stretch of continuous rock that's been covered in enough moss and algae to make it slippery to the touch. It's a giant, natural waterslide. And on the last full day of the trip, upward of one hundred Duke students (voluntarily) got naked, ran to the rock in a giant naked herd, and jumped right in. A hundred naked bodies that had been stripped of their gender; a hundred naked bodies that had been given access to nudity without immediate sexualization; a hundred naked bodies with bits flapping everywhere, all sliding down the rock together—colliding, giggling uncontrollably, flopping on top of one another in a pileup at the end. Never have I felt so unashamed or liberated. Running in a pack of people who couldn't care less about gender, never have I felt more in tune with my own identity.

By the end of the trip, I had a full beard. It was the longest I'd ever gone without shaving and, arguably, the most masculine I've ever looked. In spite of my beard and some new muscles, I'd never been more at peace with my body, my gender, or my feminine spirit. Whether it was brought about intentionally or incidentally, I'd found gender freedom in the mountains. I'd found my Walden Pond. I'd found transcendence, a natural spirit and essence beyond gender entirely. At one with the natural world, at one with my most natural self, I'd found a liberation that rattled me.

The next day, on the four-hour bus ride back to campus, most everyone was asleep. But I wasn't. My stomach churning with anxiety, I stared out the window, fast-food chains, gas stations, billboards, and exit signs supplanting mountain vistas and endless trees.

Would this freedom last? Could *this freedom last?*

Arriving back on campus, I was a mess: emotionally, but more important, physically. I was filthy, unbathed, unshaven, and grimy, with two weeks of accumulated dirt, sweat, oil, and stank for all my new classmates to behold. My hair had so much grease in it that it could stand up on its own and make lots of interesting shapes. I smelled like crotch sweat, but everywhere. It helped that there were a hundred of us who were like this, but that didn't make much of a difference when I saw my parents again for the first time.

My parents hid their revulsion, overlooking my stank and greeting me with enthusiastic hugs. Luckily, when we arrived at my dorm room, my roommate was out, so I had time to shower before meeting him. I dug around in my boxes and suitcases for a towel, pulled out my brand-new shower caddy, tossed in my electric razor and some soap, and made a beeline for the bathroom.

I breezed down the hall in my towel before pausing at the door to the bathroom. Staring back at me from the door was the usual, unwelcome sign: Men.

Oh.

Right.

The reality stung as it sunk in, burrowing its way down to my heart. That's *how this works back in the "civilized world," isn't it? I can't pee without being treated as a man. I can't brush my teeth without being treated as a man. I can't shower without being treated as a man.* Under a housing system that required every first year student to live in the gender-segregated dorms on campus, I couldn't brush my hair in a mirror, get dressed, sit at my desk to do my homework, go to sleep after a long day, bring someone home with me, or have access to any private space without being treated as a man.

The straitjacket back in place, I couldn't breathe. It felt like the last two weeks in the woods had been for nothing; everything I'd learned about myself had been for naught. I was back to being a guy, a boy, a male, a man. I was back to square one, my identity erased by the need to sleep, to bathe, to shit, to rest. Each of my basic needs became subsumed by the gender binary, packaged as things that "men do together." I was to be one of the guys again. Sure, there were some girls in my building, far down at the other end of the hall past the common room, but assumed masculinity was inescapable, and I was not to forget that I was a man. I was not to forget my proper role.

I contemplated this as I took the razor to my two-week-old beard, uncovering my smooth face; as I removed plaque from my teeth; as I stepped into the shower.

Usually, the feeling of your first post-camping shower is exquisite. The massage of the water, the slickness of soap, the heat cascading down your body, soaking into your muscles. That day, I took one of the longest showers I've ever taken in my life. I must've stayed in there for half an hour, pampering my body, bidding it to relax, praying that the heat would somehow eradicate my mounting anxiety, that my feeling of dread would wash away like the oil in my hair. How could I endure living in a boys' club for four years? Did I really have to trade the right to have my gender affirmed for the right to a bed?

When I returned to my room, clean, shaved, and "proper," I got some welcome news: I'd gotten lucky in the roommate department. I had signed up for a random roommate and was paired with a really sweet guy named Radu. Rather than the basketball-obsessed jock from New Jersey I'd feared he'd be, Radu was a nerdy, kind, athletics-agnostic guy from Romania who was studying engineering and Japanese. I don't know what I would've done if my first roommate had been some frat-star sports dude. I think I would've dropped out. But this was perfect; or at least, this was totally doable.

To add to my sense of security, my immediate neighbor was Patrick, a fellow Southern powerqueer from Texas who ended up becoming a lifelong friend, despite the fact that we spent a significant portion of our time being political rivals in student government. My anxiety slid down another notch.

Then I took a look down the hall. To my shock, the three freshman basketball players—Josh Hairston, Tyler Thornton, and *Kyrie Fucking Irving*—were only three doors down from me.

Duke Basketball* was the one thing I was trying to avoid. Contrary to seemingly everyone else on campus, it was my least favorite thing about the school. I am one of those feminists who dislikes the gender politics of commercial athletics, but cares deeply for the players. I loathe the National Football League—partly because football culture is garbage toward women, but also because it is not okay to make money off people getting concussions. I hate the fact that male athletes make three thousand times more than female athletes, the fact that NBA teams get 4 million times more sponsorship than WNBA teams, the fact that most men who like sports act like women's teams don't exist. I hate most organized sports because, as a child, they were an excuse for abuse, shame, and trauma. And while I'm not totally against the *idea* of reclaiming organized sports in my life, I certainly don't give enough fucks to actually do it.†

All my angry feminist thoughts about mainstream athletics made the

---

* Isn't it interesting that you don't even have to say "Duke *Men's* Basketball"? You just say "Duke Basketball," and everyone assumes you're talking about the men's team? As if the women's team doesn't exist? Isn't it interesting that you just say "the NBA" and everyone knows you're talking about the (*Men's*) National Basketball Association? But if you want to talk about women's professional basketball, you have to say "the *W*NBA"? Anyway.

† The one exception to this rule is my best friend Alex from high school. Once in a blue moon, he can convince me to throw around a football or shoot some hoops or watch a game. I suffer through these things, partially because he earnestly wants to show me that not all sports are bad, but mostly because his mom makes the best corn dip in the entire world. I will endure anything—even playing and/or watching organized sports—for access to good corn dip.

prospect of living right next door to the basketball players daunting. The one thing I was most trying to avoid about Duke was just down the hall.

The fan culture was immediately weird. People would leave love notes and roses and presents outside of the players' doors. They got so much free gear from sponsors that they would leave stuff they didn't want outside in the hall. And people would swarm for it. News of a fresh gear deposit would spread like wildfire by text, Facebook, and email, and would be gone within minutes. One time, because I happened to be walking by when he was putting them out, I got a pair of shorts one of the players didn't want. He was so tall that they looked like capris on me, despite the fact that I am six feet even. I could basically wear them as a dress, and did so on a number of occasions.*

Other than the daily reminder of structural inequality, living down the hall from the b-ballers didn't end up being as weird as I had expected. There were even some perks. Living near the basketball players made me seem, I dunno, cooler? And it made for a convenient talking point whenever I encountered butch dudes—my relatives, my neighbors, my dad's coworkers, you name it—who wanted to talk about Duke Basketball. They'd ask how I thought the team was doing this season, something I never had any knowledge of, and I could always defer that conversation by bragging about how I lived in the same dorm as Kyrie Irving.

But the biggest perk came on my third day in the dorm. It was a Saturday morning, and I was standing in front of the bathroom mirror brushing my teeth. In the distance, I heard the rumbling of giant footsteps. Like in *Jurassic Park*, the water in the sink began rippling as the footsteps drew nearer. I tried to act natural. I tried to play it cool. I put my toothbrush in my mouth like normal, and just as I began to brush, all three

---

* The trick is that you use one leg of the pants as a sleeve and the other leg as the body of the dress. The resulting look is a *very* short, one-shoulder dress with trendy Adidas racing stripes on both sides. It's cute as fuck; the perfect "(sloppy) day to (sloppy) night" look.

freshman basketball players burst in wearing nothing but towels. It was an erotic tempest, a whirlwind of yum, a veritable monsoon of delicious arms and muscly backs. I'd never seen so many sculpted abs in person.

In the heat of the moment, I struggled to remember both my feminist qualms about men's basketball—What *were* they? What was I so angry about, again? *Think, Jacob, think!*—and my feminist qualms about objectifying other people's bodies (even men's bodies). Attempts at jogging my memory were to no avail. In the face of so much pure sexy, all the feminist training in the world proved useless.

I tried to do that thing confident people do where they talk effortlessly to fancy people. But I also had a toothbrush in my mouth, and wanted to give the impression that I wasn't *so* starstruck as to stop brushing my teeth. So I settled on talking and brushing my teeth at the same time. As if they'd think to themselves afterward, *Wow, that Jacob is so cool. They didn't stop brushing their teeth when we came in, but* they still talked to us. *So effortless! So confident!*

"What's-shup?" I sputtered, spraying toothpaste on the mirror. *Well, this isn't working out.*

"Hey," they replied as a chorus.

I took the toothbrush out of my mouth momentarily.

"Are y'all going to that party at the Nasher tonight?" I inquired. The Nasher is the art museum on campus, and they throw the fanciest parties, complete with hors d'oeuvres, photo booths, and mocktails. Everyone dresses up. It's very chic.

"Nah, man, we're not classy enough for that party," Josh responded jokingly.

"Cool, cool," I replied and returned to brushing my teeth. *"Cool, cool"? That's ALL YOU CAN SAY? That sounds so stupid Jacob you sound like an idiot good job blowing your cover.*

Before I could beat myself up any further, it happened. Like clockwork, all three of them dropped their towels at the same time, standing buck-naked for a moment, locker room style, before stepping into the private shower stalls. I didn't even have to spy. They just did it right in front of me. Like it was no big deal. Like they weren't showing off their perfectly sculpted butts in front of a very sexually frustrated queen. Like it was something I was prepared to handle.

I was not prepared. I could, by no means, handle seeing Kyrie Irving's butt on my third day of college. My body was not ready. My mind was not ready. No part of me was ready. I was not worthy. It felt like a middle school church retreat all over again, the supposed "safe space" of a gender-segregated bathroom becoming immediately, unapologetically, aggressively sexual; the typical shame rising alongside arousal.

Instead of playing it cool, my body decided the best thing to do at that moment was to inhale some toothpaste and spend the next three minutes choking on it. Thankfully, they were all three in the shower, so they didn't realize that their sudden nudity had caused the biggest queen on campus to have a three-minute coughing fit. I still haven't recovered from that moment. I don't think I ever will. Sorry, Kyrie.

Which is how my complicated relationship with Duke Athletics began. For the duration of my freshman year, Josh, Tyler, and Kyrie were nothing but kind to me—even when I was wearing heels, even when I had on lipstick—as I went to and fro around the dorm.

But I struggled with the feeling that, even if they were nice to me in person, their very presence, the power they held over the student body, was also making it harder for me to find my way. As people, they were kind. I can't (and don't) put the blame on them as individuals. But they were also embodiments of a *larger institution* that did not treat me with that same kindness. How can you explain to someone that the foundation of their livelihood creates obstacles for you? How can you explain to someone that something innocuous to them feels awful to you? How can you explain to people who take their power for granted that their power has consequences for your life?

At a bare minimum, my proximity to the basketball players reinforced a message that became louder and louder as college wore on, one that other members of Duke Athletics would drive home repeatedly during my first year:

Masculinity has some *serious* value.

I thought all this over that night as I began to unpack. I hung my shirts, ties, and dress pants in my closet. I assembled the cheap bookshelf that I'd purchased at Target. I put up pictures of my high school friends, a few posters, some artwork. I strung Christmas lights on top of my bed.

And then, hidden beneath layers of T-shirts and cargo shorts, I pulled out a plastic bag full of my grandmother's old jewelry, all the pieces I'd been able to squirrel away without anyone noticing. I dumped her jewelry, my secret, precious, ancestral collection, on my desk. I fiddled with each piece—faux gold necklaces, rhinestone floral clip-ons, crystal pendants, pink rosettes—holding them up to a lamp, watching the rhinestones dance in the light.

I was comforted because they'd belonged to my grandmother and were infused with her love.

I was afraid because they now belonged to me, and I wasn't sure what that meant for the next four years.

The first few weeks of school were a major letdown. I'd seen on our backpacking trip how much better the people I spent every day with *could* be. But as soon as the architecture was back, as soon as everyone moved into gendered dorms on a campus, where fraternities and sororities held the lion's share of social power, I saw my peers jump immediately back into the gender molds prescribed for them.

It happened quickly. The second night we were on campus, my hiking crew decided to go to a party thrown by Wayne Manor, an all-male selective-living group that was basically a fraternity. It was our first time together again after a day of reacclimating and moving in.

The party was like any college party you'd imagine: a hallway of individual dorm rooms, with drinks flowing, lights low, people drunkenly dancing, grinding close, leaving together. I tried to have fun but couldn't, as I watched this community I'd built dissolve back into mediocrity. People went right back to their roles. The boys did what boys were supposed to do. The girls did what girls were supposed to do. They were still perfectly *nice*, but the moral courage was gone, the leave-no-person-behind mentality forgotten. Everyone returned to the script.

The problem is that there are generally no lines written for people like me. There was no role for a gender nonconforming person at Duke, hardly even a role for a gay boy. Without realizing it, just by doing what they were used to, by following the rules suggested by the structures around them, my classmates had erased me, had made my experience and contributions feel irrelevant.

By the end of the first weekend, the massive, twelve-by-six-foot benches out front of three freshman dorms were graffittied with the slogans "Drunk Bitches Love Cock," "TITS," and "HERMAPHRO-DITE."

In the vacuum that was left, I did what came most naturally: I started hanging out with the queers, joined an a cappella group, signed up for a million clubs, and tried to figure out what role, if any, existed for me on campus.

Within about a month, I'd cemented myself as *the* first-year activist queer: attending every meeting of Blue Devils United, our undergrad LGBT student organization; becoming a regular at the campus LGBT Center; and coordinating a campaign that distributed hundreds of rainbow flags to first year students. It was only natural that when the time came around for the November Drag Show Fund-raiser, I was extended an invitation not just to perform, but to be the Mistress of Ceremonies.

Enthusiastically, naively, I agreed, not realizing I was setting myself up for some very public exploration of my fledgling identity.

Before I proceed with this story, it's important to have some context. When I was a first year in college in 2010, *RuPaul's Drag Race* had been on the air for a total of two seasons and had a grand prize of only $25,000. It was still a relatively obscure/underproduced show, and while drag has been a venerable art form for centuries, drag culture hadn't become the global phenomenon it is today. This went down in the days before RuPaul, Lady Bunny, Logo, et al. transformed drag into a national commodity supported by mainstream makeup companies and media outlets alike.

Which is to say that, back then, hosting the drag show wasn't really an *honor*. It didn't make me *cool* in the queer community. It was more that no other undergrad wanted to do it, and the Blue Devils United Leadership rightfully guessed that I'd be foolish enough to say yes.

The first step was to name my drag persona and decide on a character. That part was easy—for years, I'd been perfecting a "Long Island mother" accent reminiscent of Linda from *Bob's Burgers* (actually, it was based on the original YouTube videos that John Roberts, the actor who plays Linda, made before he was ever cast in the show). I didn't work hard for a name, either; I just let it come to me. After meditating for a number of days, it came: Trudi De Vil.

Elegant name chosen, the second step was finding an outfit. I went to the two stores that I knew were great for putting together a refined, effortlessly feminine look: Charlotte Russe and Goodwill. At Charlotte Russe, I purchased my second pair of high heels ever—black lace booties with black satin laces—and at Goodwill, I managed to find a halfway decent dress and a red tulle skirt. The look was *hardly* haute couture, but it was enough for an amateur college drag show.

The last step was choosing what song I wanted to perform. I'm still proud of my choice. It was fierce; poppy, but still a bit niche; from a fabulous diva, but a more obscure, underrated element of her discography;

with a rich feminist analysis that still left opportunities to make dick jokes; erotic and Freudian all at the same time. It was a perfect selection for a budding intellectual like me who still wanted to feign that she was in touch with pop culture.

For my world premiere drag performance,* I chose to perform *Ego* by Beyoncé. If you don't know the song, do yourself a favor: put this book down and go listen to it.

To say that the song was perfect is an understatement. The song opens with Beyoncé singing about how her partner has a "big ego" (i.e., a big dick) but then pivots to Beyoncé singing about how she, *too*, has a "big ego" (i.e., a big metaphorical dick). In my opinion, it's the queerest, most transfabulous song ever written; that song enabled me, in one drag routine, to insinuate that I had a big dick while simultaneously claiming my dick as innately feminine. I was able to own the . . . umm . . . *fullness* of my masculinity without dismissing the fullness of my femininity. I saw my routine as a bold, gender-fucking piece of performance art.

Which might be *a little bit* of a stretch in terms of what the audience actually got out of it. Mostly, what they got was a B-minus performance where I attempted to do Beyoncé's choreography, lost track of said choreography, and flailed around for the remaining two minutes of the song.

The hosting routine was equally half-baked. I and my cohost, Virginia Slims (a Southern belle–type played by a grad student, who, in retrospect, I probably should've dated), opened the show by pretending that I'd forgotten to get ready. I sat onstage in a bathrobe and Virginia gave me a ring. "WHAT DO YOU MEAN, THE SHOW IS STARTING? WHY DIDN'T ANYBODY TELL ME?" I burst out, screaming into my phone before throwing it into the audience and running out. Moments later, I was back onstage, magically changed into my outfit for the show. Virginia insulted it, I retorted by insulting Southerners in general,

---

* Not counting the Miss St. Francis pageant in sixth grade.

she responded by insulting Yankees, and before you knew it, we were knee-deep in regional humor.

"Do you like barbecue?" Virginia asked.

"Yeah, I love throwing *hot dogs* on the *grill*! Who doesn't?" I responded.

"No, not *that* kind of barbecue, you idiot, I mean *real* barbecue."

"I'm not really sure what you're getting at here, Virginia. You mean burgers *and* hot dogs on the grill?"

"You Yankees are hopeless."

"Yeah, well, at least *we* have public transportation and didn't elect George Bush president for two terms!"

And so on.

At the end of the show, when Virginia and Trudi made up, I was even able to work in a killer Civil War joke: "Aw, Virginia, I'm so glad that we're making up. It's like the treaty at Appomattox! Which means I guess it's time for you to get some *reconstruction!*"

Get it? Reconstruction? As in, plastic surgery? And also as in, the era of American history when the federal government had to essentially impose martial law to stop Southern states from reinstating slavery, even *after* they'd lost the war?

Looking back, was it the most sensitive joke I've ever made? No. Did it make light of a devastating era of American history? Sure. Am I a bad person for making it? Probably. But most important, was it a brutal dig at the kind of racist assholes who, to this day, fly the Confederate flag and *still* lament that the South lost the Civil War? Yes. Yes, it was.

I'd like to think that's what America needs more of right now: drag queens dragging racists through the dirt with insensitive Civil War jokes. Or perhaps drag queens banding together and tearing down Confederate monuments? I'd like both, please.

Besides, if you're going to do drag, it's important to honor drag tradition. Being an offensive, morally decrepit asshole is a rich part of the whole endeavor. Just ask Lady Bunny—she's the stinkiest, most offensive asshole in town.*

By the end of the night, I couldn't shake the feeling that I was experiencing drag differently than many of the other performers. When used properly, drag is a radical tool that challenges the gender binary by mocking it, heightening it, exaggerating it, or rejecting it altogether, but that doesn't mean all performers experience it equally. Some performers consider drag a hobby that doesn't affect their primary identity. Some performers consider drag a separate, but equally important, identity to their day-to-day selves. Still others, myself included, experience drag as an incremental tool for gender self-exploration and evolution, a beautiful summit along our gender journey.

I left the evening conflicted. After the show, when many of the gay boys around me willingly stripped off their false eyelashes, removed their makeup, unlaced their corsets, and changed clothes, I found myself suddenly reluctant to do the same. Other than my wig—a cheap, poorly affixed clump of polyester (that, to be honest, didn't *smell* all that great) on loan from a friend—I didn't want to take anything off. While the other boys effortlessly stripped, putting their personas in garment bags, shoe boxes, and makeup totes, I found myself unable to part with mine. I wanted to wear my shitty Goodwill dress all night. I wanted to keep on my heels, leave my lipstick intact, let my earrings shimmer on the dance floor.

At the time, I felt alone, *singular* in the way that I was relating to drag. I thought I was the only one who learned something fundamental about myself that night. But as I've gotten older, I'm starting to question that assumption. Like much of my college experience, I *perceived* myself to be alone only because so few of us (myself included) had the courage

---

* Lady Bunny took a few digs at me in her recent show *Trans-Jester*, so in the spirit of good fun, I think it's only fair that I return the favor in my debut book.

or acuity to name what we were experiencing. I think that everyone was changed in some way that night. Each performer was expressing something new, powerful, and dynamic about themself. We were all learning together, fumbling our way toward liberation.

That night, I realized I didn't want what I was wearing to be a *costume*. I longed for it to be just another *outfit*—for my femininity not to be my *persona*, but my *person*. So while I eventually changed out of my dress because it was sweaty and hot, I left my lipstick and high heels on and twirled all night in my stilettos. My feet weren't entirely pleased, but my heart was imminently grateful.

I took my next gender steps gradually. I didn't know what these discoveries meant about me or my future, but more important, I didn't want to get ahead of myself. Despite my confident ethos, I was and am an exceedingly fragile creature. I break at the slightest unkind word, at the smallest look of contempt. I am socially perceptive to a fault, able to suss out the emotional and social architecture of a room with only a quick glance. When it comes to social rejection and emotional intelligence, I've never had plausible deniability. Since I was a child, I've been able to perceive exactly what most people around me are feeling. It was the only way I was able to get away with being such a little shit in middle school and still have my teachers like me. It is the only way I am able to get away with being such a big shit in the present and still manage to have a career.

While this emotional intelligence often helps me break down barriers and rip social norms apart like an industrial shredder, it also gives my heart the consistency of porcelain. One social rejection, however masked or veiled, can send me spiraling for an entire evening. One wrong look my way, however subtle or hidden, can send my heart skittering across the floor in a thousand tinkling pieces. In college, I knew myself to be highly impressionable, pusillanimous, *moldable*, putty in the hands of Duke's broader social norms.

So after the drag show, I took baby steps: unwinding my gender gradually, sounding it out letter by letter.

And what could be more gradual than wearing high heels to the Yule Ball? The Yule Ball was the Harry Potter–themed dance hosted by Duke's Quidditch team. If there's any space where you know it's going to be okay to be super queer, it's a party where a bunch of fellow nerds are already dressing up like witches and wizards.

The Yule Ball has a special magic at Duke. It's held in the Great Hall, which resembles—with an uncanny level of accuracy that the name would perhaps suggest—the Great Hall at Hogwarts. With vaulted ceilings and wood paneling, all it takes is a few flicks of a wand to make you believe you've actually been transported to a certain school of witchcraft and wizardry.

I wore the same pair of high heels to the Yule Ball that I wore in the drag show, and the evening was magical precisely because my gender was unremarkable. Sure, I got a few compliments on my shoes, but most people were too preoccupied with being nerdy to care. We spent the evening dancing, casting spells on one another, and death dropping on the dance floor any time someone had the gall to throw an *"Avada Kedavra"* our way.

That night, as I lay on the dance floor in four-inch heels, pretending to have been murdered, I thought, *Maybe college is going to be all right.* Horizontal on the floor, surrounded by wizards and witches, soaring ceiling, gothic crests, and tinkling glass spinning above me, Duke felt—for a precious moment—like home.

I went to my parents' for winter break that year feeling self-assured, confident that I could somehow make this whole college thing work.

But when I returned to campus that January, everything had changed. January at Duke University is hell. Not because of the weather—North Carolina doesn't really get *that* cold—but because the campus is overtaken by sorority and fraternity rush.

For me, the stakes of the rush process were immense, because the entire system was built around totalizing gender norms. Seemingly overnight, a two-gender system was consolidated across campus, the binary fortified in stone. People who I knew to be fearlessly individual fell in line, wearing the required salmon shorts or the requisite white dress. As they increasingly conformed to the gender binary, my slice of campus became an island.

At the time, it felt like being taken hostage, forced to endure the social effects of something that I didn't want in the first place. Even students who didn't rush were party to the madness of it. It touched everything, crawling through the consciousness of the entire first-year class. We were being sorted. We were being evaluated. If you didn't rush, you were simply admitting that you thought of yourself as a nobody.

I know this may not be fair, but to my tender proto-queer heart, it *felt* like my friends were bailing on me; deciding that my identity and happiness as a gender nonconforming person weren't worth defending; deciding that the personal cost of truly being an ally to me, of opting out of gendered social institutions that create a hostile world, simply wasn't worth it.

Watching this all go down—watching my friends join a system that would tell a girl she doesn't deserve social standing because her thighs are too big, watching my friends trade in any possibility of gender freedom in exchange for social power and shitty beer—damaged my sense of trust in the world and in other people. I'd barely begun to figure out who I was when the rug was pulled out from under me.

Two weeks into rush, when it felt like my school had hung me out to dry and my nascent identity was slipping through my fingers, I decided to fight back.

There are some decisions that are too scary to be thought through. There are some moments in life when you shouldn't look over the ledge before you jump. You can only pick at the edges of your Band-Aid for so long before you rip the motherfucker off.

Having watched one too many of my friends be fat-shamed by their supposed "sisters" and exhausted from hearing horror stories of fraternity hazing, I found myself hoofing it to the Dollar General off campus, marching straight to the makeup aisle, and purchasing the brightest red lipstick and loudest nail polish—a glittering gold—that I could find. Before I knew what I was doing, I was back in my dorm room painting my nails and adorning my lips. It was the first time since childhood that I'd done either of those things all on my own. Sure, I'd worn makeup for plays and for the drag show, but never on a random Saturday, and certainly never of my own volition.

When I was done, I stepped in front of the mirror. The reflection looking back at me was startling, yet sublimely beautiful. Staring at my own image, glorified with pigment, augmented with varnish, something struck me: I'd wanted this my whole life.

The image in the mirror conjured up memories that had lain dormant for over a decade. All at once, they were back, enveloping me in their warmth like shawls. As I gazed in the mirror, I saw my child self looking back at me. Beneath the layers of shame, cobwebs, and dust, my purest, youngest, most uninhibited form had managed to break through. My hands no longer my own, but the hands I'd always wanted. My lips no longer constituted of flesh, but of stardust.

I smiled, then broke into peals of laughter that cascaded out of me, bouncing around the room and reverberating throughout history, across time, to a place where the truth of my gender danced without confinement, without restraint, without inhibition, without fear.

Looking back at me in that mirror, I saw something I could never unsee, an image that would both support me and haunt me in the years to come: I saw myself. Truly and deeply, I *saw myself.*

But like any moment of divine vision, you have to come crashing to Earth sometime; after speaking with God, every prophet has to head back down the mountain. Unless you brought a tent, you can't stay up there forever.

More often than not, prophets are not received with kindness. Normal people don't like the fact that you spoke with God. They're jealous, because they wish they could talk to her, too. God's one cool chick, and you don't make many friends by bragging about how tight you are with her or telling people she gave you the exclusive on human truth. I mean, how would you feel if one of your friends was like, "Yeah, I already know what the next iPhone looks like—God showed me and not you." It sucks. It makes you feel left out.

En route to the dining hall for lunch that afternoon, I'd never felt more prophetic or more visible. Walking past fellow students on the quad, I felt like Moses or Jesus must've felt when they, too, returned from the mountaintop. Like Moses, I came back down from the mountain to a group of people who were praying to a false idol. Like Jesus, I came back down from the mountain a helluva lot shinier.*

The shame was overwhelming. I was imbued with divine knowledge, but all I wanted to do was keep my head down and be as invisible as possible. Involuntarily, out of instinct and fear, I looked at the ground as I walked and kept my hands in my coat pockets. It took bumping into a classmate for me to even realize what I was doing. Startled out of my daze, I resolved to keep my head up, my eyes forward, and my hands uncovered. I feigned a sense of courage: "boldly" displaying my crimson lips, letting my nails sparkle unfettered in the sunshine.

With each step, I became more comfortable with what I'd done, more fearless. People were, by and large, not freaking out. I don't know quite what I'd expected, but I certainly didn't expect people to walk by, see me wearing lipstick, and just continue walking. I thought it'd work more like a Godzilla movie or something: They'd see me stomping toward them, lips ablaze, and cower in fear, a mob of students pointing my way and screaming "QUEERZILLA!" as they fled. I'd destroy a few buildings, fight a giant squid, and leave East Campus in ruins.

---

* Okay so *obviously* it's a little arrogant to compare myself to Moses and Jesus, but at this point, it's really more about showing off my ability to cite bible stories than anything else. Can you really blame me for wanting to make my Sunday School teachers proud?

Surprisingly, things weren't like that. My classmates were either chill about it or too self-absorbed to even notice.

Entering the dining hall, I tried to distract myself from the polish coating my nails, the paint covering my lips, and the anxiety covering my heart. I tried to act normally. Slowly, I began to feel like *myself* again. I filled my tray with tofu and French fries and ice cream—my standard meal freshman year—and headed toward the seating area to find my friends.

It was at this point that my life became something akin to a sappy teen movie. It was just so *predictable*.

En route, I approached a table filled with twelve giant members of the Duke Football team (which, in 2010, was not doing very well. Just sayin'). As I was about to pass, one of the players, someone with easily a hundred pounds on me, slid out into the middle of the aisle, blocking my way. Legs spread wide, slouched real, real low in his chair—presumptively to show me just how much of a man he was or how big his dick was or something—he stared past my tray and dead into my eyes.

"You've got something on your lips," he spit menacingly, looking to his teammates for approval.

And by this point, because I'd gotten distracted by French fries and *sorta already forgotten that I was wearing lipstick*, my first thought wasn't, *"I am being bullied this is a hate crime."*

My first thought was, *"Jacob how did you ALREADY manage to get food on your face? You haven't even started eating yet!"*

I stood there for a moment, stunned.

Then it clicked.

He is talking about my lipstick.

He is bullying me.

Huh.

In my head, here's how the rest of this scene plays out:

"OH YEAH, MOTHERFUCKER?" I yelled, loud enough

for the entire dining hall to hear. The room fell silent, everyone watching with bated breath. With all eyes on me, I approached him real close, getting right between his widely spread legs and leaning in seductively, as I continued to yell:

"YOU GOT SOMETHING TO SAY ABOUT MY LIPSTICK? YOU GOT SOMETHING TO SAY ABOUT MY FASHION CHOICES, YOU PIECE OF SHIT? DOES MY LIPSTICK MAKE YOU INSECURE, LITTLE BOY? DO YOU NEED TO SHOW YOUR FOOTBALL BROS JUST HOW MUCH OF A MAN YOU ARE BY MAKING FUN OF ME? WELL, THE JOKE'S ON YOU, ASSHOLE: MEN AREN'T EVEN *REAL*. GENDER IS *FAKE*. AND THE ONLY GUYS WHO MAKE FUN OF GENDER NONCONFORMING PEOPLE ARE GUYS WHO SECRETLY WANT TO FUCK US."

I pause, taking a deep, slow breath, staring directly into his eyes. I'm not done.

"IS THAT WHAT YOU WANT, *DUDE?* YOU WANNA FUCK ME? IS THAT IT? HUH? WELL, GUESS WHAT? I WOULDN'T FUCK YOU IN A MILLION YEARS, YOU BRAT. YOU WANNA KNOW WHY? BECAUSE DUKE FOOTBALL SUCKS AND Y'ALL HAVEN'T WON A GAME ALL SEASON. MAYBE TRY ACTUALLY *BEING GOOD* AT FOOTBALL. WIN A GAME FOR ONCE. THEN, MAYBE, IF YOU'RE *REAL* LUCKY, WE CAN HAVE A CIVILIZED CONVERSATION ABOUT EXACTLY THE METHODOLOGY I WILL EMPLOY TO DESTROY YOUR DICK. *CAPISCE, MOTHERFUCKER?*"

He whimpers. He's rock hard, throbbing with desire for me. I lean in farther, slowly, excruciatingly close. I give him a gentle, barely there kiss on the cheek as I dump the entire contents of my tray onto his lap, ice-cold Diet Coke, tofu salad, and mint chocolate chip ice cream dampening his fiery crotch.

I back away, effortlessly blowing him a kiss before turning around and never looking back. Saying nothing more, I strut out of the dining hall and into the frigid January evening, where Robert Pattinson, FKA twigs, and Taylor Lautner are waiting for me in a bright pink vintage Mustang. "You're late for our double date," Taylor fusses, playfully pulling on my scarf before planting a kiss on my red lips.

"I know, I'm sorry, sweetie," I reply quietly, nestling my head into the nape of his neck. "Mama had some business to take care of."

We drive away into the night. No one comes back to campus to claim my belongings. I am never heard from again. I've simply vanished.

Years go by. Students come and go. Duke ages. Buildings rise and fall. The universe inches closer to its inevitable heat-death.

But if you look closely at the Marketplace on a cold January night when the moon is full, students will recount, hundreds of years hence, *some say you can still see the silhouette of Jacob's bright red lips whispering, "Motherfucker" into the night.*

In my head, that's what happened. If anyone asks, please tell them that version.

In actuality, I stared at him dumbstruck for approximately two seconds too long, then broke eye contact while barely managing to croak,

"Yeah, it's lipstick." It was more a puff of air than a sentence. It didn't even land as a proper retort.

Ashamed, embarrassed, and caught off guard, I shuffled sheepishly around him en route to my seat, hoping he wasn't going to try to hit me as I passed by.

That night, I sent an email to the generic email address for the football program, the only contact information I could find online. The email address was so generic I wasn't sure if anyone even checked the account, but it was all that I knew to do. I cc'ed Janie, the director of the LGBT Center who was basically my campus mom, as well as two staff members from the Women's Center.

To: dukefootball@duaa.duke.edu
Subject: Harassment by Members of Duke Football Team
Date: January 23, 2011

To whom it may concern,

My name is Jacob Tobia and I'm a first-year public policy major here at Duke. I just wanted to send an e-mail to the coaches of the football team concerning something that happened to me while I was eating dinner in the Marketplace tonight, but first a little bit of background about myself would probably be helpful. As a proud member of the gay, lesbian, bisexual, and transgender community, I am someone who doesn't necessarily operate within the gender binary, and I oftentimes engage in androgynous behavior. Tonight in particular, I was wearing lipstick. While returning to my table at the Marketplace with a plate of food, I walked past a table full of Duke football players, and one of the players—whom I can't identify—stopped me and said in a very hostile manner, "I think you have something on your lips." I replied, saying "I know, I'm wearing lipstick. I don't conform to gender norms and I'm sorry if that offends you."* The rest of the players seated at the table didn't make any effort to stop him and most of them were laughing while he did it. His comment was clearly meant to intimidate me, and I left the Marketplace feeling harassed and marginalized.

While I don't wish to file any sort of formal claim of harassment or anything like that, I wanted to make sure that I informed the football program and coaches of how members of their team had been behaving. While I know that wearing lipstick isn't for everyone, I refuse to be publicly harassed for how I express myself and my gender. From what my friend Ted, a player on your team who I know through my scholarship program, tells me of the football program at Duke, I know that the Duke football program holds respect in high regard. The behavior that I observed today in the Marketplace left me feeling anything but respected.

I hope that you will discuss this incident with your players and remind them that they should respect not just their fellow team members, but all Duke students, regardless of gender expression or perceived sexual orientation. Also, I have CC'd Janie Long, the director of the Duke Center for Lesbian, Gay, Bisexual, and Transgender Life in this e-mail

---

* Okay, so I know I didn't actually say that last sentence. I wish I had been that eloquent in the moment, but can you forgive a queen for embellishing the truth a teeny bit to reclaim a shred of her dignity?

*as well as Amy Cleckler and Erin Stephens, both of whom
work at the Women's Center.*

Regards,

Jacob Tobia

Janie replied the next morning:

*I'm very sorry you were harassed. I will definitely
follow-up with administrators in Athletics. Let's talk more in
the Center.*

Amy chimed in, too.

*you are very brave to voice your feelings and to address
this directly. please let me know how i can be of help to you,
and feel free to stop by and discuss this further.*

So did Erin:

*i think it's awesome that you are speaking up about this.
Certainly and unfortunately such harassment happens to
other students on campus and speaking up about it is the
first step for these students being accountable for their
actions and changing.*

Over the next two weeks, I took each of them up on their offer to
talk in person. I stopped by either the Women's Center or the LGBT
Center pretty much every single day of my undergraduate career. Those
spaces, and the incredible people who worked there, were the only way
that I made it through college.

After speaking with Janie, I decided to file a formal Bias Incident

Report Form, meaning that the incident would be reported to more senior-level administrators. I heard back from someone in the Dean's Office; I was assured that they would address it.

I never got a written response from the coaches. In a classic form employed by abusive institutions, they were smart enough to cover their tracks and never leave an official paper trail that acknowledged misdoing. Instead, a few days later I got a phone call out of the blue from a number I didn't recognize. It was an assistant coach on the team. Unfortunately, the call caught me off guard and I didn't have the wisdom to record it. All I can attest to is my imperfect emotional memory of the conversation:

"Hello, is this Jacob?"

"Yes, who is this?"

"Hi, I'm Coach Paulson, an assistant coach on the football team. I've received a copy of your report from the Dean's Office, but I need more information in order to address it properly."

A beat.

"Do you remember what the player who made the comments looked like? Can you identify who he was?"

"I don't remember too much about him other than what he said to me. I don't know players' names or faces, really."

"Okay, well, do you remember what he looked like?"

"I don't think I could pick him out of a crowd or anything, but I don't see how that's relevant to—"

"Well, without more information about him, we can't do very much. But I assure you this incident will be addressed."

"But what do you mean by 'addressed'? Will you be doing a training with the team or something? Will you be reaching out to the LGBT Center to set up an Ally training or whatever? Will the player face consequences? I just don't understand what—"

"We already have a training for players about this, so they already cover that when new players arrive on campus. We'll take care of it, don't worry."

I hesitated, unsure of what to say. What did he mean? *How* would they take care of it? This was a devastatingly shitty apology, if that's what he was going for. Realizing that this was going nowhere, I resigned. I gave in. I stopped pushing.

"Okay, thanks for calling."

"No problem, have a good day."

click

That was it. That was all the apology I was ever going to get. The student never had to speak with me directly, never had to take any accountability for his actions, never even had to interact with me again. I spent the rest of the school year dodging football players, unsure what had happened, what conversations the team had had without my knowledge, feeling like even more of a target than before. In their eyes, I wasn't just a fag anymore. I was a fag *who'd called their coaches*, a fag *who'd snitched*, a *tattletale sissy.*

At the end of the week, the Dean's Office reached out to check in about what had happened.

Rereading my response to them today, it's devastating. Though I was furious, though I never really got over the incident or received a proper apology, I'd resigned myself to the fact that nothing was going to happen. Made to feel ashamed for reporting what had happened to me, made *more of a target for reporting it*, I just wanted it to go away. And the easiest way to make it go away was to pretend that I was no longer angry, to put on a smile and tell them that I was okay:

Yes, I got a phone call from Coach Paulson yesterday and he told me that they were going to address the issue very soon. I'm not sure exactly what that means, but it sounds good. I also talked to him about how this incident may indicate some sort of need for more involved trainings or

workshops about LGBT issues, but he reassured me that the
football program conducts such training in-house. I'm not
sure what that training looks like exactly, but I'd be curious to
find out.

At any rate, it seems that the situation has been
addressed; I guess I was just looking for some more
substantial discussion of the systemic factors that lead to the
incident, which didn't seem to be what Coach Paulson was
focusing on. That being said, my expectations may not be
entirely realistic.

Thanks so much for all of your help in this,
Jacob :D

I even ended my email *with a smiley face.* A smiley face. My whole world had been shaken and somehow I ended up apologizing, via a smiley face, for being upset.

After that email, I hardly mentioned the incident to anyone else. I gave up. I'd learned the lesson loud and clear, one that has been re-taught to me and so many other women and femmes who have been targets of harassment and abuse: The world owes you nothing. If you are so brave as to express your gender in public, you will be harassed, you will be hurt, you may even be assaulted, and no one will have to apologize for how they treated you. They will get away with it every single time. They will make you feel ashamed of feeling hurt. They will make you feel like you are just whining.

And speaking up will only make it worse. Watching people who love you—who support you and want the best for you—try to take on the world and fight for you, only to lose, will only make it hurt more. So you stop talking about what you're facing. You stop talking about how much you're hurting. You stop telling people how shitty the world is to you because you are gender nonconforming. You end an email with a smile, take the abuse, and pretend it doesn't hurt you. You learn you have no real power, that the only power you *do* have is the power not to flinch when you are punched, not to cry when you are stung, not to acknowledge that abuse leads to injury.

I didn't realize how deeply I'd buried the incident until I sat down to write this chapter. Sitting in a café with my best friend Alex, from high school, I talked through my outline in a casual way.

"—then I'm going to write about the time when I wore lipstick for the first time on campus," I said matter-of-factly, "and that football player harassed me in the dining hall."

"Wait, what?"

"I definitely told you about that," I replied. "You know this story."

"I most certainly don't," he responded. "You never told me about that. I would've remembered that story, Jacob."

"Oh, I wonder why I never told you?"

Now that I've written it down, the reason for my silence is all too clear to me: The only thing scarier than feeling powerless to fight your bullies is the knowledge that your friends are powerless to fight them, too. The only thing worse than being hurt is being *made to feel ashamed* for being hurt.

Packing up my dorm room at the end of freshman year, I marveled at how much my wardrobe had changed in spite of everything. My grandmother's clip-on earrings and brooches were no longer alone; they were now accompanied by tubes of dollar store lipstick, vials of flashy nail polish, lacy, drapey feminine tops, and three pairs of heels: the $20 pair I'd bought in high school, the $35 pair I'd purchased for the drag show, and a $150 pair of Jeffrey Campbell LITAs that I'd purchased for myself after making straight A's all year. A trashy, flashy, beautifully curated collection of feminine silhouettes, colors, and fabrics, my wardrobe was beginning to align less with what the world had prescribed, and more with my own vision for who I wanted to be.

When I returned to my parents' house and unpacked everything for the summer, I didn't attempt to hide who I'd become. My heels were out in the middle of my bedroom alongside other shoes. My lipstick and nail polish sat unabashedly on the bathroom counter, in open air, an array of pigment and shade. I wasn't trying to hide this anymore; not from my parents, not from my friends, not from myself.

Two weeks after returning home, I began packing for a two-month trip to small-town South Carolina where I'd spend the summer doing an oral history project. I looked all over the bathroom for my lipstick and nail polish, but couldn't find them anywhere. I searched in my bedroom. The bathroom downstairs. My brother's old room. They were nowhere to be found. Where had they gone? I certainly hadn't moved them. *Interesting.*

Thankfully, I had some fairly serious indigestion that night.* Seeking gastric relief, I went upstairs to the linen closet where we keep the Pepto-Bismol. When I reached inside to grab the pink bottle, I noticed my lipstick and nail polish collection tucked away around the corner, almost out of sight.

Huh.

I certainly hadn't put them there. To this day, I don't know with complete certainty who did.

But the most likely explanation is that my dad had attempted to hide my lipstick and nail polish from me. He knew he couldn't get away with outright throwing them away, but hiding them in an innocuous-yet-undiscoverable place gave him the ability to stifle my gender while maintaining "plausible" deniability. As if that really even made sense. *"Oh, I wasn't trying to hide them—I just put them in the linen closet. You know, where every family keeps their lipstick and nail polish."*

I threw back some Pepto-Bismol, praying that my intestines would

---

* Too many beans, probably.

calm down, and quietly returned my makeup to a harder-to-find place in the bathroom.

The next day, I didn't say anything to my dad about recovering my stash. I didn't confront him or ask if he'd hidden it. I didn't yell or scream or get upset. Instead, I did him one better.

In classic, passive-aggressive Southern fashion, I didn't say a word about it; I simply wore lipstick to dinner the next night.

Chapter 7

Beloved Token

*I*n a flash, my sophomore year was beginning. But this time, I didn't come back to Duke expecting structural affirmation. I came back to Duke ready for battle—armor bedazzled; perfectly manicured nails sharpened to talons; heels spiky, long, and lethal.

I found myself slipping into an old, bad habit, one that any person of difference knows. In the absence of authentic affirmation, I let myself become a token.

Over the remaining years of college, tokenization was my curse and my saving grace. It felt like protection, a way I could be loved and supported by those around me, a way I could be included, if only as an interesting accessory. It was the easiest way to trick other people—and therefore myself—into believing that I was happy.

If you're not familiar with tokenization as survival strategy, here's how it works: When people of difference find ourselves in an institution, company, culture, or society where we are the only person like us, we become representative of *all* of us. You can be the token anything—the token black kid, the token disabled kid, the token woman, the token Jew, the token immigrant, the token queer. Your role is to be the interesting scarf, the chunky bracelet, the shawl draped on top of the model, but never the gown itself.

The whole point of being a token is that you exchange your rage at inequality for the respect and admiration of your peers. You trade in your right to be angry, to be dissatisfied, for the right to be hugged and affirmed by those around you. You stop pointing out the ways in which people are hurting you or making your identity feel impossible, and unless it is self-serving, you stop pointing out the fact that you are the only one like you.

You take the fact that there is only one of you (or, in my case, that there are *very few* like you), and instead of treating that fact as what it is—damning evidence of exclusion and discrimination—you treat it as evidence that you are special. You tell yourself that you aren't the only trans person in student leadership because Duke excludes trans people and creates a culture that is hostile toward trans success; you tell yourself that you're the only trans person because you are *that much more talented* than the rest of trans people, because you are *better* than the rest of your community.

To sincerely adopt the psychology of tokenism, you have to sell your community out. That's the dark underbelly of the thing. Instead of blaming the institutions, rules, and social attitudes of those around you for the absence of other people like you, you blame your own community. You accept that you are one of the "special ones" who "made it" through the power of their "hard work." It wasn't that Duke made it virtually impossible for trans students to live happy, self-actualized lives on campus. It's that most trans and gender nonconforming people simply weren't bright enough to make it into Duke in the first place. I was one of the special ones, the exception to the rule, the single shining star in a vacuum of trans/queer brilliance—or so the ideation of tokenization would have me believe.

The moment you adopt this psychology, the moment you give in to this strategy, you're showered in recognition. You get diversity award after diversity award after diversity award. You are heralded as a shining example of the Duke community. You are featured in the campus newspaper, in *Duke Magazine*, your existence proclaimed as evidence that Duke is great for people like you. The hard part is that some of this praise is real. Some of this recognition is deserved. But an equal part of it is toxic, insidious. Your very identity is mobilized as cover-up, the concealer hiding the blemish.

You become the evidence that contradicts your own experience. They say things like, "If Jacob can succeed here, Duke must be creating a supportive environment for trans students," when the only reason you are succeeding in the first place is because you have so dissociated from your own emotions that you no longer feel the sting of daily hostility. They will use your story to prove to themselves that they don't need to change anymore. They will use your success against your own best interest and the interests of your community. "If Jacob has managed to be happy here, then how badly do we *really* need campus-wide gender-neutral housing?"

They claim you as a success in part because they care about you, but mostly because they care about themselves more. The *I'm proud of you* is always accompanied by the *I'm proud of myself for being magnanimous enough to support someone like you.*

Over time, this strategy is devastating to your sense of self-esteem, self-love, and community. Even if only subconsciously, you have trouble spending time with your own community because you feel guilty for selling them out. You mask your anguish, your struggle, your daily pain, in order to put on a constant smile. You dissociate from your own feelings, your own heart, in order to belong.

And you work your fucking ass off. You run twice as fast and lift twice as much weight just to keep up with your peers. And if you want to *outrun* or *outlift* your peers, you triple it.

You embrace respectability, being well-regarded, as all that you have.

There is a reason that I have never made a B in my entire life. There is a reason that I have never had a GPA lower than a perfect 4.0 throughout all of high school and college. There is a reason that I was always a student leader, always took on twelve different community and artistic activities at a given time. There's a reason why I did not one, but two honors thesis projects.

Without this validation, I was afraid that everyone would abandon me.

So while many of my friends in college were alternating late-night study sessions with dating, raucous social schedules, and sex lives, I threw myself almost wholly into work, only partying on occasion to keep up appearances. Though none of my peers really knew it, I lost the ability to party, the ability to drink frequently, by my sophomore year. Alcohol was dangerous, because when I drank, that's when the feelings of otherness, of rage and alienation, would catch up with me. My fellow students drank and got horny. I drank and spiraled into self-loathing and despair.

Looking around and seeing *no one else like me*, I realized how high a pedestal I was dancing on. It was a blessing, sure, but in retrospect it feels more like height for height's sake; empty elevation. And it came with a threat: When you're on a pedestal all alone, you're the only person you have. And if you trip, if you take a misstep, there's no one there to catch you. And you can fall oh so far.

To say I was loved on campus throughout my sophomore and junior years would be an understatement. I was *adored*. I was *ubiquitous*. I was everywhere and uncontainable, a voice for the marginalized, a clarion call for a better world. I was quoted in the campus newspaper so often it became an inside joke. I was given positions of power and prestige, accolades and recognition. By almost everyone who held power, I was beloved. By a significant portion of the student body, I was beloved. By almost all my professors, I was beloved. In all its contradictory weight, I was a beloved token.

But I knew the dirty truth: As a token, much of the love I received was conditional. The moment you say you hate fraternities and wish them abolished, the love evaporates. The moment you say Duke Basketball feels like a patriarchal tool, the kindness vanishes. The moment you stop being chill about pronouns and correct an administrator in front of their superior, the affection is gone. The moment you stop being hyper-successful and just try to be a normal student instead of collecting accolades for the university, the enthusiasm fizzles. The moment you say the final episode of *The Office* felt a bit too heteronormative to you, the support disappears.

When I walked around on campus, stomping by in five-inch platforms and lipstick, I knew exactly what people were thinking about me.

How does Jacob keep going? They seem like they're happy all the time, indefatigable. How do they do it?

The recipe for success is simple, I wanted to say in my best Vanna White, saccharine smile plastered on my face. *You simply work your ass off, settle for table scraps, and give up on ever truly belonging.*

Oh, and try to get the fuck away from campus, if you can.

While I was struggling with my nascent gender identity in my own heart, unsure what it would mean for my future, I never let my peers see it. To my peers, I was a peppy, energetic, confident, and voracious activist who was changing the world, a human rights ass-kicker-slash-names-taker with a bright future in American politics. Like a luxury car, I concealed the effort, the combustion running beneath the hood, purring along quietly so everyone could focus on the smooth ride. I always tried to give a smooth ride in college. Make of that what you will.*

My sophomore year, I came back to campus with not one, not two, but four titles. In keeping with my vision for a career in politics or inter-

---

* I like to joke about having a raucous sex life in college. The *real* joke is that I had basically none.

national relations, I joined the President's Cabinet as Director of LGBTQ Policy and Affairs for Duke Student Government, was elected outreach chair for Blue Devils United, and founded two new student coalitions in that year alone.

The first was called Duke Students for Gender Neutrality (DSGN, i.e., "Design"—an organization is only as good as its acronym). It was a student coalition that advocated for gender-neutral housing and bathrooms. My best friend Sunny and I worked our asses off on it for the last three years of college, writing proposal after proposal, taking meeting after meeting, but we ultimately achieved little. Sure, gender-neutral housing was technically allowed in certain places on campus, but by no means was it encouraged or made part of the campus culture like we'd hoped. Duke didn't want to be UC Berkeley: The idea of gender-neutral, universally coed housing was just too much for the university's straight white billionaire donors to get behind, too much for their heterosexist minds to handle. We had a few victories, sure—we were able to get a coed multistall bathroom in our dorm during our senior year, and a few of our friends were allowed to live together in mixed gender roommate pairs—but that was all we had to show for three years of persistent and diligent activism.

The other coalition I cofounded that year was called Duke Together Against Constitutional Discrimination. It had one goal: to inspire the Duke community to vote against Amendment One, a 2012 state constitutional amendment that sought to prohibit same-sex couples from having legally recognized relationships in North Carolina. While the hateful amendment ultimately passed, Duke Together was instrumental in opposing it and mobilizing voters. Our efforts were so effective that the Duke campus early voting station was the busiest early voting site in the state. We were so effective that national field organizers from the Human Rights Campaign stopped by campus to learn about our strategy and efforts.

We were so effective that toward the end of May, I opened my email to find the presidential seal looking back at me. It was an official invitation from the White House to attend their annual LGBTQ Pride reception that June. I'm not sure if I cried or screamed or gasped or what, but it was, by far, the hottest invite I'd ever received. A few moments later, my friend Elena—the other co-chair of Duke Together—gave me a ring.

"Did you get the same email I just got?"

"YES I AM FREAKING OUT. WHAT IS HAPPENING?"

As plus ones, we agreed to bring our friend Adrienne, another organizer who'd been instrumental, and Janie, my campus mom and the head of our LGBTQ Center.

In order to attend, I had to fly all the way back to DC from Johannesburg, South Africa, where I was doing a summer volunteer program through my scholarship. The consummate hustler, I didn't let that stop me. I found an absurdly cheap flight and a combination of funds from multiple university and movement sources to cover the ticket.

But when I arrived in DC and unpacked at Adrienne's apartment, I realized to my horror that I wasn't *at all* prepared with the proper fashion for such an occasion. I'd been so worried about the logistics of my trip, about getting my body halfway around the world, that I hadn't thought through the absolute most important component for any event at the White House: my outfit.

In a panic, I strategized with Adrienne. *Should I just wear my suit and tie? It doesn't fit very well, but it's all that I really have. Should I wear lipstick? What about earrings? And what shoes should I wear? Can I even find heels in my size at the last minute? It's notoriously hard to find any size 11 or 12 high heels, let alone ones that are fashionable enough for the motherfucking White House.*

At Adrienne's suggestion, we took the metro to Nordstrom Rack, the only place (other than Payless, another favorite of mine) where you can reliably find cute size 11 or size 12 heels in stock. There wasn't much to choose from, but after a few minutes of digging, we found a pair of sky-high, matte black faux snakeskin heels designed by none other than Jessica Simpson, the resident favorite of all girls with big feet. God bless you, Jessica. You're my shero.

They were perfect. They had all the height I wanted to ensure I'd tower over the crowd, but were professional and sleek enough for somewhere as regal as the White House. I dropped fifty bucks on them.

The next morning, after sleeping off the jet lag, I donned my suit and threw my heels in a loaner purse from Adrienne, and we were off. We met at the East Gate of the White House complex, and queued up in the forming line. Perched on the wall that wraps around the South Lawn, I shucked off my flats, which was when it hit me:

Has anyone ever done this before? Has a sissy like me ever worn high heels to a White House reception? If so, I want to be their friend.

Those thoughts felt too grandiose, too self-aggrandizing, to say out loud. I took a cursory look at the rest of the crowd to check. Surely I couldn't be the only one.

It seemed that there were plenty of gender nonconforming women and masculine-of-center female-assigned folks, but the more I looked, the more I began to realize, *There's not really anyone else* quite *like me*. Other than a guy who was wearing a kilt (whom I of course befriended), all the other male-assigned people were so—boring. Typical. Conforming, other than perhaps wearing a brightly colored suit or a flamboyant tie. *Why do I feel like I'm the only person with facial hair and high heels here?* I pondered. *How is that possible? I mean, there are definitely trans people here, but where are the other nonbinary/genderqueer/gender nonconforming femmes like me? Where are all the other sissies?*

Before I could dwell on the matter any further, the line was moving and we were passing through security.

The reception was more lavish and beautiful than I could've possibly imagined. To this day, it's the only truly elegant queer event I've ever been to. At most gay events, you're confronted with photos of corporate logos or mostly naked men. If you're lucky, you might even get corporate logos *on* mostly naked men. Most elite gay events just sorta scream, "We know you love MUSCLES! We know you love LUXURY BRANDS! And we know you have the disposable income to BUY BOTH!"

But not this party. This party was an affair properly befitting a princess like me. An elegant party that felt like a state dinner, it was glorious. It had it all: a beautiful spread, a state band playing, an open bar. But what really stuck with me were the napkins. They were thick, beautiful, expensive napkins embossed with a gold-printed White House seal. I took twelve and stashed them in my bag as souvenirs.

And, perhaps most important, you could *sit on the furniture*! In the East Room! And in all the other rooms that were normally roped off! In fact, nothing was roped off. You could walk right up to the art; you could sit on the chairs; you could even fiddle with the curtains if you wanted to (and I did). On some level, I knew that a lot of it was just Washington posturing, a way to thank major campaign donors and supporters who happened to be queer. But on another level, it transcended all that. It was deeply meaningful; a far cry from my tokenized existence on campus; unlike anything from my wildest imaginings.

Swirling among the finery and the party guests and the champagne, you can't help but feel the weight of history. It's the portraits that do it, really. You're just minding your business when *wham*! There's JFK gazing out at you from across the hallway. The significance of the moment wasn't lost on anyone, and certainly not on yours truly, a wistful queen of nostalgia who is so delusionally reflexive that she started writing a book about her life at the age of twenty-five.

Under the gaze of people I'd only read about in history books, it was hard not to wonder what they'd think of me.

For obvious reasons, it was the First Ladies who were most memorable. When you initially walk in, Nancy Reagan greets you by the stairs. I think hers is the most glamorous portrait in the White House, no matter what anyone says.* In a floor-length draping red dress with a multitiered pearl collar, she looks like an evil empress from *Star Wars*. And rightfully so: She and her husband would've *hated* what was happening under their roof. While they were in the White House, they did their very best to ensure that people like me *simply died*. Their inaction in the face of the 1980s AIDS epidemic was nothing short of genocidal. It's fitting that she'll spend posterity draped in red, the color of blood, a color that has become the symbol of the disease she and her husband let run wild. I relished that she had to gaze out as a twenty-year-old queen like me strutted by in five-inch heels. I blew her a kiss as I passed.

Then I walked into the Vermeil Room, a first-floor room that is my favorite in the entire White House. When I entered, I found none other than Jacqueline Kennedy Onassis gazing obliquely back out at me. In a ruffled, high-collar floor-length gown, she presided over the room in solemnity, in reverence, in what struck me almost as hesitation. Far from the glamorous vision I usually associated with her, the contemplative nature of the portrait was striking. I perched on the couch in front of her to pose for a photo, blessed to simply be in her regal presence. I like to think that, while she would find most of my present fashion choices tacky, she would've given her blessing to at least *a few* of them.

It wasn't until I turned around that my breath was *really* taken away. On the far wall was none other than the bisexual/lesbian human rights goddess herself, Eleanor Roosevelt. Sporting a fleur de lis brooch, a gray suit, and pearls, she rested one pink-manicured hand on a book and cradled a yellow no. 2 pencil in the other. A woman of words, sophistication, brilliance, and diplomatic power, Eleanor Roosevelt is the closest thing we've had to a woman president. I stared at her: a symbol of queer power and brilliance, of human rights and diplomacy, of women's authority and dominion. She looked back at me with a gentle, knowing

---

* Other than Michelle Obama's, *obviously*, but that wasn't there when I visited the White House in 2012.

glance. As if to say, *You were meant to be here*. As if to say, *You belong here*. As if to say, *You should know your power*.

Just when I thought her portrait couldn't get any more fabulous, I took a look at the additional grayscale portraits of her sprinkled at the bottom of the frame. There's one of her laughing, head tilted to the side. There's another of her fiddling with her wedding ring. And there's yet another of her thinking, chin perched in her hand. Then, inexplicably, alongside the selfies are two pairs of hands floating in space. One pair of hands is holding a pair of glasses. The other is knitting.

Can you *imagine* the conversation that must've led to that portrait? When Eleanor Roosevelt, a hipster meme icon way ahead of her time, must've looked to her portraitist and said, "Hey, I don't want them thinking I'm *just* a brilliant politician. Let's make sure they know I'm a *nerdy* lesbian/bisexual, okay? What could we include in the portrait to be sure they know?"

"I dunno, maybe a pair of reading glasses?"

"Sure, but it needs *more*."

"What about a cat?"

"Too on the nose."

"What about some—um—knitting?"

"*Perfect*," she must've exclaimed. "That'll show 'em. That way they'll never forget I was crafty *and* wrote love letters to ladies."

Bidding Eleanor adieu, drunk with history, I teetered upstairs, the marble floors already making my feet sore.

When I entered the East Room and saw the presidential podium all set up for President Obama's speech, it started to sink in. All of a sudden, like a punch in the gut, my gender felt *historic* for the first time, *visionary, simultaneously ancient and ahead of its time, indelibly sewn into the fabric of the American story.*

I mused, *Am I among the first generation of sissies in American history who can dream of being here? Of flouncing about, openly gender noncon-forming, in the highest office in the land?*

My historical romanticism soaring, my self-aggrandizement at a fever pitch, I did the only natural thing for a twenty-year-old at a reception at the White House to do: I went to the open bar for a drink.

I wasn't sure if they would card me, so I watched the bar for a moment. After seeing two twinks, both with *far* less facial hair than I had, get drinks without so much as a look of hesitation, I decided they must not be carding. I mean how *tacky* would that be? To ask for ID at a White House bar *after* each guest has been personally cleared by the Secret Service? *Très gauche, mademoiselle.*

I waltzed up to the bar, ordered a gin and tonic—with Hendrick's, I believe—and proceeded to underage drink in the White House, two months shy of my twenty-first birthday. I hope that this singular fact, above all others, is what you remember me for. I don't need to be a hero. I don't need to be canonized. I don't need to meet the queen. I simply need to be remembered as the type of queer punk who drank underage in five-inch heels in front of the president. It is honestly the most important identity I have.

Badass epitaph secured, no longer afraid of death, I grabbed Adrienne and strutted to the front of the East Room where the president was to speak. On the guidance of a friend who'd been to the reception the year before, I knew that if you just stood there early, you'd be guaranteed a front-row spot. Adrienne and I stood there for an hour or so as the crowd slowly filled in.

When President Obama finally did come out to give his speech, the cheers were deafening. He spoke eloquently and with poise. But honestly, I can't say that I was altogether focused on what he was saying. If we are keeping it one hundred here, my brain kept playing one thought over and over again:

If that isn't one of the sexiest men I have ever seen.

I mean, can we talk about this? Can we? That smile? Those eyes? Those dimples? And not to mention that he is *tall*. Like, almost the same height that I was in five inch heels, and I'm six feet *without* heels on. You do the math. By the time he came around to shake hands at the conclusion of his speech, I'd been reduced to a twelve-year-old girl at a One Direction concert. I was shaking and nervous and sweating and *seriously* crushing. If it had been socially acceptable, I would've started screaming at the top of my lungs like the fangirl that I am.

I tried to hold on to my politics.

But Jacob, you have to remain critical. He still hasn't issued an executive order banning workplace discrimination against LGBTQ Americans. Statistically, he hasn't slowed deportations. You still disagree with some of this man's foreign policy decisions. And you don't like drone warfare. You must remain critical, my brain said. *It is important.*

NAH FUCK THAT! screamed my heart and girlish libido, gossiping back and forth like stylists at a hair salon. *Can you even believe how handsome he is? He is sooooo cute! Oh my God, is he looking at you right now? OH MY GOD JACOB HE'S LOOKING AT YOU!*

And he was. Before I knew what was happening, it was my turn to shake his hand and say hello. And in my panic, in my giddy schoolgirl glee, all I could muster, all I could manage to say at a gay party at the White House, was:

"We're from Duke, Mr. President! You like Duke Basketball don't you?"

"The Blue Devils are a great team!" he said back, smiling and shaking my hand before moving on.

WHAT.

Jacob. jacob jacob jacob. JACOB. You had ONE CHANCE to say something to the leader of the free world and all you could talk about was Duke Basketball, *something you* don't even really like? *I mean, you've barely gone to one basketball game, and even then it was only to sing the national anthem with your a cappella group. Why couldn't you think of something better? How about, "Do you like my shoes, Mr. President?" Or maybe "Tell Michelle I'm her number one fan!" Literally anything would've been better than that.*

Bemoaning the fact that I'd bungled my words, wishing I could've remembered how to form coherent thoughts, I consoled myself with an underage flute of champagne and sat on a fancy, historic couch in the Blue Room to rest my sore feet.

After the reception, I traveled back to Johannesburg and then to Cape Town to finish out my sophomore summer as planned.

When I returned to the US that fall, I didn't return to campus. Returning to campus would've meant confronting my demons—the tokenization, the sense of political frustration, the feeling of gender impossibility—head on, and I wanted to put that off as long as I could.

Instead, I spent my semester living in none other than New York City. I was enrolled in the Duke in New York program, so it was *technically* still Duke, but in name only. The flagship study-away program for students who were interested in media or the arts, it was self-selective in the best way, in that mostly artists, dancers, stage queens, and weirdos like me signed up.

I lived in a triple room where all three beds had to be lofted in order for us to have enough space, but it was still the most glamorous housing I've had in New York City to date. On the sixth floor of the St. George Hotel in Brooklyn Heights, my room overlooked the Brooklyn Bridge, Lower Manhattan, and, at night, the Empire State Building. In the early morning, if you woke up at the right time, the rising sun would reflect off the metallic paneling on the side of the Frank Gehry tower, lighting it up like fire. Even then, as a twenty-one-year-old, I knew I'd likely never get a view like that again.

In addition to Duke paying for us to see Broadway theater or operas at the Met, each student in the program was required to have a part-time internship. For my three-month placement, I chose to intern at the United Nations, prompting a crisis I wasn't quite ready to tackle: How was I going to navigate gender in the professional world?

Professionalism is, without a doubt, one of my least favorite words in the English language. The reason I loathe it with such intensity is because, as a word, it's *seriously* dishonest. Like three-day-old seafood, it looks *fine enough* on the surface, but the moment you ingest it and your stomach begins to pull its various components apart, it becomes oh so clear that it's actually vile. After only a few moments' digestion, your stomach rumbles, your bowels quiver, and you'd better make it to a gender-neutral bathroom *fast*.

At first glance, *professionalism* tries to convince you it's a neutral word, merely meant to signify a collection of behaviors, clothing, and norms "appropriate" for the workplace. *We just ask that everyone be* professional, the cis white men will say, smiles on their faces, as if they're not asking for much. *We try to maintain a* professional *office environment.*

But never has a word in the English language been so loaded with racism, sexism, heteronormativity, or trans exclusion. Whenever someone is telling you to "be professional," they're really saying, "be more like me."

If you're black, "being professional" can often mean speaking differently, avoiding black cultural references, or not wearing natural hair. If you're not American, "being professional" can mean abandoning your cultural dress for Western business clothes. If you're not Christian, "being professional" can mean potentially removing your hijab to fit in, sitting by while your officemates ignore your need for kosher or halal food, sucking up the fact that your office puts up a giant Christmas tree every year. If you're low-income or working class, "being professional" can mean spending money you don't have on work clothes—"dressing nicely" for a job that may not pay enough for you to *really* afford to do so. If you're a woman, "being professional" can mean navigating a veritable minefield of double standards. Show some skin, but don't be a slut. Wear heels, but not too high, and not too low, either. Wear form-fitting clothes, but not *too* form-fitting. We offer maternity leave, but don't "interrupt your career" by taking it.

And if you're trans like me, "being professional" can mean putting your identity away unless it conforms to dominant gender norms.

To this day, when I walk into an office in lipstick, a bolero jacket, and earrings, people perceive my behavior as unprofessional. My intellect, my competency, and my ability are called into question simply because my gender is different. There are countless geographic areas and professions where I couldn't even consider *having* a career because I am perceived to be so unprofessional.

Plainly put, the imperative to "be professional" is the imperative to be whiter, straighter, wealthier, and more masculine. A wolf in sheep's clothing masquerading as a neutral term, *professionalism* hangs over the head of anyone who's different, who deviates from the hegemony of white men.

Needless to say, in the formal, gendered world of professional dress, I was seriously out of my element. Up until that point, my wardrobe had been imminently casual, feminine, and borderline punk. By junior year, a "normal" outfit for me could've looked like any of the following:

Jean shorts, a chunky necklace, oversize grandma glasses, and a lacy femme camisole.

Cowgirl boots, dark wash jeans, a cut-up thrift store leather jacket, and silver chrome nails.

A shredded T-shirt, spiky stud necklace, secondhand camouflage army jacket, rhinestone clip-ons, combat boots, and a bold lip.

Or, on occasions when I had to dress fancy:

Six-inch stilettos, a vintage fascinator, and a two-sizes-too-small cocktail dress (probably ripping at the seams).

Knowing both that my present wardrobe wouldn't work in an office and that my gender identity placed me outside the bounds of "appropriate work clothes," I approached my job at the United Nations with hesitation. My bosses and coworkers were kind, empathetic people, but no amount of kindness or empathy can shake anxiety about an entire system of power overnight.

So I devised the following strategy: I would begin my time at the UN presenting in a fairly masculine way, then gradually, over time, begin to express my femininity. That way, my colleagues would have the chance to get to know my intellect, my work ethic, and *me* before they had to contend with *my gender* (as if they can really be separated). My mind made up, I packed a suit, a few dress shirts, a handful of ties, and my grandmother's jewelry for work.

But that still left the problem of shoes. I knew I wanted to wear heels to work, but from my cursory observations, work heels and party heels were very different. Because you only wear them for a few hours at a time, party heels can be as bright and as tall as you'd like. But office heels are different. They are shorter—their heels maybe an inch or two—and generally more conservative in terms of cut, shape, and material. When I looked through my closet, I realized, to my dismay, that as a college kid and full-time gender weirdo, all I had were party heels. I didn't own a single heel that was under four and a half inches.

Realizing I needed to spend good money on a new pair of shoes, I set off to find what I deemed my "Hillary Clinton heels." I found them at the Union Square Nordstrom Rack. A $50 pair of simple blue leather pumps, they had a two-inch heel and were wide enough for my caveman feet, but still narrowed to a severe, powerfemme point in the front.

Most important, they were *loud.*

Every fantasy I'd ever had about being a powerfemme involved wearing the high-heeled equivalent of tap shoes.

Click, clack, click, clack. *It's time for your three p.m. briefing, Madame President.*

Click, clack, click, clack. *Do you have the projections for next quarter, Sarah?*

Click, clack, click, clack. *The negligence of the Saudis cannot be overlooked in this case, Your Excellency.*

Click, clack, click, clack. *I said I needed that report on my desk at four, Charles. It's four fifteen and my desk is currently empty. Don't give me excuses. Just fix it.*

In my fantasy world, the loud shoes were equally important, if not more important, than what I actually had to say.

Which is why I decided that loud shoes were a must for the United Nations. It makes sense. Working at the UN, you spend an inordinate amount of time stomping across gargantuan lobbies, marching through marble corridors, and surging up and down open stairways. For this reason, the women who wore loud shoes struck me as particularly intimidating. You could hear them coming for miles. They commanded attention wherever they went, their footsteps demanding respect and admiration. I wanted to be like them.

So before I bought the shoes, I took them for a sound test, finding a long strip of tile flooring in the store. After stomping around for a minute or two, I'd made up my mind. These shoes were *perfect*. They were so loud, other customers turned to see who was wearing them. They were so loud, I inadvertently startled someone's child. I'd found my Hillary Clinton heels.

Finding the audacity to wear them to work was another story.

Even bringing them into the office in a bag, I felt hesitant. What if my colleagues weren't as progressive as I'd thought? What if they didn't think my shoes were appropriate? Or worse, what if they thought my shoes *weren't that cute*? Clandestinely, I put the shoes in my desk drawer and tried to calm down.

I decided that wearing heels was too big of a first step. So I resolved on a few baby steps to take first. I started wearing my grandmother's old brooches on my lapel. Then I started wearing earrings sometimes. So far, so good.

Six weeks into the internship, I decided that it was my moment: my main boss, Minh-Thu, was out of the country for a conference, leaving only my junior supervisor, Ryan. Ryan and I were going to a stakeholder meeting at UNHQ where I could give my new shoes a low-stakes test run.

Things went as smoothly as could be expected. The shoes *click-clack*ed like a dream on the marble floor. A few people at the UN were caught off guard at the sight of a person with a five o'clock shadow wearing kitten heels, but I received nothing worse than quizzical looks. As I went clip-clopping around the institution Eleanor Roosevelt had worked so tirelessly to create, I imagined that she would've been proud.

It was only back at the office that I began to worry. The day had been quiet. *Too* quiet. No one, not one person at the UN Headquarters building or at my office, had said a word about my shoes. I didn't hear anything *bad* about them, but I didn't hear anything *good*, either. The response had simply been silence. Not a peep. What did that mean?

I found out two days later when Minh-Thu was back. Apparently, people *had* been talking about my shoes, just not to me. After lunch, Minh-Thu breezed by my desk (and in this instance, "breezed" is literal. She's the type of powerful woman who creates her own wind when she struts down the hall. I admire her for that).

"Do you have a second to chat? Let's go to my office."

I settled in, notepad prepped, ready to give her an update on the research I'd been doing about the formation of the Sustainable Development Goals. It wasn't until she paused for a moment to collect her thoughts before speaking that I became worried—one of the most brilliant people I have ever had the pleasure of working for, Minh-Thu never paused to think. She was the type of powerhouse boss who was jumping into her ideas before you'd even had the chance to close the door, let alone sit down.

So the fact that she hadn't spoken for three seconds was alarming. A moment later, the silence broke.

"I heard that you were wearing heels around the office one day while I was out, and I wanted to talk to you about that."

"Yeah, I was," I said, dissolving into the floor.

Realizing that I thought I was being reprimanded, Minh-Thu course corrected, clarifying, "Oh gosh, no, you are *not* in trouble, Jacob! Sorry, I realize how that must've sounded. You aren't in trouble for wearing heels! I want to be very clear that we all support you wearing whatever you want around the office within appropriate boundaries. I just wanted to talk about everything, to help you think things through."

Picking myself up off the floor, the molecules of my body rearranged into human form, I started to calm down. "Yeah, I was actually hoping we could talk about it, because I really value your guidance."

"Okay, so what I'm about to say may sound harsh and it may scare you a little bit, but that is not my intention. I just—as a woman who has worked at the United Nations in one capacity or another basically since you were born, I want to give you a little perspective. It doesn't serve anybody, especially you, if you don't have context for what you're getting into."

I froze. I was already scared, but did my best to gently smile, eager to hear what she had to say.

"I know you may think the United Nations is supposed to be progressive, and some parts of it are, but by and large it's still a very conservative institution, especially when it comes to gender. I mean, we can't even get every country to agree that women deserve equal rights yet. So, in some ways, it's no surprise that gender politics at UN HQ can be backward. When I first started working here in the nineties, it was *still* fairly edgy for a woman like me to wear pants to the office. In my early career here, I couldn't wear pants, let alone be a powerful woman, without stirring up trouble."

My mind reeling, she continued, "So I guess what I'm saying is this: Walking around at the United Nations in high heels will probably be really hard for you. And whether you realize it or not, some people will discriminate against you because you are different. You may not be invited to observe sessions or take part in meetings that you deserve to participate in. You may not be given a seat at the table, even when you should have one. You may be unknowingly giving up a lot by flexing with gender like that."

"Oh, okay," I mumbled, going into shock.

"Obviously, none of this is true for our office. You should feel one hundred percent comfortable wearing whatever you want at our office. Know that we *all* respect and value you already, and that will never change, no matter what shoes you wear. Know that I respect you. But externally, in the broader UN system, expressing this side of yourself may come with serious consequences for your career advancement."

She could tell I was scared, but she needed to continue. I needed to hear it. It was important medicine to swallow, sugar be damned.

"What I'm trying to do is give you all the information I can. I want you to understand the landscape so that you can make intentional, deliberate choices about how you'd like to navigate it. If expressing your full gender at work is the most important thing right now, then you should absolutely do that. But I don't want you to make that decision in a vacuum. Does that make sense? I can't tell you how badly I wish, for my sake and for yours, that the world wasn't this way. But given the fact that, at present, this is what it's like, I wouldn't be a good mentor if I didn't share what I know."

I nodded, words evading me.

"Remember, you're not in trouble. I will back you no matter what. I will support you to the absolute ends of my ability. I will do my damnedest to protect you and help you further your career, but there are certain things that are out of my control. And I just need to be honest about that, okay?"

"Okay." I gulped, fumbling over what to say next. "Let me think about things? This is a lot of information for me to process."

"Of course, Jacob," she responded, radiating a combination of kindness, pain, and frustration. "Take all of the time you need. I'm always here to talk and strategize."

And did I *ever* take time to think about what she'd said.

At the time, it felt like she was punishing me, despite her assertions to the contrary. I was furious at her for saying those things to me—*How dare she suggest I not be myself? How dare she tell me the UN system wouldn't be receptive to someone like me? How dare she imply it might be better for me to hide my gender?*

But today, as I look back, I am able to appreciate what she was doing: She was loving, mentoring, and protecting me. The fact of the matter is that I needed to hear every single thing she had to say. I needed someone to respect me enough to shake me out of the fantasy that life as a gender nonconforming person was going to be easy. I needed someone to have the courage to tell me the inconvenient truth. In a world where people try to be polite by *not talking about* how cruel the world can be to gender nonconforming people, Minh-Thu did me the radical kindness of sharing something real. She wasn't the disease; on the contrary, she was the first person who'd respected me enough to tell me that battling this cancer was going to be a motherfucker.

Like the fabled emperor, I was running around town naked, convinced that my new gender nonconforming outfit made me special. Everyone told me so. But when it came down to it, I wasn't clothed at all; I was buck-naked, vulnerable, and unprotected. I was about to strut all over town *wearing nothing*. Minh-Thu simply had the courage to tell me that I was, in fact, naked; that the world wasn't going to protect me by default. That discrimination was going to be part of my reality, and I'd be better off if I could plan for it and make my own decision about how to maneuver.

I did not take the news of my own nakedness well. I left the office that day hurt, broken, and terrified. Clawing at my clothes, gnashing my teeth, tears burning down my cheeks, I stormed past Grand Central Terminal, past Times Square, all the way to the West Side, Gaga's "Judas" blaring angrily in my headphones, I felt my world falling apart.

It would take years for me to internalize what Minh-Thu had told me. It would take years for me to fully contemplate and process her guidance, let alone learn to appreciate her for sharing it with me.

For the moment, I decided that she was right about one thing: I needed time to think things over. I needed to think about how I wanted to proceed. How important was my gender, really? In a vacuum, I would obviously express myself however I felt comfortable, but given that I lived in the real world, a place notoriously hostile to people like me, what was I willing to give up in order to express my gender openly?

For the remainder of my time at the United Nations, I left my Hillary Clinton pumps in my desk drawer, only daring to put them on late at night when most of my colleagues had left the office.

There were two exceptions to that rule. I wore high heels—my party heels—to our foundation-wide holiday party in Washington, DC. And I wore my Hillary pumps to UN Headquarters when Ban Ki-moon and Ricky Martin spoke at a big event promoting Free & Equal, the United Nation's first ever campaign for LGBTQI rights. I couldn't help myself with that one. If there's ever a time to risk your entire career at the United Nations in order to wear a pair of two-inch pumps, it's when *Ricky Martin* is in the building.

Livin' *la vida loca*, baby.

When Hurricane Sandy struck New York City in October 2012, I didn't witness the storm firsthand. As a Southerner, having experienced at least a dozen hurricanes, I knew not to fuck around with them. I left the city and headed to Boston to visit a friend at Harvard Medical School, where the storm brought only a rainy evening and a cold day.

Back in New York, the storm was relentless.

For some, recovery was quick. My office at the UN was informally open by Thursday of that week. Subway lines from Brooklyn to Manhattan were still shut down and, feeling a bit stir-crazy having returned to my cramped dorm room, I took the East River Ferry to work. Within a week, the power was back on in Lower Manhattan.

But not all of New York was so quick to recover. As after all natural disasters, the city's poor and disenfranchised took the lion's share of the lasting damage. The Ali Forney Center, an organization dedicated to serving the needs of New York City's LGBTQ homeless youth, ran a drop-in center out of Chelsea, which had been flooded with a catastrophic three feet of water. Their main youth services center ruined, they were struggling to reopen and needed hundreds of thousands of dollars in order to do so.

When I read about the Ali Forney Center's plight, I was with my roommates in my dorm room, looking out the window at the Brooklyn Bridge, now fully reilluminated. I turned around and looked back at my closet, high heels standing at attention on my shoe rack. Inspiration struck.

"Wait, y'all, I have a stupid idea."

"Yes?" inquired my roommate sleepily. Me having ideas and wanting to talk about them was pretty much a nightly occurrence, and after two and a half months of living together, I imagine it was starting to become annoying.

"Okay, so there's this shelter for homeless LGBTQ youth in New York called the Ali Forney Center that flooded during Hurricane Sandy. I'm thinking that I want to raise some money for them as my end-of-semester project."

"How?"

"I'm going to run across the Brooklyn Bridge in high heels. I think it'd be ridiculous enough for people to want to donate money to see it.

And we all know I'm good at walking in heels—I can't imagine that running would be that much harder?"

The next day, I gave the Ali Forney Center a call to let them know what I was planning to do. They were psyched, but somewhat skeptical. Nonetheless, they walked me through how to make a fund-raising page with their online portal, and I was off.

The next week, I went down to Brooklyn Bridge Park with some friends to shoot a quick promotional video of me talking about the run. We then walked up to the Brooklyn Bridge itself to get some B-roll of me dancing in high heels on the bridge, and that's when I started to realize that I really had something. As I danced around to Janelle Monáe in my pumps, tourists passing by were *enthralled*. Some stopped to dance with me. Some asked to take photos. Some simply walked by, mouths agape, certain that this kind of thing could only happen in the Big Apple. The energy and enthusiasm I felt from those random strangers on the bridge convinced me, more than anything, that this project might just have the potential to capture the public imagination.

After we launched the video and the fund-raising page, things began to grow quickly. We raised $1,000 within the first three days. By the start of the second week, the project had write-ups in four prominent national queer blogs, catapulting donations to $5,000. Seeing that the project was really taking hold, a friend pledged that his company would match any donations I received in the next 48 hours, up to $1,500. We exceeded the match cap, pulling us up to $10,000. And that's when I got a call from Cathy Renna, a notorious lesbian publicist who was working with the Ali Forney Center pro-bono to get them press about their recovery effort. Given the runaway success of my project, she asked my permission to pitch it to a number of national outlets, and I, of course, said yes.

Which is how, by the fourth week of the project, I found out I'd been named New Yorker of the Week by NY1, the local news network for 8 million New Yorkers. As part of a special "New Yorker of the Week" series, they were featuring one person from each borough who was helping with Hurricane Sandy recovery efforts. Apparently, I was the pick for the borough of Manhattan, where the Ali Forney Center was based.

The accolade didn't come with a trophy or anything, but we did get to film a special spot for NY1 where I pretended to "train" in stilettos for the run—doing jumping jacks, stretches, lunges, sit-ups, and push-ups. In case you were wondering, yes, push-ups are *much* harder wearing heels. I'm not a physicist, but it's something about your feet being even longer than they normally are. And about most high heels having pointy toes.

The funniest part of all this was the fact that I *wasn't even a New York resident*. It was like studying abroad and being named Parisian of the Month or Londoner of the Day or something. I felt like I'd single-handedly put an end to the question "How long does it take to *really* be a New Yorker?" For some people, it can take years. But if you run across the Brooklyn Bridge in high heels, you're officially a New Yorker—in fact, you're a *lauded* New Yorker—within three short months.

Later that week, I got a call from a 212 number I didn't recognize.

"Hello, is this Jacob Tobia?"

"Mm-hmm."

"Hi, this is Rachel calling. I'm a booker at MSNBC and we were wondering if you'd like to come by on Thursday for an in-studio interview with Thomas Roberts about your Brooklyn Bridge run?"

"Um, yeah," I replied, gulping for air. "Yeah, that'd be great!"

"Okay, wonderful. I'll be in touch with more details via email. Looking forward to having you!"

"Yeah, looking forward to coming on the air!"

"Oh, and one more thing—can you bring the actual shoes that you'll be doing the run in? We want to have them in-studio for the segment."

After going downstairs to call my mom and freak the fuck out, I took a moment to Google Thomas Roberts. He wasn't an anchor who I was familiar with, but then again, I didn't really know any MSNBC anchors other than Rachel Maddow.

For those who aren't familiar, Thomas Roberts is, without question, the most gorgeous man in news (sorry, Anderson Cooper). His jawline alone could kill twelve people. They'd all just be sitting in a café or a bookshop minding their own business when *kapow!* Thomas Roberts walks through the door, they get one look at his jawline, and instantly drop dead on the floor. Add piercing blue eyes, a laser-cut smile, and a body that *might've* been stolen from Hercules, and you get what is, perhaps, the worst person I could've possibly had interview me.

I mean, if I had to sit down with Rachel Maddow or Melissa Harris-Perry, I would've been *nervous* because I love them, but I wouldn't have had to worry about accidentally giggling like a third grader with a crush. With Thomas at the helm, I had to be prepared for the very real possibility that I would step in front of the cameras, take one look into his baby blues, and melt into a glittery pink puddle on live television.

A few days later, my "running" heels at my side, I showed up to 30 Rockefeller Plaza for the interview. Sporting my new fancy dress pants from Topman, sky-high "interview" heels, a collared white shirt, my grandmother's earrings, and a blazer with a grandma brooch, I was dressed to kill. I sat down for a bit of makeup—just a touch of powder, really, I wasn't confident enough yet to wear lipstick and eyeliner on national news—and before I knew it, I was being ushered into the studio.

I didn't know quite what I'd expected, but it wasn't this. The schedule of a live news show is grueling, so Thomas and I only had about three seconds to say hello before he jumped into the segment's headlines and I waited on the side. After watching him do his thing for two minutes, they placed my "running" heels on a high table next to Thomas and sent me up to the platform for the interview.

"Now, remember, don't look directly at the cameras, just pretend they're not even there. Focus on talking to Thomas," the producer said, attempting to comfort me.

But the cameras don't make me nervous, I thought. *Thomas does! I mean look at that face, my God.*

Before I could dwell on the thought any longer, it was go time.

"In New York City in October," Thomas began, looking to camera and ignoring me, "a four-foot storm surge gushed into and through the doors of the city's leading shelter for LGBT homeless youth. That flooding utterly destroyed the Ali Forney Center's drop-in site and caused hundreds of thousands of dollars of damage. The center is now struggling to get back on its feet and one young man is offering financial 'heeling'—by putting on heels!"

They played a clip from the promotional video my friends and I shot, and before I could register how weird that made me feel, Thomas jumped back in.

"All right, and that runner is here with me now, Duke University student and LGBT activist—"

Oh my God, did he just call me an LGBT activist on the news? Like it's an official thing now? He's so dreamy . . .

"—Jacob Tobia. It's great to have you," he said, turning to me.

"It's great to be here," I managed to croak.

Do not start giggling, Jacob. Don't you do it!

"Now, your personal story is tied to this, however, you had a much more positive experience in coming out, so why did you want to do this type of stunt for the Ali Forney Center?"

Phew, a softball question, okay.

"Well, December fifteenth for me marks the five-year anniversary of coming out to my family, and I figured that there was no better way to celebrate it than to give back to youth who have not had it as easy as I have, LGBT youth who are without homes."

Then Thomas asked me a question I was *not at all* prepared for, the one question I'd sorta hoped wouldn't come up:

"What we just watched is the teaser video. You have not run across the Brooklyn Bridge yet—that's coming up on Saturday. But why do this in five-inch stilettos? I mean, you're in heels *right now*. Is this something you normally do?" he asked, quite reasonably.

Though I held my composure for the cameras, I squirmed inside. *How do I answer this? How do I talk about my gender identity on the national news when I hardly understand it myself? I mean, I don't even really wear high heels at work yet. Was it a bad idea to wear heels to this interview?*

Thankfully, I didn't have time to think. I didn't have time to doubt. I simply had to speak, to put one word in front of the other until they made a sentence. I took a deep breath and, surprisingly, formed a coherent response:

"Yeah, I mean, I wear high heels normally," I said naturally, coolly, as if it were the littlest thing in the world. "It's part of who I am. It's how I express myself. And I figured I'd take my fabulosity and put it to a good cause, y'know?"

I think Thomas might've almost been taken aback by the eloquence, concision, and thoroughness of my response. I was proud of myself. He kept it moving:

"All right, so when we talk about that, these are the shoes right here. This is the pair that you're gonna wear on Saturday? I mean, these look brutal. And dangerous."

"Ummm. My feet will be hurting a little bit, I'm sure, when—"

"Can you see these?" Thomas gestured to the camera. "Look at this!"

"Yeah, I mean, they're large. I'm not messing around. They're five-inch heels, and I'm sure that my feet will be a little sore, but it's the least I can do to help out youth who've had it a lot harder than I have."

"This is a bold move," he said, changing directions, going in for the hardest question yet. "Do you think that you're breaking stereotypes by doing this, or do you think that you're lending to stereotypes for people who might be critical of what you're doing?"

Oh, shit.

Oh shit oh shit oh shit. Now a masculine gay man is asking me live on tele-vision whether I think being feminine is an embarrassment to the gay com-munity. Crap crap crap. I know he's just playing devil's advocate, but still! I'm hardly even an adult!

But there was no time to think. I opened my mouth and, once again, was pleasantly surprised by the words that came out.

"I think that the best way to break through stereotypes is to embrace who you are no matter what, and this is who I am, so I don't think I—I—"

I fumbled for a second. Then I regained control of the ball.

"The critics can say what they want to say, but I'm proud of it."

His point about respectability politics dismissed, Thomas moved on: "What's been the response so far, and how much money are you hoping to raise?"

"It's been incredible. I was originally gonna raise $2,000, and now I'm at $10,000. And I hope that today through Saturday I'll be able to double it."

"All right, and . . . these . . . I still can't get over these shoes. I mean, look at these things, look at that heel!"

He then *picked up my shoes* from the table to show them to the camera. *I really hope he can't smell them*, I thought. *I'm not sure how clean they are . . .*

"Oh, they're not too bad," I said, attempting to assuage his worries.

"They're not bad, but I'm just saying, to run a mile is gonna be tough, but we wish you nothing but the best of luck, Jacob."

"You know, you gotta be strong. Thank you."

"You do, but it doesn't have to be by running across the Brooklyn Bridge in freezing temperatures—but he's gonna do it!"

It was like I blacked out. Like I blinked, and suddenly the interview was over. I'm grateful that I could watch the video after, because otherwise, I'm not sure I could even tell you what had happened. The combination of being on national news for the first time, warding off respectability politics, and dealing with a human being as physically perfect as Thomas Roberts was simply too much for my lil' queer heart to bear.

I was so high after the interview, had so much pure adrenaline, I could've sworn I was taller and shinier than the Rockefeller Center Christmas tree outside.

I couldn't have asked for a better day to do the run. For a mid-December day in New York City, it was warm: forty-six degrees, with crystal clear skies.

After the press junket, the actual run felt like a piece of cake; more of a celebration than a challenge. A few coworkers from the UN and friends from my Duke in New York program joined me to film the run and celebrate at the finish line. In nothing but gym shorts, a Duke T-shirt, and a Santa hat, I set off.

About two hundred yards in, a thought occurred to me for the first time: *Should I have, I dunno, like,* trained *for this? I mean, is this actually realistic? Can I run the entire length of the Brooklyn Bridge, a whopping 1.1 miles, in these shoes? And what would happen if I broke my ankle* (a distinct possibility) *when I was halfway across the bridge? Would the paramedics have to walk all the way across the bridge just to pick me up? Do they charge a special fee for ambulance pickups partway across the Brooklyn Bridge?* I'd watched countless videos of models in sky-high heels tripping on the catwalk, rolling their ankles. It looked violent enough, and they were only strutting. I was straight-up *jogging* in those motherfuckers.

With nothing but youthful ignorance and my own irrationality goading me on, I kept running. I waited for my feet to cry out in agony, waited for the inevitable moment when I'd trip and fall on my face, but those things simply never happened. Each step I took, my foot landed with grace. By divine providence alone, my feet kept going, and I passed the glitter tinsel finish line all in one piece, miraculously unscathed.

Looking back at the video, one could even say that I finished the run *strong*. My friends Michael and David, who ran alongside me to film, were out of breath from simply running in flat shoes. I'd run the mile in something like eight and a half or nine minutes, a respectable enough time for a mile *without* heels on.

Standing on the Manhattan side of the bridge, something dawned on me: This wasn't only about raising money for and calling attention to a worthy cause. This was also about *my identity*. In the wake of my conversations with Minh-Thu, in the wake of my struggle to bring my gender identity with me into the workplace, I needed to do something, to make some very public statement about who I was. I needed to reclaim my gender, to own it more loudly and with more vigor than I ever had before. I needed to tell masculine respectability politics to fuck off. I needed to reassert my right to simply be: to show others that I was strong, tougher than even the world and my own heart had given me credit for.

And if you don't think that running an eight-minute mile in five-inch heels makes me one of the toughest people you know, then I'm going to need you to prove it, broseph. Go buy your own pair of heels, run a mile, and tell me to my face that I'm wrong. Go ahead, Mr. Tough Mudder. I double-dog dare you.

Sometimes a tragedy like Hurricane Sandy can help a city find its resilience. Destruction can clear the path for audacity, adversity giving way to newfound strength.

The week after my run, I was invited to attend the opening of the Ali Forney Center's new-and-improved drop-in center in Harlem. They'd been planning to move their drop-in center uptown for years; they'd just never had the funds to do so. With the groundswell of support that the Ali Forney Center received following Hurricane Sandy, with hundreds of thousands of dollars in new donations and a huge bump in media attention, they'd been able to expedite their plan to move the drop-in center closer to the queer and trans youth—predominantly queer and trans youth of color—who they served. Because of my work and dozens of other fund-raisers, the Ali Forney Center hadn't just come back, it'd come back *stronger than ever.*

Returning to North Carolina from New York, I came back stronger than ever, too. Somewhere between the White House and the Brooklyn Bridge, I'd left behind the one thing that had always held me back: my manhood.

Okay, maybe that phrasing needs some work. I didn't leave behind my *euphemistic* manhood—my genitals hadn't changed or anything—but I had left behind *the idea of being a man.*

There wasn't a tearful, revelatory moment when it happened. Getting rid of my manhood was less like throwing away an old couch and more like getting rid of an ugly jacket that someone else bought for you that you never liked in the first place. It wasn't that I made a big decision that it had to go. I didn't heave and huff and drag a giant piece of furniture out to the curb. There wasn't one particular moment where I said to myself, *I am no longer going to concern myself with being a man.*

It was just that, after years of sitting in my closet, unworn, I decided to throw my manhood in the Goodwill bin. And by the time I finally made that decision, it hardly mattered. I had an entire identity wardrobe of texture and color at my disposal. I had labels upon labels, hundreds of identities to choose from—queer, femme, trans, gender nonconforming, genderqueer, genderfluid, gay, fabulous, gorgeous, nonbinary, cute, gender transcendental, genderfucked, unicorn, motherfucking witch—so what could I possibly need "man" for anymore? It was a frumpy, ugly, bulky old coat that I never liked in the first place. It was taking up too much room in my identitarian wardrobe, and it had to go.

And so I threw it out like any number of old things that have long lost their use and cannot be salvaged—a broken stapler, a malfunctioning blender, an old phonebook, a Shake Weight, that calendar from 2012 that you never even hung up.

But this isn't to dismiss the importance of getting rid of it. When you've seen that coat, the one you don't like, the one you never wear, in your closet for two decades, there is power in finally throwing it out. Your whole closet feels refreshed. The whole room feels different. Renewed. Cleansed.

Without the idea of manhood holding me back, I navigated the world with a new lightness of being. I found new courage. I claimed new power. And I began the years-long process of helping others get on board with my enlightened sense of self.

I started playing with new ways of talking about myself. I started using gender-neutral pronouns when people asked. I wasn't "him" anymore. I was "them." I wasn't "he" anymore. I was "they." I started to correct other people when they got it wrong.

I stopped saying I was "gay" and started saying I was "genderqueer." I stopped saying I was a "man" and started saying I was a "person." I stopped saying I was a "guy" and started saying I was a "flaming-hot mess of a queen."

And yes, while I knew on some level that these were just words, that these shifts were only semantic—imperfect approximations of far more complicated ideas—they were finally *my words*. They were words of my own choosing, begetting possibilities of my own imagining.

My newfound experimentation and courage led me to take another, more personal risk: I began the challenging process of setting things right with my church.

As it turned out, I didn't need to end things with my church; we just needed a break. I had damage that needed time to repair. In high school, I hadn't given myself the space or time to mend; I kept picking at the scab over and over, desperate for healing. College allowed me the time to properly treat my wounds. As I grew more distant, I also grew stronger in my sense of self and in the knowledge of my own power. It took my freshman and sophomore years of college, a stint in Johannesburg, and a semester in New York before I was ready to *really* go back to church.

My junior year of college, as I got dressed for Christmas Eve service, I made a decision: If my church couldn't handle me or love me as I was, I no longer needed to be a member of the congregation. I could no longer afford to be ashamed of my identity or bashful about the fact that God loves me. So, in true Jacob fashion, I strapped on my five-inch chunky platform heels—the same ones I wore across the Brooklyn Bridge— threw on a glitter-sequined vest, adorned my lips with red lipstick, and walked downstairs.

When my dad saw my outfit, he gave me his customary glare. That, I'd expected.

What I hadn't expected was the look on my mom's face. In place of the glowing smile she usually had before we went to church together, her face was stern.

"Jacob, do you really have to wear high heels to church? Can you please put on other shoes?"

My heart sank momentarily, but buoyed back up with the strength I'd been building for the past two years.

"Mom, I have been a member of this church for twenty-one years." I gestured to the floor. "I have been going to St. Francis since I was literally this tall. If they cannot love me and affirm me as I am; if they cannot handle the fact that I'm going to wear high heels to Christmas Eve service; if, after twenty-one years, they can no longer love me over *a pair of shoes*, then I don't need to continue to go there. I owe this to myself."

My mom stood trembling, her eyes watering in frustration.

"But this is my congregation, too, Jacob!" she explained desperately. "I have to deal with the consequences of your actions, too. When you show up to church in high heels or lipstick, *I* have to deal with everyone's questions and comments and stares, *too*. And unlike you, I don't get to go back to college, far away from St. Francis. This is my community *every week*—I can't get away from their judgment about my son, about my child. So please, for me, can you not wear those shoes? Please, Jacob."

I held my ground.

"It's my church, too, Mom! And I can't keep putting off who I am in search of their approval. I have spent years embarrassed of who I am, hiding parts of myself from my church, and I just can't *do* that anymore. Can't you understand that?"

Then I said the line I knew would hurt her.

"You are usually so good at loving me for who I am. Why aren't you loving me right now?"

The tears broke, falling gently down her cheeks. One thing I've learned about my mom over the years is that she cries when she's angry more often than when she's sad.

"I *do* love you. How dare you say that I don't, after everything I've done! You know, you can be so *selfish* sometimes."

She was groveling and yelling and pleading all at the same time.

"This is my community, too. I have to deal with these people, too. *This is hard for me, too!* Can't you please, just this once, do this for me? Can't you please, just this once, take off the shoes and just wear a pair of normal shoes? It's just *one* service, Jacob! It is *only. one. service!*"

I stood across the counter from her, stunned into silence. Hot tears fell onto her Christmas sweater.

"I can't, Mom. I can't take them off. I can't do that. This is *my* community, too."

"Fine, Jacob. If you're going to insist on wearing heels, then please don't sit with me at service."

A pause.

"I need to get to choir rehearsal. I'm already late."

I heard the sound of the garage door opening and my mom driving away. Twenty minutes later, I walked gingerly across the front yard toward my own car, careful not to let my heels sink too far into the half-dead grass.

The Christmas Eve service is far from somber. The sanctuary is bright, vibrant, filled with screaming children and chatting families. And *everyone* is there. When I arrived at church, the parking lot was filled to the brim, abuzz with holiday energy. The sanctuary was covered in twinkling lights, a fifteen-foot Christmas tree stood proudly behind the pulpit, and a brilliantly glowing Moravian star adorned the altar. My sequined vest sparkled in the light.

I walked slowly, sheepishly into the sanctuary. Despite my self-reported confidence, I was terrified. I didn't know how I would face yet another rejection from my church. I found my friend Daniela and asked her if it'd be okay for me to sit with her family because my mom was singing in choir. What I didn't tell her was that my mom usually came down from the choir loft to sit with me after the anthem. What I didn't tell her was that this was the first time in my life that my mom wouldn't be sitting with me at a church service. What I didn't tell her was that I was shattering inside.

Despite my nerves and anxiety about wearing heels to church, the reaction from my congregation was nothing short of a Christmas miracle. Sure, I got a few nasty glares from new members who didn't know who I was. And I got some surprised looks from young kids. But by and large, the people who mattered were wonderful about the whole thing.

My old friends from youth group were all delighted at my shoes. They thought it was badass that I had the gusto to wear them to church. And the families that had known me forever just gave me hugs and told me they were glad to see me. Some people even made cute little jokes that I must've had a growth spurt in college, because I was so much taller. "What're they feeding you over at Duke?" one of my former youth group leaders joked. "You've certainly grown!"

It seemed that the space had been good for my congregation, too. My absence had, in fact, made their hearts grow fonder.

As service began, I tried to focus on the fact that everyone was being so kind, so sweet, but all I could really think about was the fact that my mom wasn't sitting next to me like usual, holding my hand. When service ended, I stuck around to engage in the usual post-service chitchat. My mom was nowhere to be seen.

I arrived home to find her sitting at the counter. She took one look at me and her lips began to quiver. She rushed over to me, holding me as she began to cry. This time, they were tears of regret. We stood there, hugging and shaking, for a few moments before she spoke. By that point, I must've been crying, too.

"I'm so sorry, Jacob," she said through her tears. "I will never leave you alone during service again. I never want to do that to you again."

She didn't let go. I couldn't help but notice just how much taller I was than my mother. In my heels, I could perch my chin on the top of her head as she cried into my chest.

"It's okay, Mom. This is as hard for you as it is for me." After a minute, she finally pulled away, looking me straight in the eyes.

"I never, *ever* want you to think that I don't love you or accept you exactly as you are. I'm always your number one ally. It's just—this is scary for me, too. You know that."

I grabbed for the tissue box. We both needed a Kleenex at this point. She continued.

"Watching you interact with everyone at service tonight, I felt so foolish. They love you so much, and clearly are having an easier time dealing with this than I am."

"Hey there. No one has been more supportive than you, Mom." I squeezed her hand. "No one. I would never have had the courage to walk in there tonight without you."

"Can you forgive me?"

"Yes. Of course—of course I can. You're my mom, after all. I literally came from your vagina."

She hit me playfully on the arm and laughed. "Okay, now you're just being gross."

"Wanna eat Christmas cookies by the tree?"

"I'd love to, sweetie."

She smiled.

I smiled back.

"Okay, but let me take off these shoes first. My feet are killing me."

Chapter 8

Sissy, Femme, Queer, and Proud

*H*ave you ever had the misfortune of owning a perpetually itchy sweater? You know the kind: You find it in a thrift store, it likely has rhinestones on some portion of the shoulders, and it's most certainly from the 1980s. You try it on in the store, and you notice immediately that it's a bit itchy. But, against your better judgment, you buy it anyway, because it's sparkly and you like sparkles. You take it home certain that it'll get softer with time, that one day it'll become a *comfy* rhinestone sweater.

You wear it over and over, with discipline, for an entire season, only to find that it is every bit as itchy as when you bought it. You throw it in the washing machine twelve times with way too much fabric softener, but to no avail. After letting it carefully air-dry, you try it on again, only to find that the itchiness hasn't relented. So you give up and put it away, digging it back out a year later to realize not only that it is still itchy, it also doesn't really *fit* anymore.

Duke was a lot like one of those sweaters. It was something scratchy that I'd acquired in a moment of indecision, without enough thought, because the idea of a full scholarship was shiny. I spent the better part of two years trying to make it work, battling the itchiness, trying to wear it out, to find comfort, but no matter what I tried, the itchiness wouldn't relent.

So I put it away for a while and headed off to New York City. Away from campus for almost a whole year, outside the confines and social pressures that had held me back at Duke, I'd become someone different, someone bigger and stronger and taller. When I came back to campus and dug Duke out of my sweater drawer, it barely fit. I had to huff and puff just to get the damn thing back on. It was bursting at every seam, failing to contain my new and infinite sense of self.

The story of my last year and a half at Duke is the story of a sweater ripping bit by bit, unspooling to the floor, no longer able to contain me or keep me warm. In hindsight, it was a healthy, natural process; an organic shedding of an old skin that no longer fit, a necessary purging of a garment that *just wasn't me* anymore.

But while it was happening, it felt like failure. It was terrifying, because I thought Duke was the only sweater I'd ever get. I thought succeeding at Duke was my only shot at a happy, fulfilled, dynamic life. If I couldn't get it to fit, if I couldn't make this work, I worried that perhaps I'd never be warm again. Watching my life at Duke disintegrate was devastating. But so is the cost of being uncontainable, so is the price of gender ahead of its time, so is the tax levied against those who are visionary.

In some way, this period was inevitable. Having been a flamer for the entirety of my natural life, it was unavoidable that, at some point or another, I was going to burn out, crumble to ash in order to burn more brightly than ever.

During senior year, the desire to actualize my gender was counterbalanced by a force that controls everyone's life: graduation.

I was acutely aware of the fact that I would soon be cast out from the ivory tower and into the real world. This was a prospect that terrified me and, strangely, made me cling to Duke and its institutional power even as I was trying to disassemble it. Sure, I needed to ensure Duke's endowment wasn't being invested in fossil fuels or weapons manufacturing or child labor,* and yes, I wanted Duke to mainstream gender-neutral housing across campus, but I also needed to figure out how I was going to survive, to eke out a career in public policy, to maintain myself and my life after graduation.

My fear of graduation was rational. In fact, I probably wasn't scared enough. I should've been even more afraid. Yes, I felt tokenized on campus, and yes, I was politically frustrated, but my quality of life as a gender nonconforming person was actually pretty good. What I took most for granted during my time at Duke was the infinite access to public safety. Walking around on campus, I was contained in a bubble of six thousand young people and a couple thousand employees who had gotten to know me and my gender antics over the course of four years. Walking across campus in high heels and lipstick, I was completely free from street harassment. I could walk back from the library in booty shorts, pink nail polish, and espadrilles at two a.m., alone, and not think twice about my physical safety. I could wear whatever I pleased, walk to the dining hall, and pick up some *mattar paneer* without a care in the world. By the time I was a senior, I was never heckled on campus. I was never called a faggot or spit on or publicly harassed. I was treated with respect because

---

* Endowments are what schools get to have when they are so rich that *they don't have to spend their own money anymore*, and instead they get to spend *the money that their money makes for them*. Endowments are secretly invested all over the place, usually (and often *indirectly*) in companies that are involved with a lot of nasty shit: labor exploitation, state violence, war, environmental destruction, you name it. These investments are kept secret, so the campus community doesn't get to know where their money is going. Which means that Duke's endowment—and all university endowments for that matter, Harvard, Princeton, Yale, etc.—is sketchy as fuck. I mean, why would you insist on hiding your investments from the public if you *weren't* investing in unethical stuff?

everyone—librarians, janitors, faculty members, administrators, dining hall employees, Zumba instructors at the campus gym—knew me. And most even liked me.

Graduating felt like falling off a cliff, in terms of my gender. I was going to have to figure out how to navigate professional culture that made it difficult to be gender nonconforming. I was going to have to figure out how to live in a city, how to take on daily life—walking in the street, shopping for groceries, riding public transportation—as a gender nonconforming person. I was going to have to start from scratch somewhere new, and everyone would have to get to know me all over again.

I was terrified of that, of the effort it would take, of the uncertainty. And I was right to be. When I moved to DC after graduation to start what I thought would be my political career, I felt like an alien. Walking around on Capitol Hill in a skirt, I felt like a total outcast, like a public embarrassment. It was horrendous. It was so bad that I left after only two and a half months. And then, even when I moved back to New York City, things were still horrific. The catcalls were constant, the glares and heckles never ceasing every time I so much as wore lipstick. Getting dressed and leaving my house, facing the scorn of strangers and the constant threat of physical violence, became an act of superhuman courage. Some days, the anxiety would win and I wouldn't leave my apartment. One time two men on the subway loudly discussed whether they should set me on fire for being a faggot. I pretended not to hear them through my headphones.

During senior year, I didn't know concretely that I'd have to face all that, but I had a sense that whatever I was going to have to face, it wasn't going to be good.

Which is why I wanted with all my heart to be a Rhodes Scholar. It wasn't that I cared so much about studying at Oxford or living in the UK—though I certainly didn't mind the idea—it was more that being a Rhodes Scholar felt like absolute protection.

And it was what everyone told me I should want. At any top-tier school, the Rhodes is coveted as *the* symbol of academic achievement. At Duke, we had a plaque in the front of the library listing all of the Rhodes Scholars that we'd had over the years. As a scholarship student, I'd been groomed to apply from the moment I set foot on campus. I wish I could say that I was immune to this pressure, but I wasn't. Over four years, that pressure had taken its toll and what had started as a *curiosity* about the Rhodes became a full-blown *fixation*.

It also didn't help that Rachel Maddow was a Rhodes Scholar. I mean, if Rachel did it, I should too, right? She's so handsome and dapper and cute and smart and I wanted to be like that (and also maybe transition and become a lesbian so I could marry her? Are you into that idea, Rachel? Let's talk.).

The mantra that I subconsciously repeated to myself whenever my gender felt vulnerable, whenever I felt overlooked or excluded, was always, "Just get the Rhodes, then no one will ever be able to tell you to take off your skirt or lipstick or nail polish ever again."

Obviously this mantra was poison for many reasons. First of all, being a Rhodes Scholar isn't all that great and is basically irrelevant for making it in the entertainment industry—which is what I'd always *really* wanted to do but couldn't admit to myself at the time.* Secondly, Oxford seems kinda cold and dreary and lonely. Third, being gender nonconforming and a Rhodes Scholar would've ensured that I continued to be the token gender nonconforming person in my circles for at least another two or three years.

Fourth, and by far most important, *no amount of privilege earns you the right to be gender nonconforming.* Gender nonconforming people truly are the object of scorn and reprimand at every socioeconomic level,

---

* When I'm home in North Carolina and I run into someone who I haven't seen in a long time, they'll often say something like "Oh you work in the *entertainment industry* now? I always thought you were going to go into *politics!*" And in my head I'm always just like "*Girl* what do you think the entertainment industry *is?*"

among every class of people. Economic security might help you pay for therapy or medical transition, and privilege might afford some protection from physical violence, but no amount of money can protect you from emotional damage, from feeling excluded or overlooked, from depression, stigma, and a lifetime of shame.

And the idea that I could only afford to express my gender if I were a *goddamned Rhodes Scholar*, that I was *obligated* to reach such a pinnacle in order to live in my truth, is so psychologically destructive I hardly know where to begin.

As much as I do not ascribe to that ideology anymore, as much as, today, I have emancipated myself from the idea that I must collect accolades in order to express my gender, that doesn't change the fact that I deeply held those beliefs during my senior year. It was the only survival strategy I knew.

That October, I was nominated by Duke for the Rhodes as well as for the slightly-less-prestigious-but-still-fancy Marshall Scholarship. Being nominated by a top-ten school like Duke is an honor in and of itself, because you have to secure an institutional nomination to even apply. I was considered by most everyone on campus to be one of my class's top contenders: I'd *already* received one post-graduate scholarship, the Truman Scholarship, and certainly had the grades. I had been to the White House, had served on countless committees, had led too many initiatives to comfortably list on a resume, and had conducted rigorous, unprecedented historical research comparing queer organizing in South Africa to queer organizing in the United States. According to the folks at Duke who'd advised the Rhodes nomination process for over a decade, I was a shoo-in for an interview, at the very least.

Before I heard back about whether I had a Rhodes interview, I received some exciting news: I was being called to Atlanta to interview for the Marshall Scholarship.

Forgetting about the Rhodes for the span of two weeks, I underwent rigorous coaching. I went through numerous preparation interviews and hopped on a plane to Atlanta feeling confident in every aspect except one:

What the fuck am I supposed to wear?

It was the question that no one in my life really knew how to address. Unlike the advice that I'd gotten from Minh-Thu when I was working at the UN, no one at Duke knew how to be fully honest with me about this. More often than not, when I asked about what I should wear, people would say one of two things:

"I think it'd be best to go for something a little more conservative, Jacob. This is a big opportunity, and you don't want to risk it."

Which wasn't helpful because it made me feel deflated and small. But at least it was real, honest advice. Or they'd say, infuriatingly:

"Just be yourself!"

Which was *far* more useless, because which *version* of myself should I be? And should I *really* be myself? If I were *really* myself, I would wear bright pink lipstick, pink nail polish, and a grandma sweater (*sans pants*), roll in there atop chunky gold disco shoes, tell the panelists that I wanted to be America's Next Top Model, and then start crying from the pressure, mascara running down my cheeks.

At this point, I hadn't *been myself* in two decades. How in the fuck was I supposed to start now?

I ended up siding with the first group. I didn't want my gender presentation "to distract from my intelligence"—as if my gender identity and my intellect aren't one and the same, as if they could ever be separated—so I opted for a masculine look, wearing my boring suit, flat dress shoes, and a rainbow-striped tie for that "touch of flair."

At the time, presenting in this masculine of a fashion didn't feel like selling out. But that, in and of itself, is part of the problem. Throughout my senior year, when I was faced with obstacles or competitive processes or selection committees, I reverted to masculinity out of fear every time. I feared discrimination at every turn, feared that if I were to truly wear my identity on my sleeve, I would lose everything.

And that's not fair.

I was entering every competition with a psychological penalty already leveled against me. Every room I walked into in order to be judged, from auditioning to be my class's commencement speaker to interviewing for the Marshall Scholarship, I entered with the weight of a crushing double standard resting on my shoulders. Was I being authentic *enough*? Was I being *too* authentic? What was the right balance? Were these people prepared to really *see* me? Were they prepared to *hear* me?

Apparently not. My Marshall Scholarship interview was abysmal. It took place at the British Consulate in downtown Atlanta, in a conference room on the thirty-fourth floor of a skyscraper. When I walked in and saw four old white men and *one* older white woman on my interview panel, I knew my odds were slim to none. I prayed that maybe one of the dudes was at least gay or something, but didn't hold out hope. The fact that anyone could set up an interview panel for the southeast region of the United States in a black-as-fuck city like *Atlanta, Georgia,* and not even put a *single* black person (or *any* person of color) on the panel was beyond me. The Marshall Scholarship should be ashamed of themselves.

My gift and my curse is that I can read a room like a book. I can know, within twenty seconds of walking in, whether someone is going to buy what I'm selling. I am a walking spark of human energy, and it takes no time at all for me to tell whether someone is a conductor or an insulator. If I am in a room full of conductors, the electricity begins flowing immediately, sparks going off, electrons bumping and grinding all over the dance floor. But if I am in a room full of insulators, there's just nothing I can do: I can emit volt after volt, megawatt after megawatt, my nuclear reactor radiating heat and light and electricity, and it will all be for naught. No matter how electric I am, I simply cannot get insulators on board with the whole "electric current" thing.

In my electric life, if someone isn't a conductor, it's generally because they cannot handle my identity. I'm simply too queer for them, too fabulous, too gorgeously energetic for their balsa wood lives to handle. They don't know how to appreciate electricity, even if it's zapping them in the face, because they can't see through the fact that my wrists hang limply and my hips sway a bit when I walk.

I spent my Marshall interview trying my best to zap and buzz, to spark and shock, but nothing seemed to work. Trapped in a room of insulators, nothing I did seemed to get the current moving. Eventually, like any electric person does when surrounded by insulation, I just kind of shut down.

Looking back on that time in my life, I can't help but wonder if I cast a self-fulfilling prophecy. Did my fear of discrimination put me so on edge that I couldn't perform? That I couldn't fully relate to a room or an interview panel? Was it the fear of discrimination and the subsequent anxiety that made me underperform in the first place?

But that's not quite right. That's not the right way to phrase things. Saying that I made self-fulfilling prophecies makes it feel like it was somehow my fault. Which it wasn't. If you're interviewing a person of difference for a job and you don't share their identity, *the onus is on you* to go out of your way to make sure they are comfortable with you. The onus is on white people to ensure that people of color are comfortable. The onus is on cishetero folks to ensure that queer and trans folks are comfortable. The onus is on men to ensure that women know they're supported. In any situation where you have both identitarian *and* positional power—in which the interview*er* is also the person with the dominant identity—it is the responsibility of the interviewer, not the interviewee, to ensure that the interviewee feels supported and encouraged to express themselves. It is also the responsibility of any scholarship organization to put together a selection committee that represents the diversity of the applicant pool it will be interviewing.

When the Marshall Scholarship put together the Atlanta panel my year, they failed abysmally on both counts. First, by curating a panel that was 100 percent white, 100 percent over fifty, and 80 percent male, they not only failed in their responsibility to create a nurturing environment for diverse candidates, they were complicit in creating a panel that was visibly *hostile* toward diverse candidates. Even one person of color, one younger person, would've made a world of a difference, in my mind.

But if you *are* going to have a group that's 100 percent white and 80 percent male, it is the responsibility of the panel to take that into consideration when conducting interviews. It is important for them to acknowledge that diverse candidates—along literally any spectrum—may perceive the space as hostile toward them and may clam up. That is not the fault of the interviewee; it is the fault of the interview panel and the organization that assembled it. If you want to have an even remotely fair interview process, you cannot remain stoic when you see a diverse candidate shut down. Interviewers have to be empathetic and kind, affirming the interviewee actively as the interview progresses, going out of their way to ensure that the interviewee knows that *people like them are welcome.* To neglect that duty is to condone racism, sexism, homophobia, transphobia, or worse.

So no, I do not blame myself for clamming up in that interview. I do not blame myself for retreating into my shell, snail-like, when I felt threatened. I blame a scholarship organization and an interview panel that abundantly failed in its duty to ensure that I would feel welcome.

Discrimination is notoriously slippery and hard to prove, because most people, however discriminatory, are intelligent enough not to be *overt* about it.

Here's what most people think discrimination looks like:

INTERVIEWER: *What is your proudest accomplishment?*
INTERVIEWEE: *Last year, in the wake of Hurricane Sandy, a shelter for homeless LGBTQ youth called the Ali Forney Center was flooded and needed to rebuild. As part of their recovery effort, I*

raised over $11,000 for the center by doing a fund-raiser called Run
for Shelter, where I ran across the Brooklyn Bridge in high heels. The
project was featured on MSNBC and I was even named New
Yorker of the Week by NY1!
INTERVIEWER: *Wow, did I mention that I hate faggots SO MUCH?*
I'm not giving you this scholarship. Get outta here, you queen!

Here's what discrimination *actually* looks like:

INTERVIEWER: *What is your proudest accomplishment?*
INTERVIEWEE: *Last year, in the wake of Hurricane Sandy, blah blah*
blah.. . . . .
INTERVIEWER: [complete silence, no emotional response, no
follow-up question, looks down at papers uncomfortably,
completely dismisses you, just nonverbally] *So . . . why do you*
want to study at Oxford?

And, in case you're curious, here's what an ethical, nondiscrimi-
natory interview would've looked like:

INTERVIEWER: *What is your proudest accomplishment?*
INTERVIEWEE: *Last year, in the wake of Hurricane Sandy, blah blah*
blah.. . . . .
INTERVIEWER: *That's pretty incredible. What did that project mean*
to you personally?
INTERVIEWEE: *The project was deeply meaningful to me on a*
personal level. Not only was it addressing an issue that is very close
to my heart—LGBTQ homelessness and economic
empowerment—it was also about the way I did the project. I felt,
through running across the bridge in high heels, I was publicly
demonstrating the strength that gender nonconforming people like

me have. I've been told all my life that my femininity made me
weak, and this project helped me to fight back against that notion.
INTERVIEWER: *I wasn't aware that homelessness was a significant*
issue in the LGBTQ community. Can you tell us more about that?
INTERVIEWEE: *Sure. The dual forces of family rejection and structural*
discrimination—racism, poverty, xenophobia, and others—lead to
LGBTQ kids being out on the street with no safe place to turn and
no ability to safely navigate the state institutions that are
purportedly in place to protect them . . .

The differences are plain to see. Ninety-eight percent of discrimination
is not overt. Ninety-eight percent of discrimination is infuriatingly subtle.
You feel it in the lack of eye contact a person makes with you. You feel it in
a noted absence of enthusiasm. You feel it in a hesitation or a slight physical
tic. You feel it in a pause that goes on for just a moment too long. You feel
it in an uncomfortable clearing of the throat. You feel it when, out of nowhere, the air is sucked from the room as if it's a NASA vacuum chamber.
You feel it everywhere, but there is rarely any hard evidence.

A few days later, I was informed that I did not receive the Marshall
Scholarship.

A few days after that, I found out I wasn't even asked to interview
for the Rhodes.

My dreams and my hopes, however deserved or irrational, however
bougie or elitist, were dashed.

And in the days that followed, what infuriated me more than anything was just how few people were willing to say what they felt. *Everyone*
involved with my nomination was shocked that neither scholarship had
panned out. Everyone suspected that this had something to do with the
fact that I was not only queer, but *wanted to study queer things.* Everyone
who knew me felt discrimination was at play, but *no one would say it for me.*

I was left feeling even more alone than when I'd started out. I thought I might be losing my mind. Was I just paranoid to think that I'd been discriminated against? Was I just being a sore loser? Why was no one else naming it?

I should also perhaps acknowledge that the dream of a Rhodes Scholarship isn't the most *relatable* thing on the planet. It's a pretty nerdy, niche desire. The point is not that everyone deserves a Rhodes Scholarship or even that the Rhodes should matter to you (I hope it doesn't). The point is that, oftentimes, our dreams are arbitrary; that our dreaming is highly susceptible to what those around us tell us we should want. Everyone has had their equivalent of what the Rhodes was for me—that thing you yearn for and never quite get.

The award isn't the point. The accolade isn't the point. The *thing itself* isn't the point. It's the yearning and dreaming and wishing and being crushed and not being certain what's wrong with you that matter.

In the aftermath, I stopped by the Office of Scholars and Fellows—the office charged with shepherding students through the Rhodes and Marshall processes, among those for other scholarships—for a conversation with Dr. Malouf, the head of the program. Tentatively, furtively, I opened up to her about what I was feeling, how lost and hurt I felt.

"You know, Jacob," she said, "I know that this will mean little to you right now, but I need to say it. Going to Oxford to study is not in the universe's plan for you. It just isn't. If it were in the plan, it would've happened. And while right now all you can feel is devastation, I hope you can one day appreciate this for what it is: This is the universe telling you that you are meant for better things than Oxford."

She looked into my eyes knowingly, in a way that was hauntingly perceptive. I smiled softly through my tears. While my mind was skeptical and wanted to lash out at advice that seemed asinine, somewhere in my heart, I believed her.

A few weeks later, she asked me to stop by again: She had something she wanted to give me. A parting gift, of sorts. A promise of better things to come.

On the coat rack in her office hung not one, but *two* designer gowns—a black Tadashi Shoji number and a vintage velvet Bob Mackie, both handed down to her by her mother. After sitting in her closet unworn for years, she'd decided that the time was right to pass them along to me. She wanted me to know how much she believed in me, in my feminine spirit, in my beauty, in my blossoming identity. She was doing her part to welcome me into a sisterhood; a tradition of women and femmes who'd smacked headfirst into the glass ceiling; a legacy of women and femmes who'd fought for what they deserved, only to be denied because of our gender.

I whisked off to the bathroom to try them on. By complete luck, they both fit. Like a glove. They were a bit short on me, but they draped beautifully. It was nothing short of alchemy, witchcraft. I floated back to Dr. Malouf's office to show her, the hallway becoming my runway.

"Oh, Jacob," she proclaimed, "you look *stunning*!"

For a few minutes, I let her words sink in: momentary respite for an uncalm heart.

The universe hadn't finished its work. The goddess wasn't done redirecting me, steering me in a different direction through the power of devastation.

The next great defeat came in the form of a student-body-wide election for a position called Young Trustee. Each year, one Duke senior is elected to serve a three-year term as a full voting member of the board of trustees when they graduate. It is a *seriously* powerful position. I mean, Tim Fucking Cook, *the CEO of Apple*, is on the Duke board. So are Lisa Borders, the president of the WNBA, and Adam Silver, the commissioner of the NBA.

It's a big deal because, as a voting member, you have the chance to shape Duke on a core, structural level. You have the ability to tell the university president that he's not doing a good enough job. You have the ability to supervise and demand that millions—with a capital M—more dollars need to be spent on efforts to reform Duke's culture.

It was *real* power, *serious* power, and I stood a shot at it. All I had to do was convince the student body to vote for a guy in a dress instead of a frat boy. Easy, right?

Running for elected office, if only on a college campus, it felt like I was putting my gender identity on public trial. On some level, I was facing what all women and femmes face when they run for office; being made to curate a "proper" femininity, trapped in the double bind of being either "too uptight" or "too provocative," while the masculine candidate receives no scrutiny for his gender presentation whatsoever.

But in this case, the double bind was more about "authenticity" versus "relatability." If I presented as too feminine, if I let loose and truly queened out, I would alienate so many students that I'd never stand a chance. But if I didn't present as feminine, or if I put away my high heels and makeup altogether, people would be equally turned off: I'd lose votes because I wasn't being "real." Trapped between being seen as a weirdo or as a fake, I floundered, trying to figure out how to best present my gender in order to get in the door.

In the end, I opted to play what I thought was the most palatable version of myself in my campaign ads and posters. I wore a tie, a blazer— albeit with cuffed sleeves—and one small clip-on earring: a gold rosette from my grandmother's collection.

I felt naked. My main opponent had fraternity cronyism and the power of Pi Kappa Phi—the fraternity to which the previous year's Young Trustee belonged—behind him. As a South Asian frat guy in a historically white fraternity, I'm sure that he had his own baggage to deal with. But he also maintained the cultural power and the mainstream "big man on campus" status that came with being in the most politically powerful fraternity.

While he was campaigning to prove that he would be an effective trustee, I had to campaign twice as hard: I had to prove both that I would be an effective trustee and *that I was normal enough to represent Duke students*. It was a public referendum not only on my qualifications and my leadership, both of which were at that point unassailable, but also on my *normality*. Was I *really* someone capable of representing the student body on the board? Did I really share in their experiences?

My opponent didn't have to work very hard to imply that I wasn't. Each candidate received a profile in the *Chronicle*, our campus newspaper, and his headline read simply, "Candidate Emphasizes Breadth of Experience in Young Trustee Race." In the article, he was quoted as saying "The Young Trustee should be a representative of the *entire* student body, and I think that it's particularly dangerous if you have a candidate who understands one part of the school too well. Fortunately, I have a wide swath of experiences."

To this day, I'm not sure if he knew exactly what he was doing. But when I read that headline, when I saw a frat boy saying, "I have the greatest breadth of experience," in comparison to a gender nonconforming candidate like me; when I saw a cisgender, heterosexual man saying that it was "particularly dangerous" for someone to understand "only one part" of the school (i.e., the *queer* part, the *activist* part, the *non-fraternity* part) the implications rattled me:

> *I have the greatest breadth of experience.*
> *I.e., I'm a fraternity man, I can represent the average Duke student.*
> *A gender nonconforming activist who spends too much time*
> *hanging out with other activists and queers couldn't possibly*
> *do that.*
> *I.e., Jacob's identity makes them niche. I'm the true populist.*
> *I.e., You should vote for me because I'm the most traditional.*
> *I.e., Don't vote for Jacob because they're a freak.*

Whether my opponent *intended* these implications mattered very little to my tender heart. Either way, they were out there, bouncing around, jabbing my self-esteem, taunting me during the day, ringing in my ears at night. I felt them *everywhere*, and I fought them *hard*.

I campaigned incredibly and received the most endorsements from student organizations. I was the candidate-of-choice according to the Duke Partnership for Community Service, the Black Student Alliance, the LGBT Student Alliance, the South Asian Student Association, the Latinx Student Association, Duke Democrats, and even the representative body for all sororities on campus, the Panhellenic Council. My opponent received only one endorsement, tellingly from the Interfraternity Council.

I could go on and on about the hours and days I spent talking to first years at the dining hall, about the thousands of flyers I handed out, about the countless meetings I canvassed, but nothing speaks louder than the endorsements. Over four years of kicking ass and taking names in the interest of marginalized students on campus, almost every student organization representing a diverse community wanted me to be their representative on the board.

And only the whitest, most homogenous, most sexist organization on campus wanted my opponent.

The night of the election, my campaign team set up what we hoped would be a victory party. For our venue, we chose the Duke Coffeehouse. A bastion of support in my undergraduate life, the one true place on campus where freaks and weirdos were the majority, the Duke Coffeehouse was the closest thing I had to a safe space. Where most of Duke was sleek and modern, the Coffeehouse was grungy. Where most of Duke was neat and curated, the Coffeehouse was covered in murals of aliens and demons and cartoon coffee cups and David Bowie–esque starmen. It was my respite from many terrible moments, and I hoped it could be my launchpad to victory.

By eight p.m., online polling had closed, and by nine, I was gathered at the Coffeehouse with thirty of my closest friends to await the results.

If you've never run for elected office, it's hard to describe how it feels.

People think they know what it's like. They watch *Veep* or *Parks and Recreation* and feel like they get it. But it's nothing like on TV. On TV, even when Leslie Knope loses, it's still a comedy. Sure, maybe Leslie will eat one too many waffles after her loss, but she won't spiral into a three-year-long depression or lose her self-esteem because of it. She will always, invariably, have things work out for her. In a real-life election, you don't have that same guarantee.

All this results in a frenetic, anxious, terrible state of mind. The Coffeehouse swirling with anticipation around me, I sipped on a chocolate espresso milk shake to stay awake.

At ten forty-five, my cell phone rang. As discreetly as I could, I stepped outside; only my best friend Sunny came with me while I took the call.

"Hey, Jacob, it's the attorney general. I wanted to let you know that the election results are in."

"Okay," I said, bracing myself against a signpost.

"It was a very close race—the closest that we've ever seen, actually—but unfortunately, you have not been chosen by the student body to serve as the Undergraduate Young Trustee."

"Okay," I said.

"We had a very high turnout this race. A total of 3,420 students—about 53 percent of the student body—voted. And after eliminating the third-place candidate and doing an instant runoff between you and your opponent, it came down to twelve votes. Your opponent received 1,716 votes, and you received 1,704."

"Okay," I repeated, catatonic. It seemed to be the only word I knew.

"We wanted to thank you and your team for running a smooth, clean, by-the-books campaign, and while we know you must be disappointed, we hope you'll still feel proud of a job well done. It was very close."

"Okay, thanks. Do you need anything else from me?"

"No, we're all set. Have a great night."

Hands shaking, I placed my phone in my pocket, then dropped to the curb.

The tears were instant; the rebuke felt immediate.

"Oh, Taco," Sunny said, invoking my playful college nickname. She rubbed my back gingerly, encouraging me to take deep breaths.

"This hurts *so much more* than I thought it would," I managed to shudder between sobs. "How can I face everyone now? How can I go back in that room? It feels like my entire senior year's been ruined."

"I know, I know," she murmured, hand still rubbing circles on my back. "It's going to be okay, just maybe not right now."

We sat in silence for another moment, my chest rising and falling, breath returning back to normal.

"Do you want me to go in and let folks know so you don't have to?"

"No, it's okay," I said, wiping the tears from my cheeks, rubbing my eyes in hopes that they'd seem less puffy. "I need to break the news to everyone myself."

After another deep breath, I stood up, briefly reminding my body how to connect muscle to tendon, tendon to bone. I held my head up as high as I could, pulled the last bucket of strength from my well, and headed back inside.

Let me be very clear about something: My opponent was not a bad person. He's actually pretty sweet. I like him and count him as a friend, so I hope it doesn't seem like I'm shitting all over him. He didn't even really do anything *wrong*.

Which is why, when I lost, I wasn't angry *at him* specifically; I was angry at the mechanics of the election process itself, at the power dynamics of the entire campus. I didn't hate the player; but I *loathed* the game, the structure in which we were forced to compete, the fact that I had to carry so much more baggage while running the same race.

That's exactly the point: when the playing field is uneven to begin

with, you don't have to be "a bad person" to benefit from nasty institutions or unwarranted privilege. You don't have to be a bad person or even
have bad intentions to personally profit from sexism, homophobia, or
transphobia. You don't have to do *anything*. As a heterosexual, cisgender
masculine guy, you simply have to throw your name in the ring against
someone like me and *automatically* you have those forces on your side.
All you *really* have to do is say nothing against them. All you really have
to do is keep quiet, remain "neutral" in the face of fucked up power
structures, and those fucked up power structures will go on to do what
they do best: walk all over people of difference.

But just barely. What tortured me for months and years to come was
just how close the election was. Twelve votes. Twelve measly votes.
Twelve out of thirty-four hundred. My opponent won by a mere 0.18
percent. Less than one-fifth of 1 percent. That margin haunted me, if
only because of the truth it made apparent: If my gender were *even a
fraction* more palatable, if I were *just a hair* less queer, I would've *easily*
won. It only took twelve people to rob me of something so important, to
cause an identity crisis the likes of which I'd never faced before. The only
thing worse than winning by the skin of your teeth is *losing* by it.

While I cannot say exactly why I lost the election; while I can't concretely explain why I didn't so much as receive an interview for the
Rhodes; and while I can't say why, a few months later, I would be a fi-
nalist for but not chosen as my class's commencement speaker, I can say
this: These losses had to do with my gender. They were inexorably related
to the fact that I wasn't a "guy's guy" on a campus that deeply valued that
behavior, to the fact that I wasn't the "right type" of man to study at
Oxford, to the fact that my identity was "a bit too niche" for parents to
tolerate at commencement.

And, because I know you're thinking it, let me be clear about something: I am *proudly* a sore loser. I did not lose these things with grace,
and I still have not made peace with losing. Telling me to make peace
with the fact that I lost the Young Trustee election, for example—one

that I rightfully deserved to win—is like telling me to "just forget about" the fact that people like me face discrimination.

I do not have to make peace with my loss to a frat boy. I will never make peace with the fact that he beat me in part because of sexism and transphobia. And unlike Shirley Chisholm or Hillary Clinton or Carol Moseley Braun, I refuse to be classy about my loss. I am committed to being a bratty, snobby, bossy, terrible, awful, no-good, very bad, sore loser. I am committed to being the sorest loser you have ever seen. And while I may not still think about the fact that I lost an election in college—I'm much too busy these days thinking about what op-ed I need to pitch the *New York Times*, what outfit I'm going to wear on a red carpet, or what strategy I should use to beat Los Angeles traffic—I will never *get over it*.

Because the imperative to *get over it* is the imperative to erase yourself, to take your beating, fallible human heart and crush it. To take your pulsating, bedazzled, gorgeous identity and betray it. To take your glittering, shimmering, divine trauma and throw it in the trash. I will never *get over* what has been denied to me because of my gender identity. I will never *get over* the fact that people have been terrible to me because of who I am. I will never *get over* the fact that gender nonconforming people have been the target of incredible violence, marginalization, iso-lation, and neglect throughout much of the past century. I will never get over it because *it is my history*, and those who don't know their history are doomed to repeat it.

And I won't forget it because I, along with every other oppressed person on the planet, am owed. Society has a debt to me—to all of us—one they will likely never repay. I want the things that have been taken from me. I want them back. I want to have won that election and gone on to serve three groundbreaking years on the board. I want to have won a Rhodes Scholarship and attended Oxford and met Harry Potter and married him. I want to have had a happy childhood, one where I played with the toys I wanted to play with, drew the things I wanted to draw, wore the things I wanted to wear. I want to have been given the opportunity to succeed without abandoning my feminine spirit. I want to have been treated with sweetness instead of scorn when my femininity first revealed itself to the world. And for the love of God, I want a fucking partner/boyfriend for once in my life.

I will not get over these things. I will never be quiet about them. I will go down screaming, wailing, and shaking my cane to the very last breath. A goddess never forgets. She rages and thrashes and storms as loudly and as often as she can bear until she and all of her other goddess friends get what they deserve.

I will not get over it because I refuse to sabotage my childhood self. I refuse to sabotage the other living, breathing baby Jacobs out there who are trying with all their four-year-old might to hold on to a gender that is slipping through their fingers. I refuse to look my adolescent self in the face and tell them they simply need to make peace with the fact that they deserve less. I refuse.

And if acknowledging, loudly and without shame, all the ways the world has been cruel to me and to so many others makes me a sore loser, then so be it. I'll be the most glamorous, well-adorned sore loser you've ever seen. I will run up onstage like an asshole, take the mic from Taylor Swift, and cry out, for the world to hear, "We *all* deserved this award!" (even though I *love* the song "You Belong with Me"). I will do it all if that means my sense of integrity, emotional honesty, and self-love can remain intact.

And if I don't always have the courage or audacity to do that in my daily life, I will, at least, for the love of Goddess, do so in my own fucking book.

The day after the election, devastation coursing through my veins, I was filled with doubt. What did this mean for my intended career as a poli-cymaker? If I was too queer to win an election on a *college campus*, could

I ever expect to win one in the real world? Could I *ever* succeed in the political arena? Was politics even a realistic path for me?

I needed a symbolic gesture to show myself and the rest of campus that while I may have lost, I hadn't been defeated. When I finished my shower and looked through my closet, the answer was apparent. I needed to wear something killer. Having worn a suit and tie for much of the last two weeks in order to seem more electable, it was time to burst free in a big way.

Instead of dressing in the typical clothes associated with moping and loss—sweatpants, sneakers, a hoodie—I made the opposite choice. I debuted the vintage all-black Tadashi Shoji that Dr. Malouf had given me, paired it with my signature military-grade black leather combat boots, and stomped around campus that day in all black, smiling radiantly at everyone I passed.

As if to say, "You haven't crushed me—not by a long shot. If anything, you've set me free."

As if to say, "The days of mitigating my gender for you motherfuckers are over."

As if to say, *"She's baaaaaaaaaack!"*

My power was once again expanding, my self-esteem and self-love blossoming after a long winter. It propelled me into my final months of college and onto a bus bound for a retreat called Common Ground.

In a nutshell, Common Ground is a student-led diversity retreat that helps undergrads come to understand how power, privilege, and identity work. It's also notoriously hard to get into. You have to complete a lengthy application, disclose your darkest secrets, and sacrifice your firstborn to the diversity goddess in order to get a slot. Despite being one of the most visible activists on campus, I was only extended an invitation to attend the second semester of my senior year.

It's also kind of a cult. It's the sort of thing where, when you ask people who've been what it's like, they look deeply into your eyes and say something to the effect of, "It's like nothing else I've ever experienced" or "It was the most powerful weekend of my life" or "How can I put it into words? You just have to *go* to fully understand what it's like."

To be honest, I signed up for the trip for two reasons, neither of which were particularly altruistic. First off, I love camp in every sense. I love campy queens and campy TV shows and campy movies. I also love summer camp and summer camp–style trips, like Project WILD. I didn't want to be on campus as much for second semester senior year, so getting away to a cabin in the woods for a weekend, for free, was too good an opportunity to pass up.

I also went because I thought it might help me get laid. Each year, when the group of Common Grounders came back singing "Kumbaya" and hugging one another, I noticed that there were always a few new queer couples in the mix. Something about sharing your truth, being super vulnerable, and challenging privilege really seemed to get the libido going for campus queers. Dating at Duke was a slow-motion disaster for me, but I thought maybe if I went on Common Ground, some gorgeous bi-/pansexual boy would come out for the first time publicly, tell me he'd always admired me from afar, and fall right into my arms. Stranger things had happened on Common Ground.

Still hurting after the election, I thought the retreat might offer me a reprieve.

Day one of the retreat introduced me to the sixty other campers and set forth the weekend's goals. We talked about race and ethnicity and class, and it was intense. Then day two—a whole day about gender, sexism, misogyny, and, to a lesser extent, homophobia—came along. I thought I was ready for it. I had checked in with the facilitators, many of whom were my good friends, the week before. I'd asked how the gender day was structured, if it had enough space for gender nonconforming and trans folks. No one would tell me any details, but they reassured me that it would be fine; that, yes, they'd thought about this and I would be okay. Which made what happened that much more of a slap in the face.

After lunch, we all gathered in the main cabin. My friend David, one of the two co-chairs of the retreat, started:

"Okay, everyone, first of all, we want to thank you all for a great first day—and we're looking forward to an even better day two!"

The room cheered.

"As you know by now, today we'll be talking about gender," he continued. "To start with, we'd like to separate the room into two groups: women—sorry, *female*—and male participants. Female participants stay here, and all the males, please come with me!"

Sixty pairs of feet sprang into action, sneakers shuffling, flip-flops *thwack*ing, the group separating cleanly down the middle except for me. As people went to grab their jackets and notebooks, I approached the other head facilitator.

"I thought you said you'd planned for this, but there are only two groups? Where am I supposed to go? What the fuck, dude?"

"Well, technically you're male, aren't you?" he asked.

"Yes of course, I have a male body. But *why does that mean I have to go with the other males*? Are we only going to be talking about our bodies? Are we only going to be talking about our penises and beards and how weird it is when you start to grow hair around your nipples?" I asked quizzically. "Or are we going to be talking about *being men*? Because if we're talking about being men, you and I both know that I don't have much to add to that conversation."

"Jacob, you have to trust the process, okay? I promise it'll be all right. Just go."

"Fine," I relented. "But I swear to God, if people start talking about their gender instead of their bodies, I'm gonna lose it. This better be an hour-long conversation about dicks."

Frustration mounting, I went off into the woods with the male group. Much to my disappointment but not to my surprise, we did not spend the time talking about our male bodies. I wish we had. I love

talking about my dick—what it wants, what it *doesn't* want, my insecurities about it—and I'm always happy to trade best practices on mastur-
bation, prostate stimulation, or body hair grooming.

But instead, we spent the entire conversation talking about *being
men*, about masculinity, about gender. It felt all too classic, being sorted
into a group with other people because of my body and then having an
identity effortlessly imposed on that body. I resigned myself to silence,
to quiet disaffection, to sitting in the woods in a circle of men even
though I didn't belong in that circle, my distaste for rocking the boat
overruling my desire to be recognized as I am.

Halfway through the session, we were asked to generate a list of stereotypes about women, and I was such a little shit about it. We were supposed to say things like "slutty," "inferior," "bad at math," or whatever
sorts of stale tropes people hold to be true these days. Instead, I chimed
in with:

"Smarter."

"Resilient."

"Tougher."

"Rugged."

"Stronger."

"Muscular."

"Athletic."

"Politically savvy."

You get the idea.

The facilitators were less than pleased with my strategy.

"Jacob, can you please stop derailing the activity? We're supposed to
be discussing the stereotypes that we've *actually* been taught about
women, not stereotypes that we wish were true."

"I'm trying to play along, but that's kind of hard when I'm in the
wrong group."

"Would you rather go with the women's group?"

"That doesn't work, either."

"Well, those are the groups that we have. If you're not going to leave the group, can you please stop interrupting the exercise?"

"Fine," I muttered vituperatively.

But my resignation didn't last long. When we all returned to the cabin, lists of gender stereotypes in hand, the facilitators had arranged the chairs into two rows facing each other. People from the men's group were asked to sit on one side, and people from the women's group were asked to sit on the other. As if we were opposites, as if we were more different than same, as if we were opposing factions.

I was placed across the aisle from a woman classmate of mine. Immediately it felt wrong. I burned.

The facilitators asked us to scoot our chairs close enough together that our knees were touching. We were asked to make eye contact with our partner. Then the facilitators read the entire list of stereotypes made by both groups.

Gazing across the aisle at my friend Caroline, looking deeply into her eyes, it occurred to me that I was not seeing "the other." I was merely looking at my own slightly distorted reflection. I was looking at my own image, the eyes of a similar spirit transposed into a different body. I saw not an opposite but a sister looking back. We were one. We were more similar than we ever could've imagined.

And in the power of that moment, something clicked: an anger and an agony I'd learned to forget long ago. Out of my heart, my childhood self erupted, bubbling up through decades of rock and sediment and dirt, gushing forth through years of respectability and discipline and punishment and social isolation and bullying, surging through twenty years of bad habits, self-loathing, self-denial, and self-sacrifice.

I was no longer my present self. I was no longer twenty-two years old and about to graduate college. I was four years old, three, even. I was a child again. A precocious, strong, stubborn child who'd yet to give up on their gender, who hadn't yet accepted the world's edict that their gender was impossible, who hadn't yet relinquished their divine right to express themself as they pleased. I was a sapling; a tender green leaf; thriving, young, glowing, uncrushed by the world.

In the recesses of my earliest memories, when memory is more an emotion and less a series of facts, I found flashes of anger I'd forgotten. While I'd remembered my childhood as mostly confused, suppressed, and despondent, I now found precious memories of fighting back against a world that sought to erase me. I couldn't remember the exact circumstances. I couldn't remember precisely how or why. I couldn't remember what gave me the courage to fight against a world that was taking my gender from me, but I found memories of screaming, of fuming, of destroying things and slamming doors and stomping my feet and crying out. In the years before being mistreated by the world was a foregone conclusion in my mind, I remembered yelling back, clawing at those who dared cross me, resisting with everything I had.

And at that retreat, sitting knee to knee with Caroline, that child came back. That fiesty little femme who knew they deserved better, who struggled impolitely and with force, was back. And she was *furious*.

When the facilitators finished reading the lists, they asked everyone to pause for a moment of silent reflection, and then asked if anyone had any initial impressions or reflections they wanted to share. I took a deep breath and stood up.

"I have said this before, but it seems that I need to say it again, perhaps less politely this time."

Before, it had only been one pair of eyes looking back at me; now it was sixty. I was all rage and fury.

"I am not a man. I am not a woman. I am a glimmering, genderqueer, gender nonconforming, beautiful, human person, and I don't identify that way for fun. I don't identify that way because I think it makes me interesting. I don't identify that way as a hobby. I use that language to describe myself because it is fundamentally who I am."

I paused, breathing, breathing, fuming.

"For my entire life, I have been struggling against masculinity, against the imperative to be a man, against the idea that because my body looks a certain way, I must *be* a certain way. I have been struggling since the beginning of my memory. I *cannot remember* a time in my life when I have not been struggling against this, when the world wasn't co-ercing me into a gender that I wanted no part of."

The tears were starting, and for once, I understood why my mom cries more often because she's angry than because she's sad.

"I have spent my life being asked to go with the boys, to get with the program, to not make things difficult. At first, when I was three or four, I fought against people who asked me to do that. I pushed back. But they have always, always had more power than me. They won every time. So I gave up. I resigned myself to a life of being mistreated, misunderstood, miscategorized in a world that could only see gender as one of two op-tions. I gave up everything in order to fit in. In some way or another, we *all* do. I gave up my hobbies, my friends, my language, the way I held my wrists. I gave it all up."

My voice grew louder.

"Over the past few years, I have been desperately trying to get my gender back, to put my heart back in my chest. And coming here, on this retreat, I thought I would find *support* in that effort. I thought I would, perhaps, be treated *well* for once. I even asked the facilitators if they needed help ensuring that the programming was done in a way that made space for me. I was proactive about it. And each time I asked, I was assured that things would be fine, that I would be included, valued, and respected."

I crested into a full-fledged yell.

"But I *have not been respected* here today. I have not been heard or valued or *seen*. You have all, each and every one of you, done your part today in undoing me. When our facilitators separated us by gender and I noted that there wasn't a group for me, none of you stood up. None of you supported me. You just filed back into the status quo, back into what you knew, erasing me effortlessly. That is what people do to me on campus every single day. That is what people do to me in the world every single day. I am simply erased. I am asked to forget that I exist. I am asked to dispose of my gender, to dispose of myself and get with the program. But this retreat didn't have to be built this way. There didn't have to just be two groups. We didn't have to rebuild a world that only sees two types of gender, and I could've been accommodated. I could've been seen and heard. We could've done things differently. We can always do things differently, and the idea that we cannot build a different world, that the world is inevitable as it is, the idea that the gender binary is foundational and irreplaceable, is exactly what leads trans and gender nonconforming people to our demise."

And then, a bit more quietly, with something closer to calm resolve, "If accommodating me, if ensuring that my gender is respected and valued is too much work for y'all, then *fuck you*. I'm out. You don't deserve my sparkle."

I turned, whirled out of the main cabin and into the woods, where I found a comfy log to sit on and began to breathe again.

A few moments later, my gender nonconforming friend Ronnie, a junior facilitator on the trip and one of my best friends in my dorm, came out to find me.

"Hey, Mama."

Sometimes Ronnie calls me Mama.

"Did they send you out to make me come back inside?"

"No, I just wanted to come out here and sit with ya."

We sat on the log for a few minutes in silence, playing with sticks and leaves, drawing shapes in the dirt.

"I don't really have that much to say. And you don't have to say anything, either—you already said a whole lot."

"I sure did, didn't I?" I cracked a smile. "I really gave it to 'em."

A smile in return. "You got that right."

I wrapped my arms around Ronnie, and we held each other for a moment, grateful.

"Do we need to go back in?"

"Nah. I think it's good to give them the chance to process what you said. Make 'em sweat a little."

"Okay. We'll make 'em sweat."

We sat there together for a few more minutes, breathing, giggling, pointing out our favorite trees, looking for birds, human stuff.

A few minutes later, the group was on break and a few other people joined us outside. David approached me across the thicket.

"Hey Jacob, I—" he murmured, stumbling on his words a bit. "I'm sorry if the way we organized things hurt you. It wasn't our intention, I promise."

"Yeah, I'm sure it wasn't your intention," I noted, trying to stay stony, holding my ground. "But it still happened."

"For the next activity, we still have the room separated, but we thought that maybe you and Ronnie could have your own section, you know, a gender nonconforming one?"

I cut the hard-ass routine, taken aback. "That'd certainly be a step in the right direction."

When I went back into the room after break, it was still split in two, the women's group facing the men's group. But at the top of the aisle, between the two groups, there were two chairs: one for me and one for Ronnie. Common Ground's first-ever gender nonconforming group. Ronnie in tow, I walked proudly over to my new section and sat down.

I didn't say anything for the rest of the day, I simply sat in my new section with Ronnie, content with what I'd done, grateful that—perhaps for the first time in my life—yelling about my gender seemed to have worked. As I sat in the third gender section, in a chair that was properly mine, my mind was far beyond the conversation:

People actually listened to me when I said I deserved space of my own.

I have a space of my own now.
Followed quickly by:
So what the fuck am I gonna do with it?

Have you ever watched a video of an aboveground pool rupturing? If you've haven't, you should. They're funny. And sorta beautiful. And metaphorically useful.

One moment, someone is just kicking around on their floaty tube. Then a wall buckles, a seam breaks, and all of a sudden, a giant cascade of water breaks free all at once, surging across the yard and sweeping away everything in its path. Any unfortunate souls who were swimming or who were unlucky enough to be standing in the water's path are swept away, too. The whole yard is soon covered, a deluge guided by gravity, racing downhill.

That's kind of what my gender was like at the end of senior year.

One moment, it was contained, polite, and respectable: confined within its prescribed walls.

The next moment, with little left to lose, the seams burst, and my gender was all over the place, gushing forth in an unstoppable wave, sweeping me along for the ride.

I think it was that I ran out of fucks to give. While I'd found *moments* of gender freedom throughout my time in college, four years of trying to be someone else had taken their toll. I was worn out; exhausted from the effort of trying to fit the mold. The walls I'd built in my own mind, the rubrics I'd devised about which parts of my femininity could be seen by others and which parts needed to stay private, the mental mechanisms I'd constructed to hold back so-called undesirable parts of myself, the restraints I'd tightened long ago, they all gave way at once.

I found myself saying yes to things I never used to. I found myself embracing fashion that before had seemed too risqué. I attempted to show off my legs more. I explored just how much glitter I could wear on a given Thursday.

For the first time since I could remember, I let my heart lead my gender and told my brain to shut the hell up. At the age of twenty-two, I found myself in a moment of renaissance, a moment of rebirth, a moment of childlike creativity and exploration. Nothing was off-limits. Anything was possible. The world was my playroom, frat boys be damned, and I had the best dress-up bin in town.

These moments of liberation were sublime. To this day, they are my fondest memories of being on campus. The moments when, as a washed-up senior and a public failure, I stopped trying to make everyone happy and let my gender flow freely.

There was the time I went shopping with my brother and my mom at the Goodwill and bought two skirts before finding the dress to end all dresses. It was a vintage 1980s bright pink one-piece skirt suit with navy blue trim and a single oversize navy blue button at the collar. It was so short that it barely covered my underwear, but I thought I looked just like Jackie Kennedy in it. And my mom and brother agreed. I decided I was going to wear it to graduation.

Or there was the time when my friend Catherine, who lived in my quad and was also six feet tall, revealed to me that she was a serial thrifter/hoarder and needed to get rid of forty or fifty outfits. She let me come to her room and rummage through a pile of clothes double my own body weight; clothes that actually fit me because we were both six feet and we both had actual rib cages. And I left her room with probably ten new skirts, a BCBG cocktail dress, a vintage pink Lilly Pulitzer shirt, three belts, four pairs of pants, and two vintage fur shawls that hadn't been worn in over twenty years (I've been a vegetarian for a decade and would *never* purchase original fur, but when two beautiful pieces are either going to the Goodwill or to my own closet and no money is changing hands, I'll take 'em). I went back to my room and hung up all the clothes and suddenly my closet started to look like I'd always wanted it to.

Or the time that Nina Davuluri, Miss America 2014 and the first Indian American to ever win the title, came to Duke, and I was invited to a small private dinner with her because I'd made a YouTube reaction video supporting her when a bunch of people said vile racist shit on Twitter after she was crowned. And my friends gathered in the Student Government office to help me squeeze into a borrowed size 2 Hervé Léger cocktail dress for the dinner. It barely fit and I was popping at the seams and kinda couldn't breathe, but I looked killer and felt beautiful and had never worn a $2,000 dress like that before in my life. And then when I saw Nina, she said, "Is that an Hérve Léger?" and I blushed and said, "Why, yes it is! It's on loan from a friend," and I felt smart in every sense of the word.

Or during spring break, when I ran away to New York City to hang out with my friend Alok and we went to parties together and wrote and performed poetry and I stomped around town in my cute new wardrobe and got to see Janet Mock interview Laverne Cox at NYU and took a selfie with Laverne after the talk and started to grasp just how much I was, in fact, part of the trans community.

Or when I decided I wanted to start using gender-neutral pronouns *everywhere*, not just at queer conferences. And I started telling people on campus—professors, students, administrators, everyone—that they shouldn't call me "he" or "him" anymore, that I wanted to be called "they" and "them." I felt a new sense of power because I was finally learning to stand up for myself; because I was finally acknowledging that my gender deserves to be accommodated and treated well by other people, even if it requires them to use language and pronouns they aren't used to.

Or the time when Sunny and I performed a drag routine to Tony Bennett and Lady Gaga's rendition of "The Lady Is a Tramp" for Lavender Ball, the annual queer formal. And we started off with me singing Tony's part in a suit and Sunny singing Gaga's part in a gown. Then we got naked onstage and by the end I was singing Gaga's part in a gown and Sunny was singing Tony's part in a suit.

Or when Student Affairs had their annual Leadership & Service Awards, the fanciest awards ceremony for undergrads, and I wore the black velvet Bob Mackie gown from Dr. Malouf and won so many diversity and leadership awards that it was kind of embarrassing and pretended I was walking the red carpet at the Emmys and felt gorgeous, albeit sweaty.

Or on the last day of classes, when we had a big music festival on campus and everyone drank all day and I ran around drunk in a neon pink tutu and bodice with a smaller purple tutu around my neck to round out the look, then met up with Sunny and Ronnie and other friends and we all painted our nails in the common room at the end of the night.

Or, most memorably, the time Gloria Steinem came to campus and gave a lecture to a standing-room-only crowd at Duke Chapel, and I got up to the mic during the Q&A and asked her what we could do to ensure that sissies like me can be happy, and she threw a power fist in the air and proclaimed, "Sissy!" And as her voice reverberated throughout the church, I threw my power fist up in the air, too, and shouted back, *"Sissy, femme, queer and proud of it, dammit!"* And for a moment both of our voices echoed together, bouncing off the stone walls, dancing about the gothic cathedral, blending and reverberating until the entire chapel erupted in applause and I felt somehow ordained.

As quickly as it had started, it was over.

Graduation weekend came before any of us were ready. We turned in our theses, blinked, and presto—we had to get the fuck out. Our tuition money run dry, our grades posted, it was time to go.

Now that I'm a "proper" lady, I look back at graduation weekend and just think, *Oh my God, why did I want everyone to see my underwear all the time?* But when I really reflect on my state of mind at the time, it makes sense.

Let me justify myself. When you are compelled to hold back your gender identity for twenty or thirty years, you have a *lot* of catching up to do when you finally come around. And it's awkward for everyone. Oftentimes, when you come out, you go back to being a child. You want to relive your life all over again, reclaim the femme childhood you never got to have, which means you have to learn all the awkward lessons your friends already learned in middle school.

I didn't get to cover my whole body in fluffy pink garments as a child, didn't get to wear the cool Disney Princess–themed hair clips or chronicle my thoughts in a *That's So Raven* notebook. I never got to have my Claire's years. Nor did I get to have my Hot Topic goth-chick phase in high school. I never got to listen to too much Evanescence, strut around in fishnets, paint my nails black, and cover my eyelids in purple glitter. I never got to wear slutty dresses to prom or winter formal and grind with boys to the Black Eyed Peas. I wasn't given the opportunity to get my scandalousness out of my system in senior year of high school or freshman year of college like many of my ciswomen counterparts.

Because I'm trans, I had to do all those things as an adult. I'm still kinda cycling through the phases. I mean, I'm twenty-seven and I am *just* buying my first tube of black lipstick. I bought a pair of Spice Girls–style four-inch platform sneakers just the other day. I'm wondering when I'm going to get to my pretty princess phase, when I'll dress like Sleeping Beauty on a normal Wednesday. I think it's coming. It's unpredictable and erratic, but equally fun and fabulous.

All this is to say, by the time I graduated college, I was learning fashion lessons and flexing with boundaries that are usually reserved for fifteen-year-old girls—namely, lessons about skirt length.

I just didn't get it. How short was too short? Could any slit ever be too high? Did the limit even exist? And why did dresses seem to get *shorter* when I sat down? Also, how comfortable with my frontal bulge was I *really*? I'd written a 120-page history thesis, but all I wanted to really explore were the mechanics of pleather miniskirts.

In my gender rebirth, I cut all my shorts twice as short so that I could show off my legs. I started wearing tiny dresses and skirts that barely covered my thighs when I sat down. I felt glorious and cute and sexy and all the frat boys couldn't stop staring even though they knew they shouldn't. One European exchange student even asked me why I didn't shave my legs, because he thought I had nice legs and should show them off more. And I was annoyed at him for policing my body hair but thrilled that he'd acknowledged some facet of his desire for me.

I spent most of senior spring in short shorts, miniskirts, and teeny dresses because it was my way of saying fuck you to everyone. You wanna make me feel like an outcast? Well, then you're going to have to see my leg hair in all its glory. You wanna make me feel like a freak? Well, then I'll just have to take three inches off all my hemlines. You don't want me to represent you on the board? No worries. Here's my ass. Kiss it if you must.

I don't think that you have to actually succeed at having a lot of sex in order to be a good slut. These days, sluttiness is more of a political mind-set, a rebellious declaration of sex positivity, than an activity. During graduation weekend, I was at my peak. I used the unruliness of my body, its immodesty and irreverence and lack of discipline, to fight back. I was a dignified social-justice slut who never actually succeeded in getting laid.

For graduation weekend, I planned five outfits.

The first was for my final board committee meeting. While I wasn't elected to serve as Young Trustee, as a vice president in student government, I was a non-voting member of Duke's Business and Finance Committee. It was a good committee for me to be on while I was working on endowment transparency, because it was the committee with the highest density of very rich people.

To my final Duke board meeting, I wore a white top, bolero blazer, and black skirt that went down to mid-calf, but had a slit that came up to mid-thigh. I called it my Angelina Jolie skirt because it showed so much leg. I strutted into the board meeting in my heels and confidently sat down next to my fellow committee member Gao Xiqing, the outgoing president and chief investment officer of the China Investment Corporation, China's sovereign wealth fund, worth around $800 billion at the time. We chatted for a moment before getting down to business. When the meeting ended, I was thanked for my service on the committee and congratulated on my upcoming graduation that weekend. I smiled politely and stood up, revealing the full extent of my skirt to the room. *Bet you're gonna miss these gams*, I thought as I strutted out.

The second outfit was the most dramatic. Not in terms of fashion, but because of the drama that it caused. It was a simple enough BCBG dress with a blue floral pattern. It was still too short, but not as bad as some of my other outfits at the time. I wore it to the graduation celebration that was held for members of my scholarship class and their parents.

When I walked out of my dorm onto the main quad to meet my mom and dad, their reactions could not have been more different. My mom immediately began tearing up, proud that her baby was graduating and nostalgic for the old days, overcome by the feelings that a mother usually has. My father, on the other hand, broke into a deep, serious scowl. As I hugged my mom, my dad pursed his lips, trying and failing to contain his rage.

"Is *this* what you're wearing?" he spat. "You're going to wear *this*?"

"Yes, this is what I'm planning to wear," I responded matter-of-factly, with perhaps a *touch* of snark.

"I can't believe this." His voice was rising. "I can't frakin' believe this!"

Frak is the word my dad uses when he is angry instead of saying "fuck." For the longest time, I did not know where he picked up this habit. It was just a strange tick he'd developed over time, one that made it really hard for me to take him seriously when he was mad and cursing. I've since learned that saying *frak* instead of *fuck* is a reference from the hit sci-fi series *Battlestar Galactica*. Knowing this does not make it any easier to take him seriously when he is mad and cursing.

"I can't frakin' *believe this!*" He was yelling now. A few students walking by were concerned, but no one stopped.

Then, "You *liar!*"

"When did I lie to you?"

"I asked you not to wear any of this crap for graduation, I told you that for *one weekend* I didn't want any of this *San Francisco* shit. You *promised me* that you would just be *normal* for this weekend and now you're going back on that frakin' promise. You *liar.*"

I thought back to our recent conversations. I really tried to remember the moment when I'd *promised* him that I wouldn't wear a dress for graduation. The conversation when I'd "promised" him had likely gone more like this:

DAD: *You're not going to wear any of that weird crap to graduation are you?*

ME: *What do you mean, "weird crap"?*

DAD: *You know, dresses and women's shoes and that.*

ME: *I dunno. I haven't really thought about it.*

DAD: *Well, I want to ask you one thing, as your father. I want you to dress normally for graduation. Please do that for me, okay?*

ME: [nervously, noncommittally, trying to change the topic, but absolutely in no way agreeing to those terms] *Okay, we'll see. Anyway, what do you want to watch on TV?*

According to my father, that constituted a promise. Sometimes, my dad remembers more with emotions than with facts. Sometimes, I remember more with emotions than with facts. Make of that what you will re: this book.

"I never promised you that, Dad. I wouldn't've. I've had my graduation dress picked out for *months.*"

"Graduation *dress? Jesus*, you're going to wear *a dress* on Sunday?"

"That's my current plan, yes."

"I can't frakin' believe this."

"Look, Dad, it is *my* graduation, not yours."

I might've been yelling by this point, too, and my mom was *definitely* crying angry tears.

"You didn't even *pay* for my college. If you remember, I got a full ride so that you and Mom didn't have to. So I *am going to wear what I want*, and if you want to be a part of my graduation weekend, then you're going to have to deal with that. But you are *more* than welcome to leave if you're too uncomfortable. I don't need you here if you're just going to be nasty. This is my weekend to celebrate with my friends and you are *the only person on campus* who is even mad about my dress at this point. I literally just sat next to the president of the fucking Sovereign Wealth Fund *of China* in a skirt and he couldn't've cared less. Everyone else here thinks I'm fabulous, Dad. From Dee, my friend who's a custodian in the library, to the provost. Perhaps you could join them?"

I paused for effect as my father fumed.

"Now, if you're done having a fit about this, we are late to the celebration for my two hundred thousand dollar scholarship. You can come or not, Dad. Your choice."

He didn't respond, glaring angrily, then proceeded to do the most awkward thing he possibly could've. He went to the reception, but refused to walk beside me and my mom, instead trailing a few paces behind us. Then he *refused to talk to me or acknowledge my existence* at a reception filled with parents gushing about their kids. They had an official photographer at the event and my dad wouldn't even take a professional photo with my mom and me.

By this point in my life, I'd gotten used to how my dad's temper worked, which is that he gets *really, really* mad for a period of a few hours, gives you the silent treatment for a day or two, and then goes back to being generally kinda sweet. So I wasn't devastated by the fact that he wouldn't be seen with me at my own reception. It made me look courageous, or perhaps gracious, and just made him look like a profound, insufferable asshole.

But let me defend him for just a second. First off, for my graduation trip, my dad took the entire family to *San Francisco*, a city that is, to him, the gayest in the world. So it's not like he was opposed to *every* facet of my identity or anything. I mean we wandered around *the Castro* together for like three hours *the very next week*.*

And while he may have been a jerk on graduation weekend, he was climbing a *fairly steep* hill. Not only was I making him be seen in public with me in a dress for the first time, I was making him be seen in public with me in a *slutty* dress, which was fabulously too short and might've shown a bit of bulge at the right angle, for the first time.

It was truly a double whammy, because we were combining a big cis-father/trans-child fight with a separate, more classic fight that most girls have with their parents at the age of fourteen: the "you can't go out in that skirt, it's too short" fight. So I was having my gender-affirmation *and* my sex-positive-femininity fight with my dad *at the same time*.

Dad, I'm gender nonconforming and you have to get used to it. And I'm also kinda slutty and you have to get used to that, too. Now come to the ceremony—I'm graduating summa cum *laude with distinction!*

I like to think of this as *efficiency*. Why have two small fights when you can just have one really big one?

My baccalaureate service in Duke Chapel the next day was easier. My outfit involved a pair of bright vermilion shorts, red lipstick, a kinky glitter vinyl bow tie made by my friend,† and brown leather espadrilles.

---

* Have you ever been to the Castro *with* your parents? In addition to the giant rainbow flag billowing over the street and the endless sea of posters featuring half-naked nineteen-year-olds in kinky puppy outfits, there is a bakery that sells cookies shaped like *literal dicks*. My dad deserves major kudos for not only keeping his cool there, but *financing the excursion*.

† Check out @gnat_glitter_kink on Instagram. I promise you will not be disappointed.

For some reason, inexplicably, my dad can deal with heels, especially wedges. He can even kind of deal with lipstick and makeup. It's just the dresses and skirts that drive him over the edge. Day two of graduation weekend passed without incident.

The next day was the big one. While I didn't get to speak at graduation, I did get to sing as part of the octet that performed the National Anthem and the Alma Mater. So I had to get up early that morning to head to rehearsal and line up under the stadium for our procession onto the stage. Groggy but buzzing with anticipation, I put on my fourth and arguably most iconic graduation weekend outfit: the Jackie Kennedy–inspired bright pink skirt suit that just barely covered my underwear, my navy blue Hillary Clinton pumps from my time at the UN, and a pearl-lined navy pillbox hat that would've made even Kate Middleton jealous. I looked *incredible*, perfectly representing Duke by adeptly straddling sluttiness and refinement.

Strutting around campus the day of graduation was a whirlwind and, in a way, my first taste of celebrity. Parents, my classmates, and administrators alike couldn't stop staring at me, not only because my outfit was impeccable and outlandish in equal parts, but because most of them, parents and siblings included, already *knew who I was*. I'd begun the (self-aggrandizing, delusional) transition from student to legend.

Have you heard the story of Jacob? They were a student here once. Legend has it that their legs were five feet tall. They once sent an administrator to the hospital because their skirt was so short.

Sitting onstage at graduation, staring out across the thousands of students and parents gathered before me in Wallace Wade Stadium, sweating my face off, a more heroic narrative began to dawn on me. I hadn't just survived this place, I'd demanded and maintained my right to exist. I hadn't let Duke crush me or walk all over me. If anything, I'd done my damnedest to walk all over Duke.

And while the changes I wanted to see take place during my four years on campus hadn't *really* happened, while the culture hadn't fundamentally shifted to make Duke a place where someone like me could succeed and thrive *in step* with the university rather than *in spite* of it, something much more important had happened.

While I hadn't irreversibly changed Duke, Duke had irreversibly changed me. I left Duke knowing, more categorically than ever, exactly how resilient I was. If I could end four years at Duke standing firmly on-stage in slutty Jackie Kennedy drag, singing the Alma Mater in front of thousands, I could take on *anything*.

Duke may have been a trial by fire. But I am a flamer of the highest order. I'm a motherfuckin' phoenix. And you can't kill a phoenix with fire, honey, because we're *made of the stuff*. When confronted with fire, when faced with adversity, we shine *brighter*.

Or at least that's the optimistic telling.

That's what I tell myself on the good days when I feel strong and whole.

On the days when I feel broken, on the days when I feel worn down or empty, the story changes.

The truth is that my time at Duke was a paradox.

A cold fire.

A salty cradle.

A beautiful wound.

A pair of Louboutins.

On the one hand, they elevate you. They make you taller and bigger and higher. They give you a sense of power and purpose and fashion and ferocity. They give you a whole new attitude and an unstoppable sense of confidence. They *make* the outfit. But the whole time you're wearing them, you're struggling to balance. You teeter on the edge, liminal, un-certain, never quite comfortable.

The act of wearing them—the contortion of the foot, the crushing of the toes, the breaking of the back—leaves damage that *lingers* long after you've taken the shoes off. Just one evening leaves blisters that last for a week. If you wear them most every evening for four years, the damage becomes visible, the shape of your foot changes. The bunyons and ingrown toenails and back pain are inescapable.

Duke was a gorgeous pair of dangerous shoes. For four years, it made me who I am. Astride elite private school prestige, I looked effortlessly perfect. I was privy to opportunity and opulence that I'd never dreamed possible. I felt bigger and stronger and *better*. I could get into any party in the world, light up any room that I pleased, open any door. I spent four years trying to convince myself that the shoes weren't *that* painful, that I'd broken them in and they were unique to me, that the leather had molded to my foot and was now comfortable.

But at some point, I had to look myself in the mirror and decide that the glamour was no longer worth the damage.

I had to put the shoes away and it was hard. I felt shorter and less powerful in flats. I didn't know who I was without my Blue Devil stilettos, and it took a long time to figure that out. As often as I was tempted to, I tried my best not to wear those shoes anymore. I tried not to mention Duke or talk about my pedigree. I had to find other ways to define myself and earn my place in the world.

Sometimes, I catch myself looking at my Duke blue pumps with rose-tinted longing. There are moments when, perched on the shelf, I still find them beautiful in spite of the pain that they caused. There are moments when I yearn to twirl on the dance floor in them one more time.

For years after college, I felt perpetually underdressed. To this day, I'm still trying to fight off that feeling. It's an unfinished seam in this story, visible to anyone who cares to look.

After an exhausting four years, I needed a *break*. But not before I could get in one more epic night on campus with my mom in tow. The night after graduation was parents' night at Shooters, the trashy country-western bar frequented almost exclusively by Duke students. My mom agreed to go.

A few hours later, I changed into my fifth and final graduation weekend outfit: a sleeveless black button-up vest, black pleather mini-skirt, black cowgirl boots (*sans* heel), and bright red lipstick.

My mom met us outside Shooters in a pink striped shirt and jeans. She took one look at me, at my teeny skirt and my sleeveless shirt and my gaggle of tipsy friends, and broke into a smile, then a laugh.

"My, that outfit is *something*, Jacob!" She beamed at the friends surrounding me, supporting me just as I was. "I can't say it's my *favorite* look of yours, but you look adorable!"

The night went by in a blur, partially because I was tipsy, but mostly because I was in heaven. My friends and I took the club by storm. We pulled our moms up to dance on the bar. I rode the electric bull in a miniskirt. My mom and I even danced in the cage perched two stories overhead. We tore. the. place. up.

And there was *no* negative commentary on my gender from *anyone*. Everyone was chill. Everyone was fine. It wasn't just respectful, it was affirmational. There was much to celebrate, and my gender got swept up in the revelry, as much a part of what we were celebrating as anything else.

At around ten thirty or eleven, the moms were tired and decided it was time to leave their children to properly begin our final evening of debauchery.

That's when it happened. In the eleventh hour, I spotted Bruce Springsteen in the flesh. His daughter, Jessica, was in my graduating class, and though we never really hung out, I spent four years praying that I could be at the right place at the right time when Bruce happened to be around. And after four years of waiting, on the final night of my life as a student, The Boss himself passed me on the stairs at Shooters, and I was *just* sober enough to remember it. We made eye contact for approximately half a second, and then it was over.

Which begs the question: How much are you allowed to crush on your classmate's dad? Like, at what point, if any, is that acceptable? Because damn, Bruce ages *well*. If you're reading this, I'm sorry, Jessica, but it has to be said: Your dad is still *fine*. I'll have what he's having.

I spent the rest of the evening celebrating four years of identity development and work well done in the only fashion truly befitting a revered institution such as Duke: by accidentally flashing everybody my underwear. The more drinks I had, the less I seemed to notice the exact geometry of my legs and their intersection with my skirt. I danced on the bar: probably flashing everybody. I danced in the cage: probably flashing everybody. I danced on the giant sculpture of a rearing white horse: *definitely* flashing everybody. I have photographic proof of that one, a picture of me proudly standing on the horse's rump, holding on to its mane, perching the leg closest to the camera at an upward angle so you can perfectly see my dark blue briefs.

It was one of my prouder moments. I'd like to think that flashing people my Hanes was just my drunken way of saying, "I'll miss some, but not all, of you. Here's to a (sorta) great(ish) four years!"

We ended the evening in a giant circle of seniors, arms draped over one another as we sobbed and drunkenly sang "Wagon Wheel," the infamous song originally written by Bob Dylan and fleshed out/popularized by Old Crow Medicine Show. The Southern version of "Closing Time," it was the Duke student body's official party-ending music.

Only in this case, it wasn't just ending the party. It was ending everything.

And it was only then, in a circle of drunken crying, that I realized what I'd missed. While I was excited to leave Duke and get the fuck out of North Carolina, there was something here worth mourning, a glittery baby in all the bathwater I was about to throw out.

As much as I had loathed the place, I'd earned my right to exist there. I'd earned my right to walk around campus in any outfit I could imagine, free from harassment, free from aggression, free from any questions about my gender at all. I could walk into any room on campus and simply *be*. My existence, my identity, and my self-expression were all a fact of life at Duke.

After that drunken circle of seniors was broken, all that security would be gone. I'd have to do it all over again. This time, in the real world.

Going forth into adulthood, I couldn't help but remember how I felt before my high-heeled run across the Brooklyn Bridge. The truth is, when I set out to do the run, I *had no idea* if I could actually pull it off. There was no road map. There were no best practices. I just had to set out, put one foot in front of the other, and, in spite of all the odds against me, have faith that I'd make it to the other side unharmed. I had to look the raw, cruel numbers about high heels, physics, and ankle injuries in the eye and say *fuck 'em*. I had to take a risk, to bet big in full knowledge that the deck was stacked against me.

Being gender nonconforming as a college student felt easy enough. People expect you to play with gender and sexuality while you're in school, to experiment a little. But the unsaid expectation is that, after you graduate, those experiments will come to an end. *It's okay to try hooking up with girls in college, Tina, just so long as you settle down with a good man in the end.*

But I'd discovered something about myself that was irreversible. I couldn't "grow out of this phase" when I graduated, because my gender *wasn't* a phase. There was no tidying up this mess. In a shower of glitter, confetti, and sequins, my identity had *exploded everywhere*, and no vacuum or broom in the world could clean it back up. It was out in the open; ubiquitous, uncontainable, coating everything.

There was no manual for how to be gender nonconforming in the real world, away from my friends, outside of the Ivy League(ish) campus bubble. There was no guidebook on how to be gender nonconforming as an adult. No *Idiot's Guide to Coping with the Fact That Your Gender Is Fucking Ridiculous*. Like running across a bridge in high heels, applying lipstick for the first time, or dressing like Jackie Kennedy, it was un-charted territory for me. All I could do was throw caution to the wind, publicly commit to my gender, and pray for the best.

At the time, the doubts felt inescapable: Was my identity even pos-sible? Could I exist after graduation? Could I find happiness? Could I still be *me*?

Standing on the beer-covered floor, arm in arm with a hundred of my sweaty classmates, I decided I could go one more night without asking the big questions, could go one more moment without the exis-tential terror setting in.

Instead, I let the song take me away. We all did. We belted in a drunken stupor, nostalgic tears streaking down our cheeks. Arm in arm, we swayed; rocking, cradling one another.

All sweaty bangs, sniffly nose, and smeared lipstick, I braced myself to weather the impending doom of adulthood, to face a glamorously un-certain future, to take on the miraculous, life-changing bullshit to come.

Chapter 9

Dear Mom and Dad

DAD,

I want to start with you. The unfortunate thing about memoir is that you have to tell the truth and you have to talk about the messy stuff and the parts when people you love were not always their best. The whole premise of this book is that I'm trying to recount what actually happened; I'm not sugarcoating anything or shaving down the rough edges or paving over the bogs. And what results is a complicated picture, a portrait of real, writhing, vulnerable, open people. People who are not perfect, who don't always know how to handle everything that's being thrown at them. What results is a book that you might feel set you up as a villain, an antagonist.

But my intention was only to show that things were complicated. Too often, in the quest to make our identities and lives easily digestible, understandable, and squeaky clean, queer and trans folks sidestep telling the complicated stories. Our parents are reduced to one of two tropes: the acceptor or the rejecter. We either tell the story where our parents immediately stepped up to affirm our identities, or we tell the story where we overcame our parents even though they rejected us.

The story we don't tell is the story that's more often true: the story where we go back and forth between those two poles for years, oscillating between acceptance and rejection in a pendulum dance.

So I have to tell the stories of when we didn't agree, Dad, because I need other parents out there to know that this is not black-and-white. That things like acceptance and love and coping and rejection and complication are all part of this process. If I pretend you've always been a perfect dad, if I erase the parts where you were a little bit of a jerk (or the parts when *I* was a little bit of a jerk), I would be doing a disservice to other dads out there who are struggling to get through their own ideas of masculinity in order to love their gender nonconforming kids.

The reality is that you were not raised to understand a child like me. You were not brought up in a world where someone like me was deemed possible. And yet, after you married Mom and had kids, you found yourself contending with the impossibility of my gender. You fought it for a spell. There were moments when you made things harder for me than they had to be. But you ultimately broke through to a world in which I am very much possible, if still sometimes insufferable, in your mind.

For all the other dads out there who have a kid like me, *you* are the hero of this story. Sure, you've never sat me down and said verbatim, "Dearest child of mine, I affirm your gender and love you for it, and I am proud that you are changing the world through your feminist activism and lipstick." But you don't have to say that, because *talking* isn't how you generally show love.

You show love through actions, not through words. And the way you've changed, the way you've figured out how to love me even when I come home from church in a red dress, lipstick, and chunky-heeled boots, is no small feat. Your transformation of love is nothing short of miraculous.

I've written a lot about the moments when we disagreed, but there are other stories—stories that are less "relevant," less "on topic"—that haven't made the cut.

Like when my back spasmed for the first time when I was alone in a hotel room in Dallas for a speaking engagement and I was terrified. One moment I could move, and the next moment, I couldn't. Scared and crying, I called you first. You helped me push through the pain and get up out of bed. You talked to me for thirty minutes as I tried to stretch, to do small movements, to walk up and down the hallway outside my door a few times. You told me exactly how much ibuprofen to take and in what order to stretch, take a hot shower, and lay back down.

Like the way that every day, until I was at least thirteen or fourteen, no matter how tired you were, you gave me a back scratch before bed. And we'd talk about my day for a few minutes and I would be almost asleep when you'd say, "Jacob, I'm proud of you," and I'd say, "Why?" and you'd say, "I don't have to have a reason," and I'd drift off.

Or how, two years after I first came out as gay, we went on a walk through the neighborhood and you told me you were sorry that you'd said all those hurtful things, and I told you that it was okay and that I loved you.

Like the fact that on my most recent visit home, when Mom was slammed at work and I was busy writing my face off, you cooked dinner for us basically every night. And when I started eating vegetarian, you not only learned how to properly cook tofu, you started eating it yourself.

Like the fact that right now, as I'm at our kitchen table writing this, you came downstairs to say hello. I'm sitting here, wearing my grand-mother's old earrings and blowing my nose a bunch because I'm getting over a cold, and you're sitting across the table from me sipping your black tea.

I love you. And while we still may have a few fights about my gender left in us—perhaps what I wear to my wedding? If *that* ever happens—I'm happy *almost* all of them are in the past.

I'm proud of you, Dad.

I don't have to have a reason.

MOM,

Plain and simple: I couldn't have gotten any luckier than you.

It almost feels silly to shower you with any more accolades, because everyone who follows me online already knows that you're an ally icon. In college, you were almost as much of a celebrity on campus as I was, known far and wide for your brilliant acceptance of your trans-fabulous kid. My favorite picture of us will always be from North Carolina Pride in 2013, when we rode on the Duke float together. You perched on the front of the float, waving a rainbow flag while I stood on top in Sunny's old Duke-blue prom dress, proudly wielding a trident and holding my hand-painted sign: "Not GAY as in HAPPY, but QUEER as in FUCK YOU!"

I love that you've always had a gender-bending edge yourself, though there are times when it makes me question whether we are, in fact, re-lated. When I think about our divergent fashion sense, I can only scratch my chin. You prefer understated earrings for Christmas; I haven't worn an understated earring in my entire life. You look dapper in your blazers; I look like Barbara Bush in mine. Just the other day, you said you wished you could wear your hiking boots every day; I do not fully understand this desire.

Despite our sartorial differences, we make a great team. Remember when I got my first job in Los Angeles but it was super-last-minute and we had to drive across the country in three and a half days? The first day of our trip, we drove 1,200 miles straight from Raleigh, North Carolina, to Oklahoma City because we are both road warriors who would probably do well in a lesbian biker gang. We made such good time that we were able to add a visit to the Grand Canyon. When we arrived at the South Rim, it was snowing and we stared out in silence for a whole minute before turning to each other, tears brimming in our eyes.

I know that reading this book is hard for you. You've told me over and over again that you wish things could've been better. As much as I tell you not to, I know you beat yourself up about my childhood. You wish you could've done more, could've done things differently, could've done something to make it easier for me. It's hard enough for *me* to look at the past and acknowledge that things weren't perfect. I can't fully understand how hard it must be for *you.*

I've said this before, but I want to say it again: So few of my scars have anything to do with you. And in the moments when you were unsure, in the moments when you weren't certain what to do and perhaps made the more conservative choice, I know you were only trying to protect me as best you knew how. After all, it's not like anyone gave you a guidebook for how to best support a feminine male child. It's not like there were resources out there for you. There were no expert maternal road maps for navigating my fledgling identity.

What matters most is what happened when, in late adolescence and early adulthood, I began to express my identity anew. You were there *every step* of the way, holding my hand, providing a sympathetic ear, giving me a shoulder to cry on, reading every article I wrote (and a bunch that I didn't) so you could always be up to speed. We've easily had sixty different conversations about trans people, queer identity, and gender politics in the last year alone. You've come to every one of my workshops and keynotes and speeches that you possibly could've, beaming proudly as I stood at the podium. You like and comment on literally every single thing I post on Facebook, even when I'm posting pictures in tiny skirts or with no shirt on or being a little raunchy.

I don't think we need to spend any more time worrying about how things were when I was a kid, because we're building a different world together. We're building a world where no parent with a gender nonconforming kid has to feel alone or out to sea; a world where no parent has to ever choose between keeping their child safe and encouraging their child to express their heart. Through your love for me, through your unqualified affirmation, empathy, and support, you are changing the world for thousands of other little Jacobs out there. I hope you know that.

MOM AND DAD,

I'm starting to understand what it's like to be far away from home. Los Angeles is *far* from North Carolina. I'm no longer a hop, skip, and jump away; I'm thousands of miles hence, perched on the other edge of a continent.

I miss being close to home; I miss both of you more than I let on. The two months I spent living back in North Carolina while I finished this book were sublime. Having dinner with both of you almost every night, taking walks around the lake, crashing in my childhood bedroom, spending time with my brother when he could sneak home from Asheville, visiting with friends who have known me my entire life—what could be more wonderful?

I hope this book can serve as something like closure for all of us. The adversity has officially been reclaimed, the challenges overcome and chronicled, the pain transformed, the lead turned to gold. We no longer have to live in the past, in the "what ifs" and the "should'ves." We're done with those things because we've done them justice. They're behind us, and all you two have to think about now is normal boring parent stuff that stresses me out. Stuff like, "Is Jacob saving for retirement?" "Did Jacob remember to sign up for healthcare next year?" Or, my personal favorite, "When is Jacob going to settle down with someone? You know the neighbors already have *grandkids*."

And I, in turn, will only think about the normal boring kid stuff: Dad, have I called you in the last few days? If not, I'll give you a ring. Mom, have I texted you a cute video of an animal eating fruit this week?

If not, I'll go find a video of an opossum eating some grapes. I know those always make you laugh.

I don't always understand how, but we made it. I love y'all.

Your weird lil' queer kiddo,

Jacob

P.S. Don't worry, Mom, I promise I haven't forgotten that you want to go on *Ellen* with me someday.

P.P.S. Ellen, the ball's in your court now.

Epilogue

Notes to Self

*H*ey you.

I know you just graduated college and are terrified about the world beyond school, but I wanted to drop in to give you some reassurance and a touch of spiritual guidance. I'm gonna do my best to be Oprah for you: to hold your hand and comfort you with my life wisdom, to let you cry against my perfect, billionaire bosom.

I want to start with lipstick, because where else would I start? These days, you keep a compact in your book bag so you can apply makeup on the go. You've started doing this new thing where you put a little Chapstick down and *then* lipstick, because the resulting red is a touch more subtle. Subtlety is something you're learning, by the way. You're cool with being more subtle about your gender now, not because your gender means less to you, but because you've emancipated yourself from the idea that you always have to prove something to other people. You've finally begun to realize that you don't owe anyone shit, and you don't have to wear bright lipstick all the time in order to demand to be seen and heard and validated. You only wear bright lipstick when you damn well please—which, to be fair, is still pretty often.

It's surprising how well you're doing these days. I mean, your life is still messy because you're changing careers for the fourth time in as many years, but you're holding it together pretty well, all things considered. Weathering the turbulence like a pro.

The coolest thing about where you're at now is that your identity has begun to feel sorta, I dunno, natural? You've done the internal work of naturalizing your own gender *to yourself*. You've told yourself enough times that you are beautiful and worthy of love, and at some point recently, you started to actually believe it. It'll take a few more years for you to understand this, but the thing about humans is that we have to learn everything at least three times. First, we learn it intellectually in our brains. Then, often months or years later, we learn it emotionally in our hearts. And then, sometime after that, we learn it instinctually in our guts. Your brain knew that your gender was beautiful in college. Your heart learned it a few years after that. And at the tender age of twenty-seven, your gut, your instinctual self, your subconscious thoughts, have started to get on board with the idea, too. Which means you're actually starting to feel happy on the regular.

You've learned that strength doesn't look like never getting hurt; it looks like being able to recover more quickly when you do. It's not about *whether you fall*—it's about *getting better at picking yourself back up*.

Writing a book has helped immensely. You were holding on to a lot of unsorted, messy baggage when it came to your identity. In the process of writing a book, you've forced yourself to pull those old suitcases out of the attic, dust them off, dump them out on the carpet, and begin the arduous process of sorting it all out. It's been helpful, edifying, cathartic. You've cried in cafés on at least a dozen occasions; the intensity of your (re)discoveries surprising even you.

But it's also been a bit discombobulating. Thinking about your gender for too long can be like spelling. If you write out any word and then look at it for too long—*tomato, paucity, preponderance, disintegrate*—the spelling will start to look funny. Are you sure tomato doesn't have an "e" at the end? Are you sure you put all those vowels in the right spot? Does something look weird to you? It looks weird. I don't know why it does, but it does. *Does.* That's a weirdly spelled word, too. Hm.

There will still be days when you aren't sure if you've gotten everything quite right when it comes to your gender, but the beauty of who you are now is that you're not really worried about it anymore. So what if you didn't get everything right in this book? So what if your gender changes tomorrow and then changes again twelve years from now? So what if you didn't describe every single facet of your being perfectly? Who you are changes. Humans are messy. Gender is even messier.

You've let go of a lot of your anger, too. You're less *angry* at people who still believe in the gender binary and more *exasperated* by them. Like, if they're not gonna get on board, can they at least have the courtesy to get the fuck outta your way? You feel this way toward casting directors and producers and editors and politicians and a lot of people. But fewer people than you think, actually.

Because the world's learning to be better to you. Sure, you still get catcalled when you walk around in New York, but there are literally and figuratively way more people on your team than there used to be. Figuratively, it feels like people are coming around to a world where gender nonconforming people are an accepted part of daily life. Literally, you have an actual team: a literary agent, an editor, two acting agents, two TV writing agents, a movie writing agent, a branding agent, an agent for breathing, an agent for eating, and a separate agent for bowel movements.

You finally stopped fighting the fact that, above all, you are a storyteller. And after a tough stint in DC and a few challenging years in New York, you've admitted to yourself that creating better culture is as important (if not *more* important) than creating better policy. Policy is formal and on paper, but culture; culture you can feel. So now you make

TV and art and written work (including this book) that change hearts and minds and reach further than you fully understand. You're still kicking ass and taking names on behalf of trans and gender nonconforming people, but instead of doing it on Capitol Hill, you're doing it in the Hollywood Hills. Sure, they're both narcissistic cesspools, but at least the Hollywood Hills come with *actual* pools, too.

Which is to say that your life is kinda, dare I say it, *glamorous* now? You know lots of really incredible people. You've been to lots of fancy parties. You haven't just walked red carpets, you're actually kind of *good* at it now. You get seriously texted questions like "hey are u going to Sundance this year?" or "what's ur Golden Globes weekend plans—u going to anything?" and you respond to these questions without your head blowing up. One time, you chatted with Neil Patrick Harris about leg hair.

The bleak news is that your dating life is still a disaster. Gay boys won't touch you with a twenty-foot pole and you don't have the right equipment for straight guys, so you're stuck trying to find all the beautiful bi-/pansexual dudes out there, and even though, statistically speaking, millions and millions of people are bi/pan, bi erasure is real, and finding actual bi/pan guys on dating apps is really hard. So you haven't gotten laid in a *lot* longer than you'd care to publicly admit.

At this point, your only hope dating-wise is to Mindy Kaling it. You just have to become a national sensation and write a show for yourself where you get to date Chris Messina and Glenn Howerton and Seth Meyers and a bunch of other traditionally gorgeous guys and *then* everyone will figure out that they actually wanted to fuck you this whole time. That's how it works, right, Mindy? *Right?*

Every now and then, you will still struggle with silly gender stuff, like going into women's stores on your own. Even in New York City, the supposed center of the queer universe, some women remain supremely uncomfortable when they see you browsing the gowns beside them at

Saks Fifth Avenue or Bloomingdale's. They see a male person looking at dresses and immediately think, *What are* you *doing here?*

The irony of their *what are you doing here* glares is that they are actually pretty deserved, but not on account of your gender. They are deserved on account of the fact that, though you talk a good game and pretend very well, you still do not actually have enough money to purchase anything at Saks or Bloomie's off the rack. I mean, you *could* buy a three-thousand-dollar gown if you wanted to. You'd just have to skip paying rent for a few months. Maybe your landlord wouldn't mind, if you looked pretty enough?

And, obviously, some things about femininity will still annoy you. Like the fact that, even though you only put it on an hour ago, you're already taking off your lipstick because you want a snack, and if you don't take off your lipstick, you'll end up eating it. You're fairly good at preserving your lipstick while eating these days, but sometimes—like when eating a giant Rice Krispies treat, for example—it's not worth it to try.

They say that the moral arc of the universe bends toward justice. You're not sure if you always agree with that idea. There are some moments when that feels ridiculous, when it feels like all the evidence is indicating otherwise. But on the good days—when the world is gentle with you and you've managed to avoid hearing about tragedy through the internet—there are certain things in your life that compel you to think it might be true after all.

These days, you feel more connected to your herstory and your community than ever before. You celebrate, claim, and live in community with your *trans*cestors. Their spirits dance in your head, encouraging you, leading you forward, reminding you that you are loved. With each passing day, you are more and more grateful for all the trans and gender nonconforming people who have come before you, how they poured love out of their souls and into the world, often at great personal cost, so you could be surrounded by it. You owe everything you are to Marsha P. Johnson and Sylvia Rivera and Flawless Sabrina and Miss Major Griffin-Gracy and Bamby Salcedo and Joan of Arc and Walt Whitman and Christine Jorgensen and Holly Woodlawn and Candy Darling and Mary Henly and Joseph Lobdell and Jennie June and Billy Tipton and Virginia Prince and two-spirit people and every gender nonconforming person who rioted at Compton's Cafeteria and every trans person who rioted at Stonewall and thousands and thousands and thousands of others.

While you may not have learned their names until adulthood, your trans elders have informed *everything* in your life. You carry their mantle proudly. They are with you every step of the way. Their brilliance and courage and love are baked into every single word of this manuscript.

Through reconnecting with your community, you've also begun to reconnect with spirituality. Today, you are stronger in your faith than you've ever been. You don't exactly know whether Jesus was the child of God or whatever, and you don't really know if the word *Christian* is exactly the term you should use to describe yourself, but here's what you do know:

You know that Jesus was dope as fuck. Jesus was a radical hippie who hung out with a band of working-class weirdos, hated the Roman Empire and corrupt religious leaders alike, embraced sex workers and saw their humanity, and wore flowy-fabulous robes perfectly accessorized with strappy leather sandals.

You also know that Jesus was nonbinary. It's kinda obvious to you, actually, at this point. God is clearly too big, too wise, too omnipotent to have an easily discernible binary human gender. I mean, God made *all* the genders, so clearly God isn't just one. God is genderless, or rather, genderful.

And, according to Christian theology, Jesus is the child of God—God's spirit manifested in a human body that just happened to be male. So Jesus was a genderless, divine soul living inside a male body. Which means that Jesus was nonbinary and a member of the trans community.

The way I see it, either you believe Jesus is the child of an omnipotent, genderless God and was therefore trans, or you're denying the full divinity of Jesus Christ. Boom. Take that, haters.

You also know that going to church when you're back in North Carolina is something you adore, and that you have the best congregation ever. Going to church with Mom when you're home kinda rocks now. She's still singing in the choir, so she heads in thirty minutes before you do to rehearse. Then you roll in five minutes before service and sit in section B, near the middle aisle. You save Mom a spot, and when the choir finishes the anthem, she joins you in the pew. She usually makes it to you in time for the New Testament reading, and she's always back in time to hear Pastor Donna—your black, female pastor (and fellow Dukie!)—give the sermon. The other Sunday, when one of the pastoral interns was giving the sermon, she discussed Eric Garner and #BlackLivesMatter as an example of our duty as Christians to stand with oppressed people. It was fuckin' awesome.

Mom has even learned to goof off a bit during service. You whisper jokes to each other, make each other laugh, and hold hands on and off throughout. Even if you didn't believe in God, you'd still go to church with her, just to make her happy. At this year's Christmas Eve service, she even tolerated your recent edits to "Joy to the World":

> *Joy to the world*
> *The Lord has come**
> *Let Earth receive her Queen!*
> *Let every heart prepare Her room*
> *And heaven and nature sing*
> *And heaven and nature sing*
> *And heaven and heaven and nature sing!*

---

* *Get it?*

What's remarkable about the routine is just how normal the whole thing has become. That you can come to church in a Sunday dress and wedges, pick a seat, and simply enjoy the time with Mom is a reality that you don't take for granted. You know it hasn't always been like this. Church wasn't always a fun place for you to be or a welcoming place for your budding queer spirit. But it also could've been so, so much worse, and for many of your queer/trans friends, it still is.

These days, church is a celebration. Each time you sit together in church—you in your lipstick and dangly earrings, Mom in her choir robe—you are celebrating your love, your perseverance, how hard you've worked and how courageous you've been in transforming your congregation.

The greatest gift is that your sense of self and your spirituality no longer feel oppositional; instead, they feel inexorably linked. In one way or another, you've always understood yourself to be the gorgeous creation of some higher power, and nowadays you know for a fact that She doesn't make mistakes. The words you wrote when you were seventeen ring more true with every passing day: You are fearfully and wonderfully made.

With that spiritual peace comes the ability to reclaim your pain, and the pain of your community, as a blessing. Because, in fact, trans and queer people *aren't* normal.

Whenever we are afflicted, whenever we fight, whenever we are hurt, we don't bleed blood: We bleed *glitter.* Arteries bursting with sparkles, our injuries blanket the world around us in shimmering bits of crystal. Our wounds are never in vain, because the moment pain escapes our bodies, it is transmogrified into flecks of gold, of silver, of diamonds and ruby, pearl and opal and sapphire cascading, emerald and tourmaline and amethyst encrusting everything in sight.

So even when we're at our weakest, even if we don't make it, even when the world gets the best of us, it gets *the best* of us. We are never really gone. We leave so much glitter in our wake that no one can ever hope to fully clean it up.

To this day, your divine conviction in your own self-love makes you kinda arrogant and a little bit of an asshole. Right now, as you're sitting in Cup A Joe in Raleigh finishing up this chapter and listening to "PYNK (ft. Grimes)" by Janelle Monáe, there are three teens who just came in and are being loud and taking up too much space at the table where you're sitting.

And because you are an arrogant, millennial asshole writing your book in a coffeehouse, all you can think is, *Y'all need to go be annoying somewhere else. Can't you see that I'm doing* the Lord's work *right now? I am literally writing gospel.*

Arrogant, divinely ordained, radical self-love is not always a flattering look, and it certainly doesn't make your life any easier.

But goddammit, is it *ever* fierce.

ACKNOWLEDGMENTS

I am acutely aware of the fact that this book is, in many ways, a historical accident. Not so much the fact that the book *exists*, but the fact that *I, of all people,* was given the opportunity and support to write it. For generations, gender nonconforming people like me have been compelled to be invisible, to hide, to downplay our identities or put ourselves away. We have been criminalized and thrown in prison. We have been threatened with violence if we let our true colors shine.

Which is to say that the contributions and brilliance of gender nonconforming people have not always been widely recognized by the world. The fact that *my* contributions, in specific, are allowed to be printed in these pages feels like an accident, if only because gender nonconforming people like me have *always* offered so much to the world but have rarely been given credit for our work. This book is the very tip of the iceberg in terms of what gender nonconforming people have already contributed.

So, first and foremost, I want to thank my own community. It is only because of gender nonconforming and trans people who have struggled on the margins that I'm able to exist as I am today. I want to thank every little boy who rummaged in their grandmother's jewelry box. I want to thank every little girl who was rebellious enough to reach for the construction helmet during dress-up. I want to thank every gender nonconforming or trans person who has taken a look in the mirror, known that their choice in clothing would result in being mistreated by the world, and made the courageous choice to set foot outside anyway. Your existence supports my existence. Your strength makes me strong.

I want to thank every gender nonconforming musician and artist and theater performer and costume designer who has used performance and the arts to make the world safer for me. I want to thank every trans person who's ever mustered the courage to tell people to fuck off, who's ever mustered the audacity to demand better treatment and rights. I want to thank every gender nonconforming, trans, and queer person who, after being erased or overlooked because of who you are, has continued pushing and creating and building and moving. Your sacrifices and very existence have made my life possible. I hope that, in these pages, I've returned the favor; that this book being in print will help make your life feel more possible in turn.

Sitting down to write this book was a challenge. Typing out and fine-tuning these sentences took more heart and guts and tears than I realized it would. But getting the audacity to *start typing* in the first place, to believe that my story *mattered*, that my life mattered in general, was much more difficult than actually writing this. And so I want to thank each of the people in my life who have taken the time to remind me, in myriad, often tearful ways, that my life matters. I didn't always know that and it has taken practice to get it right. Thank you for being with me, encouraging me to hold on when I wasn't sure I had any more strength left. You know who you are. And I love you.

In the interest of helping fellow powerfemmes get ahead in their careers and access much deserved clout, I also want to mention a few people by name. Thank you to my agent Katherine Latshaw for emailing me out of the blue and asking if I had something I wanted to say to the world because *did I ever*. Thank you to Megan Hogan for stoking this flame when it was only an ember. Thank you to Kerri Kolen and Sally Kim for investing (literally) in my future and for initially taking this project on. Thank you to my editor Helen Richard for taking the ball and running farther than we both imagined (see? I *can* make sports metaphors!). Thank you to my agent Val Champeau for letting me cry on the phone on a weekly basis (and for sending me ice cream cake with extra sprinkles when assholes harass me in public for being trans). Thank you to Kim Yau, Marissa Fine, Dana Spector, and the whole team at Paradigm for helping me see that this book could turn into anything I wanted it to be. And to Natalie Viscuso, Nick Pepper, Eric Brassard, and Fola Goke-Pariola at Legendary, let's hope that the whole "turning this book into a TV show" thing works out! Even if it doesn't work out, y'all are a dream come true.

I'd be remiss if I didn't also thank the many independent coffeehouses that have allowed me to post up for hours and hours writing and have tolerated me being "that weird crying girl in the corner" when I was writing the hard parts or "that giggling trans lady who just spit out a little bit of her coffee" when I was writing the funny parts. Thank you to Java Jive in Cary, North Carolina, Cup A Joe in Raleigh, Common Grounds Coffee House in Apex, Stone Creek Coffee in Milwaukee, Wisconsin, H Coffee House in Los Feliz, California, Bricks & Scones in Larchmont, and Vineapple in Brooklyn Heights, New York. I couldn't have done this without you, your coffee, and your sweet treats.

Lastly, and most importantly, I'd like to thank every person who has ever looked at a bold print or a sequined garment and thought to themselves, "Yeah, I guess I don't *really* need to keep that. It's pretty tacky. Let's just give it to Goodwill." It is only through your terrible decision-making, your lapses in sartorial judgment, and your complete inability to appreciate beautiful garments that I have been able to amass such a magnificent wardrobe today. I will be forever grateful that you didn't keep your great aunt's sequined dress from the eighties. It has found a happier, less judgmental, more affirming home in my closet.